Dark Pools & Flash Crashes

Understanding Liquidity Crisis and Market Fragmentation

Noble Trex

Published by NobleTrex Press

For permissions and other inquiries, write to:
P.O. Box 3132, Framingham, MA 01701, USA

Contents

Introduction

On the afternoon of May 6, 2010, the financial world witnessed a phenomenon that defied the conventional logic of economics. In the span of mere minutes, the Dow Jones Industrial Average plunged nearly 1,000 points-wiping out roughly one trillion dollars in equity value-only to recover most of those losses just as rapidly. Traded companies with solid fundamentals saw their stock prices briefly trade at pennies, while others skyrocketed to absurd valuations, all without any significant news event or change in their underlying business operations. This event, now known as the "Flash Crash," was not driven by human panic in a crowded trading pit. It was a silent, digital failure, a cascading interaction of algorithms and market structure that revealed a startling truth: the modern stock market is no longer a collection of people shouting in a room, but a colossal, high-speed network where the rules of engagement have fundamentally shifted.

This book, Dark Pools & Flash Crashes: Understanding Liquidity Crisis and Market Fragmentation, is an exploration of that shift. It is a journey into the invisible architecture of modern finance-market microstructure. While the nightly news focuses on *what* prices did-whether the S&P 500 went up or down-this text focuses on *how* they did it. We aim to pull back the curtain on the "black box" of the exchange, revealing the gears, levers, and hidden wires that determine the price of assets in the twenty-first century. To understand the volatility of today's markets, one must look beyond the headlines and economic indicators to understand the mechanics of liquidity, the fragmentation of trading venues, and the complex interplay between human intent and machine execution.

Our journey begins by stripping away the intimidating jargon that often acts as a gatekeeper to financial understanding. We start with the foundational premise of what a market actually is. In the opening chapters, we distinguish the vital difference between an asset's fundamental value and its market price. We introduce the cast of characters-from retail investors to massive institutions and the intermediaries who connect them-and define the central concept of this book: liquidity. Crucially, we redefine liquidity not merely as the volume of shares traded, but as the ability to transact immediately without significantly impacting the price. This distinction is the key to understanding why markets that appear healthy can suddenly become fragile.

From these foundations, we descend into the engine room. We dissect the anatomy of a trade, moving beyond the simple click of a "buy" button to visualize the Limit Order Book. By understanding how orders are queued, matched, and executed, the reader gains insight into the friction of trading-spreads, slippage, and market impact. We explore the critical tradeoffs between aggressive orders that demand speed and passive orders that prioritize price, and we examine the specific rules exchanges use to decide who wins the race when milliseconds matter.

However, the modern market is not a single location; it is a fragmented archipelago of trading venues. We traverse this fractured landscape, explaining how trading is split across dozens of public exchanges and private alternative trading systems. This brings us to one of the most provocative and misunderstood subjects in modern finance: Dark Pools. Often cast in popular media as nefarious cabals where the elite exploit the public, we dismantle these myths to reveal the mechanical reality. We explain the legitimate institutional necessity for opacity-how pension funds and mutual funds use these venues to shield large orders from predatory detection-while frankly addressing the risks of adverse selection and the impact of "dark" trading on public price discovery.

As we navigate this fragmented world, we inevitably encounter the dominant species of the modern ecosystem: the algorithm. We explore the rise of automation and High-Frequency Trading (HFT). Rather than vilifying speed, we analyze it as a commodity. We clarify the role of electronic market makers who provide the grease that keeps the wheels turning, while also introducing the concept of latency arbitrage and the feedback loops that can occur when machines interact at speeds beyond human comprehension.

The narrative then pivots to what happens when this complex system comes under stress. We examine the anatomy of a liquidity crisis-the moment when the music stops. We detail how leverage, crowding, and forced selling can create a vacuum in the order book, leading to a "run" on the market. This theoretical framework sets the stage for a detailed analysis of the Flash Crash and other historic dislocations. Through these case studies, we observe the terrifying speed at which liquidity can evaporate and how a single spark-be it a "fat finger" error or a large sell program-can trigger a cascade of automated selling that overwhelms the system's resilience.

Yet, this is not a story of hopelessness. We dedicate the latter portions of the book to the guardrails that have been erected to prevent total systemic failure. We discuss the evolution of regulation, from circuit breakers to kill switches and risk checks, evaluating the constant arms race between market innovation and regulatory safety. We weigh the trade-offs of transparency and the ongoing debate over how to best structure a market that is both efficient for traders and fair for the public.

Finally, we translate this high-level theory into a practical toolkit for the reader. Whether you are a student of finance, an aspiring trader, or a curious investor, understanding market structure is a form of self-defense. We provide mental models to visualize market dynamics and offer concrete safety tips-such as the dangers of Stop orders during volatility and how to interpret the "tape" when markets are under stress.

The goal of this textbook is to provide a comprehensive, elegant, and mechanically precise understanding of how trading actually works. By the end, you will look at a stock chart not just as a squiggly line of prices, but as the output of a dynamic, breathing ecosystem-a constant struggle for liquidity between buyers and sellers, lit exchanges and dark pools, humans and algorithms. Welcome to the machine.

Chapter 1

The Invisible Engine: How Markets Actually Work

Most people view the stock market as a casino or a wiggly line on a TV screen. But beneath the flashing numbers lies a mechanical engine designed to solve a specific problem: matching strangers who want to swap risk. Before we can understand why this engine sometimes explodes in a flash crash, we need to open the hood. We will look at how the gears-buyers, sellers, and the hidden middlemen-actually mesh together, and why the price you see on your screen is rarely what an asset is truly worth.

1.1 The Purpose of Markets

To see what markets are actually *for*, you must separate two different arenas that share the same tickers and the same headlines but do very different jobs:

- the **primary market**, where companies raise new money, and

- the **secondary market**, where investors trade existing ownership claims with each other.

They connect—the health of one affects the other—but they are not the same machine.

The Primary Market: Funding the Real World (Occasionally)

The **primary market** is the part of the financial system where money flows *into* a company in exchange for newly created securities (shares or bonds). It is called "primary" because the security is being sold *at the source*. The company is on the other side of the trade.

Common primary-market events include:

- **IPOs** (initial public offerings): a private firm sells new shares to the public for the first time.
- **Seasoned equity offerings**: a public company issues additional shares later.
- **Corporate bond issuance**: a firm issues bonds to borrow money from investors.
- **Private placements**: securities are sold directly to a small set of investors rather than the public.

In the primary market, the intuition people have is correct: if you buy *newly issued* shares, the company receives cash (minus fees). That cash can fund factories, software development, hiring, marketing, acquisitions—the real-world activities that ultimately determine long-run value.

But here is the key point for understanding day-to-day trading:

Most trading you see on screens is not primary-market funding. It is investors trading *with each other*.

An IPO is a major event, but it is also relatively infrequent for any given company. A mature public company may go years without issuing new equity. Yet its shares trade every day, sometimes millions of times a day. That constant churn is not "funding the company over and over." It is something else.

The Secondary Market: Trading Ownership (Constantly)

The **secondary market** is where already-issued securities are bought and sold among investors. When you buy 100 shares of a company in the market at $50 per share, the $5,000 does not travel to the company's bank account. It goes to the person (or institution) that sold you those shares.

The company is not absent from the story–its prospects drive why the shares are worth anything–but the company is not your direct counterparty in the trade.

This is where the stock market spends most of its life: **rearranging who owns what, at what price, and at what moment**.

This can feel abstract, even pointless. If the company doesn't receive money when shares trade, why does the secondary market matter so much?

Because a functioning economy needs three things that the secondary market provides:

1) Price Discovery: Turning Opinions into a Number

The market price is a constantly updated consensus about "what this claim on future cash flows is worth *right now*."

That consensus is not formed by debate or a committee. It is formed by trades.

Every time someone buys, they reveal: "At this price, I think it is cheap enough." Every time someone sells, they reveal: "At this price, I would rather hold cash or something else."

Out of that tug-of-war comes a price. This is **price discovery**. It is one of the most important public signals in capitalism, because it influences decisions far beyond trading desks:

- a company's perceived cost of capital,
- whether managers issue stock or buy it back,
- whether employees accept equity compensation,
- how lenders view creditworthiness,
- how competitors and acquirers value strategic moves.

A good price is not "correct forever." It is merely the best clearing price available given current information, beliefs, and constraints.

2) Risk Transfer: Moving Exposure to Those Who Want It

People and institutions do not all want the same risks at the same time.

- A retiree might want to reduce equity exposure to stabilize spending.
- A pension fund might want to increase long-term equity exposure.
- A market maker might want to hold inventory for minutes, not months.
- A hedge fund might want to express a specific view quickly and then exit.

The secondary market allows these transfers of risk. It is less a "casino" than a gigantic, continuous system for reallocating exposure to uncertainty.

3) Incentives and Governance: Ownership Must Be Tradeable to Matter

Shares are not just pieces of paper; they are *control rights* and *claims*:

- voting,
- dividends,
- residual claim on assets if the firm is liquidated.

Those rights have power partly because they are tradeable. If owners could not easily exit, ownership would be sticky, and control would be less contestable. Tradeability supports accountability: poorly managed companies tend to see selling pressure, depressed prices, activist interest, and sometimes takeovers.

Why Liquidity Is the Lifeblood of the Secondary Market

Now we can name the central idea that will echo through the rest of this book:

The secondary market can only do its job if it is liquid.

Liquidity sounds like a technical word, but the intuition is simple. In the secondary market, investors are constantly asking two questions:

- 1) *Can I trade when I need to?*
- 2) *Can I trade without getting punished by the price moving against me?*

If the answer to either becomes "no," the entire purpose of the secondary market begins to fail. Price discovery breaks (prices become unreliable), risk transfer breaks (people cannot reduce exposure when they need to), and confidence breaks (participants back away, making liquidity worse).

To see why, imagine two versions of the same world.

World A: Liquid Markets

In a liquid market:

- A buyer who wants to buy can usually do so quickly.
- A seller who wants to sell can usually do so quickly.
- Trading a moderate amount does not drastically change the price.

When a new piece of information arrives—an earnings report, an economic shock, a geopolitical event—the market can digest it through many small trades across many participants. The price adjusts, but the process is relatively orderly.

World B: Illiquid Markets

In an illiquid market:

- There may be few standing buyers at the moment you need to sell.
- The available buyers may demand a large discount.
- Your own trade can move the price sharply against you.

In this world, trading is no longer a routine activity; it becomes a negotiation under pressure. The market price stops being a calm summary of information and becomes, at times, a stress signal.

A Crucial Clarification: Trading Activity Is Not the Same as Funding

Because the primary and secondary markets share the same assets, people naturally blend them together. This leads to common misconceptions that matter during crisis events:

- **Misconception:** "When trading volume is high, companies are getting lots of money." **Reality:** High volume usually means ownership is changing hands rapidly. The company receives money only when it *issues* securities (primary market).

- **Misconception:** "If markets are volatile, companies lose money." **Reality:** Volatility changes the *price of ownership claims*. It can affect corporate decisions and financing conditions, but the cash in the corporate bank account does not mechanically rise and fall with every tick.
- **Misconception:** "If I sell, I'm taking money out of the company." **Reality:** You are taking money from the buyer in exchange for your shares. The company's operations continue; what changes is who bears the risk and who holds the claim.

This matters because liquidity crises (including flash crashes) happen in the *secondary* market. They are not primarily about companies suddenly losing their factories or their customers. They are about the trading system's ability to continuously match buyers and sellers at reasonable prices.

The Secondary Market as a Continuous Auction

A helpful mental model is to treat the secondary market as a **continuous auction**:

- Every moment, there is a best available price to buy and a best available price to sell.
- Orders are constantly arriving, being cancelled, or being executed.
- The "market price" you see is often the last traded price—the last point where a buyer and seller agreed.

In calm times, this auction feels smooth. Prices drift, and trading seems effortless.

In stressed times, this auction can become fragile. If participants step back—or if automated systems withdraw—the auction still exists, but the gap between willing buyers and willing sellers can widen dramatically. That widening is not just a cost; it is a symptom of the market losing its ability to perform its core job.

Why This Distinction Sets Up the Rest of the Book

- The **primary market** is about **raising capital** (important, but episodic).
- The **secondary market** is about **trading ownership and transferring risk** (constant, and systemically sensitive).
- **Liquidity** is what makes the secondary market functional; without it, prices can become unreliable and moves can become violent.

From here, the natural next question is: *who* provides that liquidity, *who* consumes it, and *what incentives* keep the system stable—until, sometimes, they don't.

1.2 The Cast of Characters

In the previous section, we separated two jobs the financial system performs:

- the **primary market**, which raises money for companies, and
- the **secondary market**, which continuously transfers ownership and risk among investors.

That distinction sets up a practical question: *who, exactly, is doing all this trading?*

When people say "the market," they often imagine a single crowd with a single motive. In reality, modern markets are an ecosystem. Different participants show up for different reasons, operate on different time horizons, and use different tools. Some are trying to invest. Others are trying to provide liquidity (and earn a spread). Others are trying to keep prices aligned across venues. And a few are simply trying to get out of the way fast enough not to be run over.

Understanding this cast of characters is essential for the rest of this book, because liquidity crises and flash crashes often occur when **the wrong players are left holding the responsibility for liquidity at the wrong moment**.

A Market Is an Ecosystem, Not a Monolith

A helpful metaphor is a food chain—not because markets are cruel by nature, but because **participants interact**, and the behavior of one group can change the survival conditions of others.

In a calm market, the ecosystem is balanced:

- long-term investors supply patient capital and opinions about value,
- institutions move large size carefully,
- market makers and high-speed firms provide immediacy, keeping trading friction low,
- arbitrageurs keep prices aligned across many venues.

In a stressed market, that balance can break. Participants who look like "liquidity" in normal times may *pull back* when risk spikes, and the ecosystem can suddenly feel like a crowded theater with exits that got smaller at the exact moment everyone wanted to leave.

The Ecosystem Trophic Pyramid (Speed vs. Size)

Before we define each group, anchor yourself with a simple organizing principle:

> **The fastest players tend to trade small and often. The biggest players tend to move slowly and trade carefully.**

Speed and size pull in opposite directions. If you are moving $10 million, you cannot behave like someone moving $1,000. You must plan, hide your intentions, and avoid moving the price against yourself. If you are trading thousands of times per second, you cannot do deep fundamental research on each trade; you are operating a different kind of business.

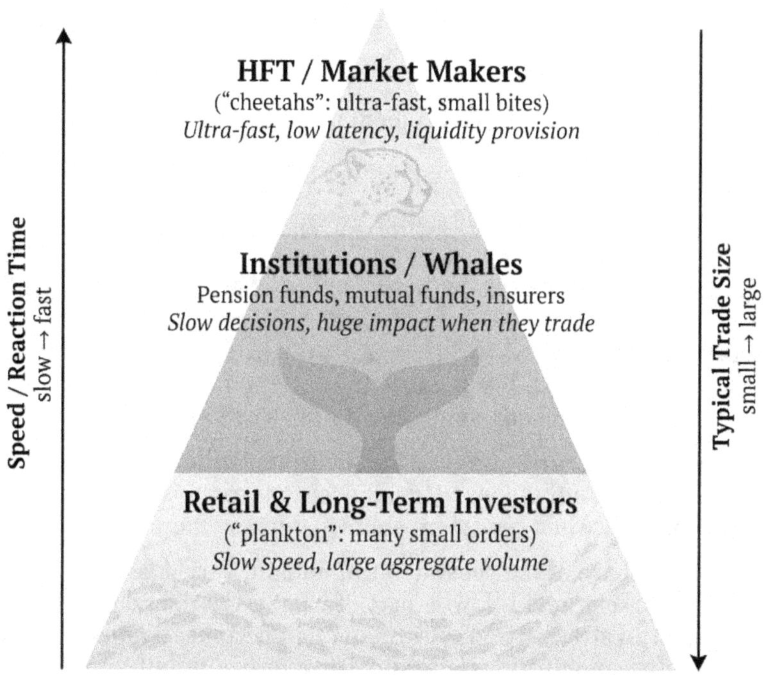

Different participants specialize in different combinations of speed and size.

This pyramid is not a moral ranking. It is a *mechanical* ranking: who can move fastest, who can move biggest, and what role each plays in keeping the secondary market liquid.

Retail Investors: Slow, Diverse, and Often Underestimated

Retail investors are individuals trading through brokerages: a parent investing for retirement, a young professional buying an index fund, someone rebalancing a portfolio, someone day trading, someone following a headline.

Retail is not one strategy. It is a category defined by *scale and access*. Retail orders are typically smaller, arrive throughout the day, and come with a wide variety of motivations:

- long-term investing (retirement accounts, index funds),
- shorter-term speculation ("I think this stock will pop"),
- cash needs (selling to pay tuition, a house down payment),
- behavioral impulses (fear, excitement, chasing trends).

Retail tends to be "slow" in reaction time. Not because individuals are unintelligent, but because they are human. They read news, place orders, and are not competing for microseconds.

Retail can be large in aggregate. One retail order is tiny relative to an institution. But millions of small decisions can move markets over time, especially when sentiment shifts in one direction.

Retail is the base of the ecosystem: abundant, varied, and persistent. In calm markets, retail flow is part of what gives the market texture and depth. In stressed markets, retail often becomes a *liquidity taker* (selling into fear or buying into a spike), which can amplify moves when other liquidity providers step back.

Institutional Investors: Whales That Must Swim Carefully

Institutional investors include:

- pension funds,
- mutual funds and ETFs (and their underlying portfolio managers),
- insurance companies,
- endowments and foundations,
- sovereign wealth funds.

Institutions are defined by **size**. They manage money measured in millions, billions, or trillions. This size creates a problem that is central to liquidity:

> If you are big enough, you can move the market simply by trying to trade.

Suppose a pension fund wants to sell $200 million of a stock. Even if the stock is "liquid" on most days, that order is too large to dump at once without pushing the price down. Institutions therefore use techniques designed to **minimize market impact**:

- breaking orders into smaller pieces,
- trading over hours or days,
- using algorithms (VWAP/TWAP and other execution strategies),
- seeking venues intended to reduce information leakage (including dark pools).

Institutions are "slow" in two senses:

- **decision speed**: investment committees, risk limits, mandates, compliance.
- **execution speed**: even when the decision is made, the actual trading must be paced.

This is why institutions are often called **whales**. A whale cannot sprint like a cheetah. But when a whale turns, the ocean notices.

Dealers and Market Makers: The Merchants of Immediacy

Now we reach the group that many casual investors rarely think about, even though they touch nearly every trade.

A **market maker** (or **dealer**) is an intermediary willing to quote Bid (price they buy) and Ask (price they sell).

Conceptually, market makers sell you immediacy:

- You want to buy *right now*? They sell to you (from inventory or by hedging).
- You want to sell *right now*? They buy from you (and manage the risk).

They are not doing this out of charity. They are running a business whose survival depends on managing two things:

1) Inventory risk. If a market maker buys shares from you, they temporarily hold them. If the price drops before they can sell or hedge, they lose money.

2) Adverse selection. If a better-informed trader buys right before good news (or sells right before bad news), the market maker is more likely to be on the losing side. Market makers therefore adjust prices, spreads, and sizes based on perceived risk.

This is the first place where liquidity begins to look conditional:

> Market makers provide liquidity when they believe they can manage the risk of providing it.

When uncertainty rises, they often:

- widen spreads,
- quote smaller sizes,
- reduce activity or step away entirely.

Those actions are rational for them individually. But system-wide, they can produce a sudden **liquidity air pocket**—the kind of environment where small shocks become large price moves.

High-Frequency Trading (HFT): Speed as a Business Model

High-frequency trading refers to firms that use automation and low-latency technology to trade extremely quickly, often holding positions for very short periods.

It is crucial to separate *how* HFT trades from *why* it trades.

Many HFT strategies are a form of modern market making:

- posting many small quotes,
- updating them rapidly as conditions change,
- earning tiny margins repeatedly,
- keeping inventory near neutral via hedging and rapid turnover.

Other HFT strategies focus on:

- **arbitrage** (capturing small price differences across venues),
- **latency advantage** (reacting faster to public signals),
- **order anticipation** (trying to infer and respond to large hidden demand).

To the casual observer, HFT can look like "noise." But from a market-function perspective, HFT is important because it often supplies a large fraction of displayed liquidity during normal times.

That comes with a trade-off:

- **Benefit:** Tight spreads and fast price alignment when conditions are stable.
- **Fragility:** Liquidity that can be rapidly withdrawn when models detect rising risk.

This is one of the central themes behind many flash-crash narratives: liquidity that is plentiful at 9:35 can be scarce at 9:36, not because investors changed their minds slowly, but because machines changed their quotes instantly.

Arbitrageurs: The Predators That Keep "One Price" Across Many Places

Modern markets are fragmented. The "same" stock can trade on multiple exchanges and off-exchange venues. In a healthy system, prices across venues remain tightly linked.

Arbitrageurs are the participants whose business is to enforce those links:

- If Stock X is $50.00 on one venue and $50.02 on another, an arbitrageur can buy at $50.00 and sell at $50.02 (in principle).
- Their actions push the cheap venue up and the expensive venue down, restoring alignment.

Arbitrage sounds like free money, but it is not frictionless:

- fees,
- latency (the price may change before you complete both sides),
- limited liquidity at the quoted prices,
- sudden volatility that turns a tiny spread into a loss.

In calm times, arbitrage is a stabilizer. In stressed times, arbitrage capacity can shrink, allowing temporary dislocations—"one stock, many prices"—that feel surreal to anyone expecting a single unified market.

Liquidity Takers vs. Liquidity Providers: A Role You Can Switch Without Noticing

A final lens ties these characters together: at any moment, a trader is either **taking** liquidity or **providing** it.

- If you use a market order ("buy now"), you are **taking** liquidity.
- If you post a limit order ("buy, but only at $X or better"), you are **providing** liquidity—you are offering to be the counterparty for someone else.

Retail can provide liquidity with limit orders. Institutions can provide liquidity when they patiently work orders. HFT firms can take liquidity when they detect an opportunity. Market makers can take liquidity to hedge. Roles switch continuously.

What matters in a crisis is not labels, but the balance:

When too many participants want immediacy at once, and too few are willing to warehouse risk, liquidity becomes scarce—and prices can jump.

Why This Cast Matters for Flash Crashes and Dark Pools

The ecosystem becomes unstable when several forces align:

- **whales** (institutions) needing to trade size under pressure,
- **cheetahs** (HFT / market makers) pulling back or repricing rapidly,
- **arbitrageurs** struggling to keep venues aligned,
- **retail** reacting to headlines and price moves, sometimes all in the same direction.

When the cast is clear, the plot of a liquidity event becomes easier to follow. You can ask the right diagnostic questions:

- Who needed to trade *immediately*?
- Who was supposed to provide liquidity, and did they step away?
- Did fragmentation create multiple prices or confusing signals?
- Did the fastest players amplify a move that began with a slow, large order?

1.3 Price is Not Value

By now we have two essential building blocks.

First, most trading happens in the **secondary market**: investors exchanging ownership claims with each other, with **liquidity** as the system's lifeblood.

Second, that trading is not performed by a single "market mind," but by an **ecosystem** of participants—from slow, diverse retail investors, to massive institutions that must move carefully, to fast intermediaries who specialize in providing immediacy.

With those pieces in place, we can tackle one of the most common (and most expensive) misunderstandings in finance:

The market price of a stock is not the same thing as the stock's value.

They are related, but they are not synonyms. Confusing them leads people to interpret every price move as a change in the underlying business—and to be shocked when prices behave in ways that seem irrational. To understand flash crashes, liquidity vacuums, and sudden dislocations, you must become comfortable with the idea that **prices can move violently even when value has barely changed**.

Two Words, Two Jobs

Let's define the terms in plain language.

Value: A Slow, Fundamental Concept

Value (or **intrinsic value**) is an estimate of what an asset is *worth* based on fundamentals.

For a company, fundamentals might include:

- expected future profits and cash flows,
- growth prospects and competitive position,
- balance sheet strength (debt levels, cash),
- risk (how uncertain those cash flows are),
- the broader economic environment (interest rates, demand).

You can think of intrinsic value as a "business reality" concept. It tends to move as information about the business changes—new products, new competition, regulatory shifts, recessions, breakthroughs, scandals. These things matter, but they usually do not change *every second.*

In other words: value is often **slow**. It can jump (an unexpected bankruptcy, a surprise acquisition), but most of the time it evolves gradually.

Price: A Fast, Mechanical Concept

Price is not "what something is worth." Price is simply:

the number that clears the market right now.

A trade occurs only when a buyer and a seller agree. The price is the compromise that allows the trade to happen at that moment, given:

- who urgently wants to buy or sell,
- how much size they want to trade,
- how much liquidity is available right now,
- what other venues are quoting,
- what intermediaries are willing to warehouse risk.

This is why price can be fast. It responds not only to fundamentals, but also to **order flow** and **liquidity conditions**. When the ecosystem shifts—when market makers widen spreads, when institutions execute large orders, when algorithms retreat—prices can change quickly even if the underlying business has not.

A Simple Thought Experiment: Same Company, Different Prices

Imagine a company that owns a stable business: it sells toothpaste. Nothing dramatic is happening. No new competitor. No scandal. No revolutionary product. If you were forced to estimate intrinsic value, your estimate might be roughly the same on Monday and Tuesday.

Now imagine two different market situations.

Situation 1: Calm and liquid. Many buyers and sellers are present. Market makers are quoting tight spreads. Institutions are trading gradually. In this environment, a small imbalance in buying or selling is absorbed easily. Price changes, but moderately.

Situation 2: Stressed and thin. A macro headline hits, volatility spikes, and intermediaries reduce their quoted size. A large fund needs to sell quickly. Suddenly, there are fewer bids available at nearby prices. The same "toothpaste business" is now trading in a different *micro-environment*. The clearing price can drop sharply as the market searches for buyers.

In the second situation, the company did not become a worse toothpaste company in five minutes. The trading system simply demanded a lower price to attract immediate buyers.

This is the first intuition behind liquidity-driven events: **price can be a referendum on market conditions, not merely a referendum on fundamentals.**

Why Returns Are About Price, Not Value

In investing, what you *earn* is measured using **returns**. A return is computed from *prices*, because prices are observable and executable. You cannot trade at "intrinsic value"; you trade at prices.

For a simple one-period return:

$$R_{t\to t+1} = \frac{P_{t+1} - P_t}{P_t}.$$

If a stock goes from \$100 to \$110, the return is:

$$R = \frac{110 - 100}{100} = 0.10 = 10\%.$$

Notice what is missing from the formula: value. Returns are agnostic to whether the price move was driven by:

- genuine new information about the business (a value change),
- changes in risk preferences ("risk-off" selling),

- liquidity conditions (spreads widening, depth vanishing),
- forced trading (margin calls, redemptions, rebalancing),
- mechanical feedback (stop orders triggering more selling).

This matters because many of the most dramatic returns—especially over short horizons—are dominated by the latter forces.

The Voting Machine vs. the Weighing Machine

A classic way to express the price–value distinction is to say that markets behave like:

- a **voting machine** in the short run, and
- a **weighing machine** in the long run.

The short run is a vote: it aggregates preferences, fears, urgency, and positioning. Votes can swing quickly. The long run is closer to weighing: over time, cash flows and economic reality tend to matter more.

This metaphor is not a promise. "Long run" is not a guaranteed deadline where sanity returns by Friday. But it is a useful compass: short-term price moves can be dominated by the market's *mechanics*, not just its *analysis*.

Financial Noise: The Gap Between Information and Motion

If value is the signal, price is the signal plus a lot of other stuff. That "other stuff" is what we will call **financial noise**.

Noise does not mean "random" in the sense of meaningless. It means price moves that are not primarily explained by changes in intrinsic value.

Noise can come from several sources:

1) Differing Time Horizons

A long-term investor might buy because they believe the business is undervalued over five years. A day trader might buy because they expect a momentum move over five minutes. A market maker might buy because they sold a millisecond earlier and need to rebalance inventory.

All three are "rational" within their horizon. But their coexistence means today's price can be pulled by forces that have little to do with long-term fundamentals.

2) Constraints and Forced Trading

Institutions often trade due to constraints, not conviction:

- a fund faces redemptions and must raise cash,
- a risk model forces de-leveraging when volatility rises,
- an index fund must rebalance,
- a margin call forces liquidation.

These trades are not statements about value. They are *statements about necessity*. In thin conditions, necessity can dominate the tape.

3) Market Structure Friction

Modern markets are fragmented and automated. Price formation is shaped by:

- the availability (or withdrawal) of liquidity across venues,
- the behavior of intermediaries managing inventory risk,
- the speed at which quotes update,
- routing and matching rules.

Noise increases when the plumbing matters more than the news.

4) Human Emotion and Narrative

Even in a world of algorithms, humans are still in the loop:

- fear makes investors demand a discount,
- greed makes investors pay up,

- narratives spread ("everyone is buying this"),
- regret and panic accelerate selling into falling prices.

Emotion is not merely psychology; it affects liquidity. When fear rises, fewer participants are willing to provide bids. That makes prices jumpier, which increases fear—a feedback loop we will revisit.

A Useful Mental Model: Price = Value + Liquidity Conditions + Pressure

One way to keep yourself grounded is to treat price as the result of multiple layers:

$$\text{Price} \approx \text{Value} + \text{Liquidity/structure effects} + \text{Order-flow pressure.}$$

This is not an equation you can plug numbers into. It is a diagnostic model.

When prices move, ask:

- Did fundamentals truly change (value)?
- Or did the ease of trading change (liquidity)?
- Or did someone need to trade fast (pressure)?

In a liquidity crisis, the second and third terms can dominate. That is how you can get extreme prices that look disconnected from any reasonable estimate of value.

Why This Matters for Flash Crashes

Flash crashes and sudden dislocations are, at their core, stories about the separation between price and value.

During a flash crash:

- value does not have time to meaningfully update,

- but price can "gap" because the market is searching for liquidity,
- and the fastest participants may reduce exposure simultaneously.

In that moment, the price is not a careful valuation. It is the output of a stressed auction.

This is why a flash crash can be terrifying: it feels like reality is breaking. But what is really happening is more specific:

The market is temporarily struggling to perform its secondary-market job—matching buyers and sellers smoothly.

In the next section, we will name and quantify the concept that determines whether this auction feels smooth or violent. We will define **liquidity** precisely—not as "a lot of trading," but as the ability to trade meaningful size without moving the price.

1.4 Defining Liquidity: The Water in the Pool

So far, we have built three ideas that fit together:

- Markets are mostly **secondary markets**: places where ownership is exchanged and risk is transferred.
- Those markets are an **ecosystem**: slow investors, large institutions, and fast intermediaries all interact.
- **Price is not value**: prices can move for reasons that have little to do with the underlying business.

Now we can define the concept that determines whether the secondary market behaves like a smooth highway or a narrow bridge in a storm:

Liquidity is the ability to trade meaningful size quickly without moving the price too much.

This definition is deliberately more practical than a dictionary definition like "ease of buying and selling." It contains the two parts that matter when markets suddenly go wrong:

- **Size**: how much can you trade?
- **Price impact**: how much does the act of trading change the price you get?

If you remember only one sentence from this section, make it this:

High trading volume does not guarantee high liquidity.

Volume tells you that trades happened. Liquidity tells you whether a trade *could* happen *now*, in size, at a reasonable cost.

The Theater Exit Analogy: Liquidity Is About the Bottleneck

Imagine a crowded theater.

- The number of people in the building is like **market interest** (lots of people own the asset).
- The number of people *moving around* is like **trading volume**.
- The width of the exits is like **liquidity**.

On a calm day, people can leave in an orderly way. But if something frightens the crowd, what matters is not how many people are inside—it is whether the exits can handle the flow *without panic turning into crushing pressure.*

Liquidity works the same way. In quiet markets, it *feels* abundant. In stressed markets, the exits can suddenly look very small.

The Order Book: Where Liquidity Actually Lives

Liquidity is not a vibe. In modern markets, it is embodied in a concrete object: the **limit order book**.

A **limit order** is an instruction like:

- "Buy 100 shares, but only if I can pay $50.00 or less,"
- "Sell 100 shares, but only if I can get $50.10 or more."

These orders sit in a queue waiting to be matched. The collection of resting buy and sell orders (at many prices) is the order book.

The book has two sides:

- **Bids**: buy orders (demand)
- **Asks** (or offers): sell orders (supply)

The **best bid** is the highest price someone is willing to pay right now. The **best ask** is the lowest price someone is willing to accept right now.

And between them sits the most important friction in everyday trading: the **spread**.

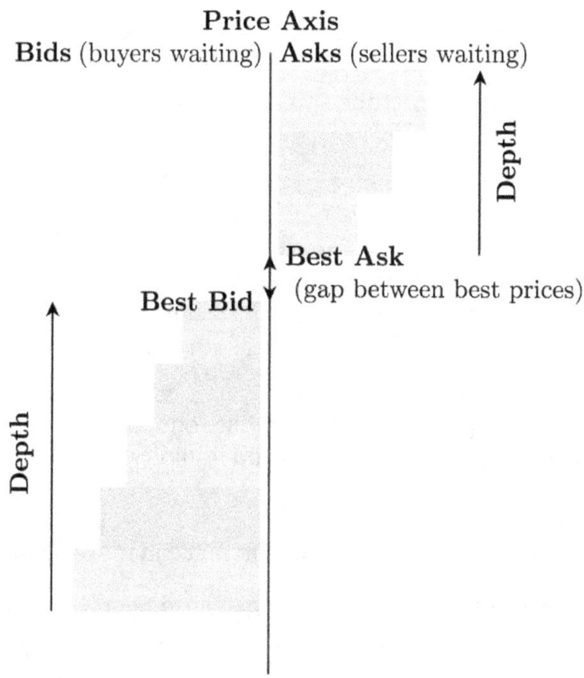

Mid-price lies between best bid and best ask

The diagram is intentionally abstract: no decimals, no queue priority rules, no exchange-specific quirks. But it contains the two building blocks that will reappear throughout the book: **spread** and **depth**.

Spread: The Cost of Immediacy

The **bid–ask spread** is the gap between what buyers are willing to pay and what sellers are willing to accept *right now*.

If:

$$\text{Best Bid} = \$50.00, \qquad \text{Best Ask} = \$50.05,$$

then the spread is:

$$\text{Spread} = \$50.05 - \$50.00 = \$0.05.$$

A simple way to interpret the spread is as a "toll" you pay to trade immediately:

- If you buy immediately, you typically pay the ask.
- If you sell immediately, you typically hit the bid.

So if you buy at $50.05 and then instantly sell at $50.00, you lose $0.05 per share (ignoring fees). That loss is not a mystery; it is the market charging for immediacy.

Why does the spread exist? Because someone has to take the other side and bear risk. Market makers and liquidity providers are exposed to:

- **inventory risk** (holding assets that can move against them),
- **adverse selection** (trading against someone who knows more),
- **volatility risk** (prices moving quickly while quotes are posted).

When risk rises, spreads tend to widen. That is the market saying: "Immediacy is more dangerous right now, so it costs more."

Depth: How Much You Can Trade Without "Falling Through" the Price

If the spread is about *cost per share*, **depth** is about *quantity available.*

Depth answers questions like:

- "If I want to sell a lot, how many shares are waiting to buy near the current price?"
- "If I want to buy a lot, how many shares are waiting to sell near the current price?"

A deep market has a thick stack of orders near the current price. A shallow market has a thin stack.

Depth matters because large orders do not execute at a single price. They "walk the book."

Walking the Book (A Non-Technical Picture)

Imagine you want to sell 10,000 shares immediately. The best bid might represent only 500 shares. After you sell those 500, you must sell the next shares to the next best bid, and then the next, and so on.

If depth is strong, those levels are close together and plentiful. The average price you receive stays near the current price.

If depth is weak, the book might have "holes"—not much demand at nearby prices. Your order can push the price down rapidly simply because there is not enough standing buying interest.

This is why liquidity is not "lots of trading." A market can have huge trading volume but still be fragile at a particular moment if the book is thin *right now*.

Liquidity Is Not Volume: Three Quick Contrasts

To make the distinction concrete, consider three scenarios.

Scenario A: High Volume, High Liquidity

A major stock trades actively all day. The book is deep, spreads are tight, and large orders can be executed with little price impact. This is the idealized "liquid" picture.

Scenario B: High Volume, Low Liquidity

A stock is in the news. Trading volume surges. But quotes are nervous: spreads widen and displayed size shrinks. Many trades occur, yet each additional trade moves the price more than usual. Volume is high, but liquidity is poor.

This often happens during stress: lots of people want to trade, but few want to provide resting orders.

Scenario C: Low Volume, Adequate Liquidity

A quiet period: not many trades. But the order book is stable and reasonably deep. If you want to trade a moderate amount, you can do so without much impact. Volume is low, but liquidity is not necessarily terrible.

Resilience: Liquidity Over Time, Not Just At One Snapshot

Spreads and depth describe the book *at a moment*. But markets are dynamic. Orders appear, disappear, and move. A crucial (often overlooked) dimension is **resilience**:

> **Resilience is how quickly liquidity returns after a shock.**

In a resilient market:

- a burst of selling may push the price down,
- but new bids arrive quickly,
- spreads tighten again,
- depth rebuilds.

In a non-resilient market:

- selling pushes the price down,
- liquidity providers retreat,
- spreads widen further,
- depth fails to replenish,

- and price can cascade as the auction searches for buyers.

Resilience is where market structure and participant behavior become critical. When fast intermediaries pull quotes and slow institutions pause execution, the book can stay thin longer than people expect.

The Practical Definition (What You Should Picture)

If you want a practical mental image of liquidity, do not picture "a lot of trades." Picture this:

> A liquid market is one where the order book is **deep near the current price** and the spread is **tight**, *and* where both recover quickly after being hit.

That is the water in the pool. In normal times, it supports swimmers. In stressed times, it can drain—sometimes quickly enough that the market feels like it has dropped out from under your feet.

Once you understand liquidity as depth, spread, and resilience, the next question becomes unavoidable:

> What happens to prices when that liquidity disappears?

That is where volatility, gaps, and the illusion of smoothness enter the story.

1.5 Volatility, Jumps, and the Illusion of Smoothness

In the previous section, we defined liquidity in operational terms: **depth**, **spread**, and **resilience**. Liquidity is not "a lot of trading." Liquidity is the market's ability to absorb trades *right now* without prices lurching.

That definition leads to an uncomfortable conclusion:

Prices are not guaranteed to move smoothly.
They move smoothly only when liquidity is continuously available.

Most of the time, charts make markets look like a flowing line. But that smoothness is partly a visual illusion. Under the surface, markets are discrete auctions that can go from "many nearby bids and offers" to "almost none" in moments. When that happens, prices can *jump*.

This section explains why.

Volatility Is Not Just "Nervousness"

In casual conversation, people use *volatile* to mean "wild" or "emotional." In market mechanics, volatility has a precise meaning:

Volatility is the degree to which prices vary over time.

In practice, we often measure volatility using returns. If P_t is the price at time t, the return from $t-1$ to t can be written as:

$$R_t = \frac{P_t - P_{t-1}}{P_{t-1}}.$$

A highly volatile asset is one whose returns swing widely—big ups and downs. A low-volatility asset is one whose returns are small and steady.

But measuring volatility is easier than understanding its *cause*. To understand flash crashes and liquidity crises, we must connect volatility to the order book.

The Continuous-Motion Myth (and Why It Persists)

If you watch a price ticker, it feels continuous: \$100.01, \$100.02, \$100.00, \$99.98. Even daily charts look like a smooth curve.

That perception persists for two reasons:

- **Lots of trades create lots of dots.** With frequent trading, the gaps between trades are tiny, so the line looks smooth.

- **Charts connect points with ink.** Your charting software draws a line between two prints even if there were no trades in between.

But the market itself does not promise a continuous path. It promises only this:

At any moment, you can trade at the prices *currently available* in the order book.

If there are no orders at intermediate prices, the market can move from $100 to $90 without ever trading at $95. There is nothing mystical about it. It is simply a property of a thin book.

Gaps: When the Market "Teleports"

A **gap** is an empty region of prices where no trades occur. Gaps can happen on a daily chart (overnight news), but the same idea applies inside the day and even inside a second.

Think back to the order book.

- In a deep book, there are many bids at many nearby prices.
- In a thin book, bids might exist only at a few scattered prices.

If a wave of selling arrives, the market will execute against the best bid, then the next, then the next. If the book is thin, "the next" might be far away. The price doesn't glide; it *steps*.

A Concrete Micro-Example (No Advanced Math Needed)

Suppose the best bids (buyers) look roughly like this:

Bid Price	Shares Willing to Buy (Depth)	Cumulative
$100.00	200 shares	200
$99.90	200 shares	400
$99.50	200 shares	600
$98.00	200 shares	800
$95.00	200 shares	1000

Now imagine a sell order for 1,000 shares that must execute immediately (a liquidity-taking order). That order will *consume* each bid level until it fills. The last shares will trade at $95.00.

Notice what happened:

- The market did not trade at every price between $100 and $95.
- It jumped across missing levels because there were no resting orders there.
- The seller didn't "decide" $95 was fair value; $95 was where the next available buyers were waiting.

That is a gap in action: price moves because the book is being eaten, and the spacing between liquidity levels determines how violent the move looks.

The Inverse Relationship: Low Liquidity, High Volatility

Now we can state the key relationship in plain language:

When liquidity is low, small imbalances in order flow can cause large price moves.
Low depth and wide spreads make prices jumpier, which shows up as higher volatility.

This is not a philosophical claim. It is mechanical.

Why Depth Matters

Depth is the book's shock absorber.

- **High depth** means many shares are available near the current price. Selling pressure is absorbed across many orders with small price concessions.
- **Low depth** means the next available buyers are far away. The market must move the price substantially to find enough demand.

In deep conditions, a 10,000-share sell order might move price by a few cents. In shallow conditions, the same order can move price by dollars.

Why Spread Matters

Spread is the market's friction.

- **Tight spreads** mean the auction is competitive: buyers and sellers are close to agreement, and small trades do not cause large quote changes.
- **Wide spreads** mean agreement is hard: liquidity providers demand compensation for risk, and the price you get for immediacy is worse.

Wide spreads can also worsen jumps because they are often accompanied by reduced displayed size. When spreads widen, you are frequently seeing a market that is already pulling back.

Why Resilience Matters

Resilience is the market's ability to heal.

Even if depth is temporarily consumed, a resilient market replenishes: new bids appear, spreads tighten, and the price path becomes smoother again.

In a non-resilient market, liquidity does not refill quickly. The book stays thin. That makes every new order more impactful. Volatility becomes self-reinforcing.

The "Jumpy" Market Is the Normal Market Under Stress

It is tempting to think of jumps as rare glitches. But jumps are a natural consequence of the market's design:

- Orders are discrete.
- Liquidity is finite.
- Liquidity providers are allowed to cancel or reprice.
- Participants have different speeds and different constraints.

When conditions are calm, these features fade into the background and the market looks continuous.

When conditions are stressed, those features become visible. The market looks like a staircase.

How Jumps Create Feedback Loops

Once prices begin to jump, they can trigger further instability. Several common feedback mechanisms are especially relevant for flash crashes:

Stop Orders and Forced Execution

Many traders use stop-loss orders designed to sell if price falls below a level. Stops are often implemented as market orders once triggered, meaning they *take liquidity*. In a thin book, this can accelerate downward moves: a drop triggers stops, stops trigger selling, selling consumes more depth, which causes a larger drop.

Risk Limits and De-Leveraging

As volatility rises, risk models can force firms to reduce positions. That reduction often happens via liquidity-taking trades. The more volatile the market becomes, the more forced selling can occur, further increasing volatility.

Liquidity Provider Retreat

Market makers and fast intermediaries manage adverse selection and inventory risk. When prices start moving abruptly, they may widen spreads or reduce quoted size. Individually rational behavior can collectively reduce liquidity, which makes prices even jumpier.

These loops are why sudden events often feel nonlinear: the first push is small, but the response grows rapidly.

A Practical Rule of Thumb: Smoothness Is Borrowed From Liquidity

If you want an intuitive, durable takeaway:

A smooth price path is not guaranteed; it is "borrowed" from available liquidity.

When the order book is full and resilient, the market has the resources to produce smoothness. When the book empties or stops replenishing, smoothness disappears, and volatility rises. Prices do not "choose" to become erratic; they *are forced* to search for counterparties.

Why This Sets Up Flash Crashes and Market Fragmentation

A flash crash is, in many ways, what happens when the market experiences a sudden shortage of the very thing that normally creates smoothness: **nearby liquidity**.

In the chapters ahead, we will examine how this shortage can be amplified by modern structure:

- liquidity split across many venues (fragmentation),
- hidden liquidity that may not be visible until it trades (dark pools),
- speed advantages that cause simultaneous quote updates and cancellations,
- cascades driven by automated execution and risk controls.

For now, keep the chain of logic tight:

- Prices are set by the auction in the order book.
- Liquidity (depth, spread, resilience) determines how smoothly that auction clears.
- When liquidity is low, the market clears through jumps and gaps.
- Jumps and gaps manifest as higher volatility—and can ignite feedback loops.

That is the bridge from "how markets work" to "how markets break."

Chapter 2

Under the Hood: The Mechanics of a Trade

When you tap 'Buy' on a trading app, it feels instantaneous, but behind that button lies a complex, high-speed digital arena. We often imagine the stock market as a single price ticker moving up and down, but it is actually a massive, competitive queue where milliseconds dictate winners and losers. This chapter lifts the lid on the exchange's 'black box' to reveal the machinery that turns your decision into a trade, defining the rules of engagement that underpin every flash crash and liquidity crisis we will explore later.

2.1 The Limit Order Book

To understand how a flash crash can happen, or why prices can suddenly "gap" when everyone tries to exit at once, we first need to understand the everyday machine that produces prices in the first place. That machine is the **Limit Order Book (LOB)**.

Most people talk about *the* price of a stock as if it were a single, precise fact—like the temperature outside. But in real markets, the "price" you see on a screen is better understood as a **negotiated truce** between two crowds:

- **Buyers** stating what they are willing to pay.
- **Sellers** stating what they demand to sell.

The limit order book is the continuously updated list of those intentions.

Two Sides of One Market: Bid and Ask

At any moment, the book has two sides:

- **Bid:** The **highest price** that someone is currently willing to pay to buy. Think: *"I'll buy it, but only up to this price."*
- **Ask (or Offer):** The **lowest price** that someone is currently willing to accept to sell. Think: *"I'll sell it, but not for less than this price."*

The market's most important "headline numbers" come from these two values:

- The **best bid**: the top buy price currently available.
- The **best ask**: the top sell price currently available.

Here is the key point: **these two numbers are usually different**. That difference is not a bug; it is the normal state of a functioning market.

The spread (the gap in the middle).

The distance between the best bid and the best ask is called the **bid–ask spread**, or simply **the spread**:

$$\text{Spread} = \text{Best Ask} - \text{Best Bid}$$

You can think of the spread as the market's *friction* or *toll* for trading immediately. When markets are calm and liquid, the spread tends to be small. When markets are stressed, the spread tends to widen—sometimes dramatically.

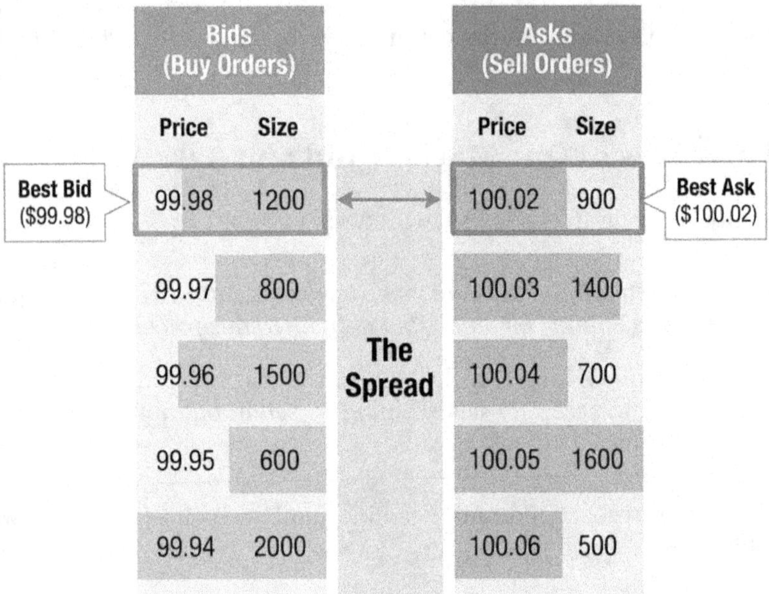

Orders closer to the middle are more likely to trade.

Why "Price" Is Not a Single Number

Suppose you look at a quote and see something like:

99.98 bid / 100.02 ask

What is the stock "worth" right now?

In the strict, mechanical sense, the market is telling you two different truths at the same time:

- If you insist on **selling immediately**, you can likely sell at about \$99.98 (you hit the best bid).
- If you insist on **buying immediately**, you can likely buy at about \$100.02 (you lift the best ask).

So the "price" depends on *which side you are on* and *how urgently you want to trade*. The spread is the price of that urgency.

The midpoint is not a tradable promise.

People often compute the **midprice**:

$$\text{Mid} = \frac{\text{Best Bid} + \text{Best Ask}}{2}$$

This midpoint is a useful *reference* (many charts and models use it), but it is not automatically a price you can trade at. The book does not offer you the midpoint unless someone actually posts an order there and another party agrees.

The Book as a Ladder of Choices

A limit order book is not just one bid and one ask. It is a **stack** (a ladder) of prices on each side.

On the **bid side**, you might see:

- someone willing to buy at \$99.98,
- someone else willing to buy at \$99.97,
- then \$99.96, and so on.

On the **ask side**, you might see:

- someone willing to sell at \$100.02,
- then \$100.03,
- then \$100.04, and so on.

Each step has a **size** (how many shares are offered at that price). This is why traders talk about **depth**: the book is deeper when there are many shares available across many price levels, and it is shallow when only a small amount is available near the current bid and ask.

Market Depth: Liquidity You Can See (and Liquidity You Can't)

The simplest way to picture liquidity is: **how much can you trade without moving the price much?**

In a deep book:

- the spread is usually tight, and
- there is meaningful size sitting at many nearby levels.

A moderately sized market order can trade without "walking" far up the ask ladder (if buying) or down the bid ladder (if selling).

In a thin book:

- the spread may be wider, and/or
- the visible size near the best prices is small.

Now even a normal-sized order can chew through the nearby levels and force the trade to happen at worse and worse prices. This is the mechanical seed of sudden air pockets and sharp, discontinuous price moves.

A preview of where crises begin.

Liquidity crises rarely start with a mysterious force. They start with something very concrete: **the book is not as deep as people assumed**. When stress rises, some participants cancel orders, others step back, and the gap between bid and ask can widen quickly. Once that happens, every urgent trade effectively becomes more "expensive," which can trigger even more urgency. The limit order book is where that feedback loop becomes visible.

A Mental Model: The Book Is a Waiting Room, Not a Forecast

It is tempting to read the book as a prediction: "There are lots of bids, so the price will go up," or "There are many asks, so the price will fall." Sometimes those intuitions work, often they fail.

The limit order book is a waiting room of conditional promises. Each order says, "I will trade *if* the price comes to me."

Those promises can be cancelled, modified, or replaced in milliseconds. The book is real, but it is also dynamic. That dynamism is why markets can look stable for long stretches and then, under stress, re-price violently in a short time.

The One-Sentence Definition You Should Keep

If you remember only one sentence from this section, make it this:

The limit order book is the live list of buy and sell intentions, and the "price" is the gap between the best buyer (bid) and the best seller (ask).

That gap—the spread—is small when liquidity is plentiful and confidence is high, and it can explode when liquidity evaporates. In later sections, we will build directly on this structure to explain how different order types interact with the book, why speed matters, and how ordinary trading mechanics can turn into extraordinary breakdowns.

2.2 Aggressive vs. Passive Orders

In the previous section, we built the central mental model: the market is not a single price, but a *two-sided book*—bids on one side, asks on the other, separated by the spread. Now we can ask a practical question:

> When you want to trade, do you *wait* for the market to come to you, or do you *cross the spread* and trade right now?

Almost every order you place is, at its core, a choice between two styles of behavior:

- **Passive (Liquidity Providing):** place an order *in* the book and wait.
- **Aggressive (Liquidity Taking):** place an order that *immediately* matches with what is already in the book.

These aren't moral categories—they are mechanical categories. They describe how your order interacts with the limit order book.

The Two Roles: Makers and Takers

Markets often describe participants as **makers** and **takers**:

- **Maker:** A trader who **adds** an order to the book (typically a limit order) and therefore **provides liquidity**. They are "making" a market by offering to buy or sell at a stated price.
- **Taker:** A trader who **removes** an order from the book (typically via a market order, or a marketable limit order) and therefore **consumes liquidity**. They are "taking" what is available right now.

This maker/taker language is widely used because it points directly to what matters in calm markets *and* in crises: **liquidity**. In stressed moments, the number of willing makers often shrinks, while the number of urgent takers rises. That imbalance is one of the simplest mechanical explanations for spread explosions and sudden price jumps.

Passive Orders: "I Will Trade, But Only at My Price"

A **limit order** says:

> Buy (or sell) *up to* (or *down to*) a specific price, but do not give me a worse one.

Examples:

- **Buy limit at $100.00:** "Buy, but do not pay more than $100.00."
- **Sell limit at $100.50:** "Sell, but do not accept less than $100.50."

If your limit price is not immediately compatible with the other side of the book, your order **rests** in the book. Resting is the signature of passivity: you are willing to trade, but you require the market to come to your price.

What passive orders give you. Passive orders give you:

- **Price control.** You set the worst price you will accept.
- **Potentially better execution.** If you buy at the bid or sell at the ask, you are not paying the spread in the same way a market order does.

What passive orders risk. Passive orders also risk:

- **Non-execution.** You may simply not trade.
- **Adverse selection.** This is the subtle one: sometimes the moment you get filled is *exactly* when informed or faster traders want to trade against you. In plain English: you may get filled right before the price moves against you.

That last point matters later when we discuss fast markets and fragmentation. For now, keep the intuition: **passive orders are not "free lunch."** They are a trade: you exchange immediacy for price control.

Aggressive Orders: "I Need It Done Now"

An **aggressive** order is one that executes immediately against the best available prices already sitting in the book.

The most direct example is the **market order**:

> Buy (or sell) *right now*, at the best prices available, whatever they are.

If you send a market buy order, you will match with the current best ask (and if your order is large, with the next ask, and the next, "walking the book"). If you send a market sell order, you hit the current best bid (and then lower bids if needed).

What aggressive orders give you. Aggressive orders give you:

- **Execution certainty (usually).** In normal conditions, if the stock is trading, your order will fill quickly.
- **Speed.** You don't wait in line; you step to the front by accepting what is offered.

What aggressive orders cost you. Aggressive orders cost you:

- **The spread.** If you buy at the ask (instead of bidding) or sell at the bid (instead of offering), you pay the gap.
- **Price uncertainty.** You do not control the exact price, especially when the book is thin or moving quickly.

This is the central tradeoff of trading mechanics:

Passive (Limit)	Aggressive (Market)
More price control	More execution speed
May not fill	Usually fills quickly
Can earn the spread (in a sense)	Pays the spread (in a sense)
Can be "picked off" when conditions change	Can suffer slippage when depth is thin

The Book Is a Queue: Aggression Is "Crossing the Spread"

Using the book picture from the prior section:

- Passive buyers typically post at or below the current bid.
- Passive sellers typically post at or above the current ask.

Aggressive trading happens when you are willing to **cross the spread**:

- To buy immediately, you accept the ask.
- To sell immediately, you accept the bid.

This is why spreads matter so much. In a calm, liquid stock with a one-cent spread, "crossing the spread" is a small concession. In a stressed market where spreads widen sharply, crossing the spread becomes expensive, and the very act of seeking immediacy can magnify price moves.

A Crucial Nuance: A Limit Order Can Be Aggressive

Beginners often equate:

$$\text{Limit} = \text{Passive}, \qquad \text{Market} = \text{Aggressive}.$$

That's a good first approximation, but it is not always true.

A **marketable limit order** is a limit order priced so that it executes immediately. For example:

- If the current best ask is $100.02 and you submit a **buy limit** at $100.05, your order is willing to pay at least $100.02. It will typically execute immediately (like a market order), *but* with a cap: you won't pay above $100.05.
- If the current best bid is $99.98 and you submit a **sell limit** at $99.95, you are willing to accept at most $99.98 (and possibly lower). It will typically execute immediately, with a floor at $99.95.

Mechanically, these are **aggressive** because they consume displayed liquidity right away. The difference is that they add a safety rail: a maximum (for buys) or minimum (for sells).

Why This Distinction Matters in Fast, Fragile Markets

The maker/taker split sounds like jargon until you see what happens during stress.

In a panic, many participants who normally provide liquidity become cautious:

- They cancel resting limit orders.
- They widen their quotes (posting farther from the middle).
- They reduce size (showing less depth).

At the same time, urgency rises:

- more traders become takers (they demand immediate execution), and
- their orders eat through the remaining depth.

This is the mechanical skeleton of a liquidity event: **fewer makers, more takers, wider spreads, thinner depth, more slippage**. Later chapters will add important complications (fragmented venues, hidden liquidity, algorithmic feedback loops), but the starting point is simple and concrete: *how orders touch the book.*

A Practical Rule of Thumb (Not a Guarantee)

For a casual investor, the cleanest way to remember the logic is:

- If your priority is **price**, you lean passive (limit).
- If your priority is **immediacy**, you lean aggressive (market or marketable limit).

Neither is "right" in all cases. The market forces you to choose which risk you prefer:

- the risk of **not trading** (passive), or
- the risk of **trading at a worse price than you expected** (aggressive).

In the next section, we will put a dollar sign on that choice by breaking trading costs into what you can see (commissions) and what you often can't see until after the fact (slippage and market impact).

2.3 The Cost of Trading

In the last two sections, we built the mechanical picture of trading:

- The market is organized as a **limit order book** with bids, asks, a spread, and varying depth.
- Every trade is a choice between **passive** (waiting in the book) and **aggressive** (crossing the spread to execute now).

Now we put numbers on those mechanics. Many new investors start with a simple belief: *"Trading is basically free now."* After all, many brokers advertise zero commissions.

But even when commissions are zero, trading is **not** free. The real costs often hide inside the execution process itself. They show up as the difference between the price you *thought* you would get and the price you *actually* get.

This section breaks trading costs into two categories:

1. **Explicit costs:** visible fees you can point to on a statement.
2. **Implicit costs:** costs embedded in prices and execution (spread, slippage, and market impact).

Understanding these costs is not just practical advice—it is foundational for understanding flash crashes and liquidity crises. When markets become stressed, implicit costs can explode even if explicit costs remain unchanged.

Explicit Costs: The Easy-to-See Part

Commissions and fees

Commissions are the classic explicit cost: the broker charges you a stated amount per trade (or per share). Today, many retail platforms charge $0 commissions for stock trades, but that does not mean there are no costs at all. There can still be:

- **Exchange and regulatory fees** (often tiny, sometimes passed through),
- **options contract fees**,
- **margin interest** if you borrow to trade,
- and other account-level charges.

For our purposes, the key point is simple: explicit costs are *line items*. If you want to know whether you paid them, you can usually find them written down.

Why explicit costs are not the main story in fast markets

In normal conditions, explicit costs are often small relative to the more important (and less obvious) costs created by the limit order book. In stressed conditions, explicit costs might be unchanged while implicit costs become enormous. That is why the rest of this section focuses on the hidden side.

Implicit Costs: The Costs You Pay Through the Market

Implicit costs are not a fee charged by your broker. They are the cost of interacting with a two-sided, finite-depth order book.

There are three core implicit costs to understand:

1. **The spread** (paying for immediacy),
2. **slippage** (getting a worse price than expected),
3. **market impact** (moving the price against yourself by being too large or too urgent).

These concepts are closely related, but not identical.

The Spread: The Toll for Immediacy

Recall the basic quote:

$$99.98 \text{ bid} \quad / \quad 100.02 \text{ ask}$$

If you submit a market *buy* order, you likely pay about \$100.02. If you submit a market *sell* order, you likely receive about \$99.98.

Even if the "true value" of the stock is somewhere in between, your execution is pulled to one side because you demanded immediacy. In that sense, crossing the spread is like stepping onto an express lane: you go first, but you pay a toll.

A simple way to quantify spread cost. A common benchmark is the midprice:

$$Mid = \frac{Bid + Ask}{2}$$

If you buy at the ask, your immediate cost versus mid is roughly:

$$Cost \approx Ask - Mid = \frac{Spread}{2}$$

If you sell at the bid, the cost versus mid is also about half the spread.

This is why spreads matter so much: they are a direct, mechanical cost of aggressive trading.

Slippage: "I Tried to Pay X, But Paid More"

Slippage is the gap between an expected price and the realized price. It is often described casually as "bad fills," but the deeper idea is: the book moved, or the available liquidity was thinner than you assumed, *during the time your order was trying to execute.*

Slippage can happen for multiple reasons:

- **The quote changes before you execute.** In fast markets, prices update many times per second.
- **Your order is larger than the best price level.** You consume the top of the book and continue into worse levels (you *walk the book*).

- **Other traders react to your order.** Your activity reveals urgency; the book can thin out as others cancel or reprice.

Small order vs. large order intuition. If you buy 10 shares in a deep, liquid stock, you might fill entirely at the best ask. Slippage may be near zero. If you buy 500,000 shares, you cannot reasonably expect all of them to be sitting at the best ask. You will likely fill across many price levels, producing a higher average price than you initially saw on the screen.

This leads to a critical idea:

> **The displayed best price is not a promise for large size. It is a price for a small quantity.**

Market Impact: When Your Trade Becomes the News

Market impact is slippage with a cause: *your own order* pushes the market price in an unfavorable direction.

How buying pushes price up against you

Imagine a simplified book on the ask side:

- 5,000 shares offered at $100.02
- 8,000 shares offered at $100.03
- 10,000 shares offered at $100.05

If you submit a market buy for 20,000 shares, you will:

1. take the 5,000 at $100.02,
2. then take the 8,000 at $100.03 (total 13,000),
3. and then take 7,000 more at $100.05 (total 20,000).

Your **average price paid** is above \$100.02, even though that was the "headline" ask when you started. The book did not deceive you; it simply did not have infinite depth at that price.

Why impact is the precursor to liquidity crises

Market impact is not just a nuisance; it is the key to understanding why panic can feed on itself. In a stressed market:

- depth shrinks,
- spreads widen,
- and impact per share rises.

That means every aggressive trade moves the price more, which creates worse prices, which can trigger more forced trading (margin calls, stop orders, risk limits), which creates even more aggressive trading. The cost mechanism becomes the crisis mechanism.

A Useful Accounting Framework: Implementation Shortfall

Professionals often summarize implicit costs with a concept called **implementation shortfall**: the difference between the price you wanted (often measured at the decision time) and the price you actually achieved, including opportunity costs from not getting filled.

For a buy order, a simplified version is:

$$\text{Implementation Shortfall} \approx (\text{Average Fill Price} - \text{Reference Price}) \times \text{Shares}$$

For a sell order, the sign flips accordingly.

You do not need to compute this to be a thoughtful trader, but the framework reinforces the central point: **execution is part of the trade**. The decision "buy" or "sell" is only half the story; the path you take through the order book determines your true outcome.

Putting It Together: A Practical Taxonomy of Trading Costs

To keep the mental model clean, separate costs as follows:

Cost Type	What It Means in Plain English
Explicit costs (commissions/fees)	The broker/exchange charges you a stated fee. You can see it.
Spread cost	The built-in toll for trading immediately: buying at the ask or selling at the bid.
Slippage	You get a worse price than expected due to movement or limited depth during execution.
Market impact	The part of slippage caused by *your own* size/urgency pushing the price against you.

The Core Lesson for the Rest of This Book

When markets are healthy, implicit costs are often small enough that they feel invisible. When markets become fragile, implicit costs become the headline.

That is why liquidity crises are so psychologically shocking. People do not just see prices fall; they discover that the *cost to trade* has changed. The spread widens, the book thins, and executing becomes expensive exactly when everyone most urgently wants to execute.

In the next section, we will look inside the matching engine and answer a question that matters far more than most casual investors realize: when multiple orders want the same price, *who gets filled first*? The answer—and the incentives it creates—is one reason modern markets can become a speed contest under stress.

2.4 Winning the Race: Matching Rules

So far, we have treated the market like a set of visible shelves: bids on one side, asks on the other, and a spread in the middle. We then added behavior: some traders **provide** liquidity with passive orders, others **consume** liquidity with aggressive orders. And we put a price tag on it: spreads, slippage, and market impact.

Now we zoom in on the part most people never think about until something breaks.

> If many people want to trade at the same price, who goes first?

This is not a philosophical question. It is a rule coded into the exchange's **matching engine**. The rule determines who gets filled, who waits, and who misses. And because money depends on milliseconds (and sometimes microseconds), the rule creates powerful incentives that shape modern market structure—including the technology arms race that shows up in flash-crash stories.

The Matching Engine: The Market's Referee

An exchange is not just a place where people meet; it is a computer system that:

1. receives orders,
2. stores them in the limit order book,
3. and matches compatible buys and sells according to a strict priority logic.

Think of the matching engine as the *referee* of the market. When a buy order and a sell order can trade, the engine decides:

- **whether** they trade (are the prices compatible?),
- **at what price** they trade (usually the resting order's price in continuous trading),
- **and crucially: which resting order gets filled first** when many are waiting at the same price.

The last bullet is where "winning the race" enters the story.

Price-Time Priority (FIFO): The Default Rule

Most continuous limit order books follow a principle often summarized as:

> **Price is king; time is the tie-breaker.**

More formally, this is **price-time priority**, also called **FIFO** (first-in, first-out).

Step 1: Price priority

First, the matching engine chooses the **best price**. For buys, the best price is the *highest* bid. For sells, the best price is the *lowest* ask.

So if there are bids at $100.00 and $99.99, a sell order that arrives will match with the $100.00 bid first. Even if the $99.99 bid has been waiting longer, it is at an inferior price.

This is why traders improve their prices by a penny: stepping ahead on price often moves you to the front of the line.

Step 2: Time priority (the queue)

If multiple orders are waiting at the *same* price, the exchange must pick an order. Most of the time, it picks the oldest one: the one that arrived first.

That means that within a single price level, the book is a **queue**. And like any queue, your position depends on **when you got in line**.

A concrete example.

Suppose the best bid is $100.00 and three traders are waiting to buy at $100.00:

- Trader A bid $100.00 at 09:30:00.100
- Trader B bid $100.00 at 09:30:00.250

- Trader C bid $100.00 at 09:30:00.900

If a sell order comes in for 200 shares and Trader A is waiting for 200 shares, Trader A gets filled first. If the sell order is for 300 shares and Trader A is only bidding for 200 shares, then:

- Trader A gets 200 shares, and the remaining 100 shares go next to Trader B, and so on.

This seems almost too obvious to mention—until you realize what it implies in a high-speed market: **time priority turns small speed advantages into persistent queue advantages.**

The Queue Intuition: A Grocery Store Checkout

The easiest way to remember price-time priority is to picture a grocery store checkout:

- **Price priority** is like choosing which checkout lane you're allowed to use.
- **Time priority** is like standing in line once you're in that lane.

A trader posting a limit order at the best bid is like joining the shortest, fastest-moving lane in the store—but once you join, you still have to wait your turn.

Why the queue matters even if you are "at the best price."

Many casual investors assume that being at the best bid (or best ask) guarantees a quick fill. Not necessarily. If you are *behind* a lot of size at that price, you may wait a long time and never get filled if the market moves away.

In other words, there is a difference between:

- the **best price**, and

- the **best position** at that price.

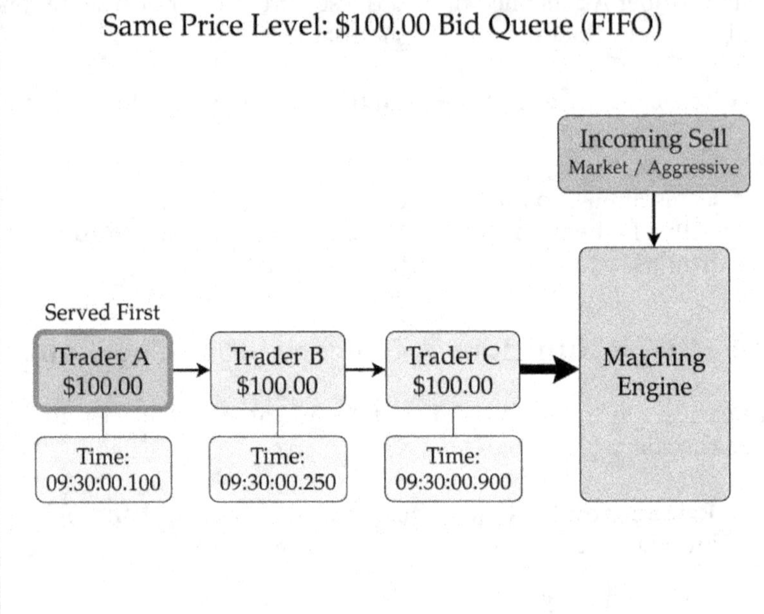

All three bid the same price. FIFO means the earliest timestamp gets priority.

Why Speed Matters: Queue Position Is Economic Value

Price-time priority makes markets feel fair in a commonsense way:

- better prices go first, and
- for equal prices, earlier orders go first.

But it also creates a very specific incentive:

If you can be slightly faster to post, cancel, or replace orders, you can systematically improve your queue position.

That queue position can translate into real money in several ways.

1) Getting filled (or not) during fast moves

During a quick move, the best bid or best ask may be hit by a wave of aggressive orders. If you are near the *front* of the queue at the best price, you may get filled before the market moves away. If you are near the *back*, you may get little or nothing.

This matters to passive traders in particular. You can be correct about the price you want, but wrong about whether you will actually get it.

2) The arms race of cancellation and replacement

In modern electronic markets, many traders constantly adjust orders:

- cancel if conditions change,
- re-post at a slightly different price,
- or rejoin the queue to avoid being "picked off."

But there is a hidden consequence: **when you cancel and re-enter at the same price, you usually lose your time priority.** You go to the back of the line.

So participants face a tension:

- Stay posted and keep queue position (but risk adverse selection), or
- cancel to reduce risk (but give up your place in line).

If you are fast enough, you can try to do both: stay posted when it is safe, pull away when it is dangerous, and re-enter quickly enough to regain priority on the next opportunities. That is one reason speed became so valuable.

3) Why microstructure matters in liquidity events

In a liquidity crisis, the book can thin out and update rapidly. When that happens:

- the value of being first in line rises (because fills become scarce),
- the value of being able to cancel quickly rises (because being passive becomes riskier),
- and competition for queue position intensifies.

This doesn't mean "speed causes crashes" by itself. But it does mean the *rules of matching* shape behavior under stress. When the environment becomes fragile, incentives that are harmless on a normal day can become destabilizing.

A Simple Summary You Can Carry Forward

At the level of mechanics, most matching engines answer the "who goes first?" question with a clean hierarchy:

1. **Best price wins.**
2. **At the same price, earliest time wins (FIFO).**

Everything that follows in modern market structure—competition to be first, to cancel quickly, to manage queue position across fragmented venues—rests on this basic logic.

2.5 Auctions vs. Continuous Trading

Up to this point, we have described a market that feels like a *stream*:

- orders arrive one by one,
- the matching engine applies price-time priority,

- and trades happen continuously whenever a buyer and seller overlap.

That is **continuous trading**, and it is how most of the day works.

But markets are not *only* streams. At two of the most important moments of the trading day—the **open** and the **close**—many major exchanges switch to a different mechanism: an **auction**.

This change is not cosmetic. It is a deliberate design choice that helps markets discover a fair price when information is arriving all at once and the order book is most fragile.

Two Different Machines for One Goal

Both continuous trading and auctions try to do the same thing: match buyers and sellers and produce prices. They differ in **how** they do it.

Continuous trading: a real-time queue

In continuous trading:

- Orders are processed **one at a time**, in arrival order.
- Prices can change **trade by trade**, second by second.
- **Time priority** matters: being early (or fast) can be valuable when many want the same price.

This system is excellent for a normal flow of trading. But it has a vulnerability: when a shock hits and many orders arrive at once, a continuous stream can become chaotic. Quotes can gap, depth can vanish, and speed competition can intensify.

Auctions: batch the orders, then pick one price

In an auction:

- Orders are **collected over a window of time** (seconds to minutes, depending on the venue and auction type).

- Instead of matching immediately, the exchange treats the orders as a **batch**.
- The exchange computes a single **auction clearing price**: the price that best balances supply and demand for that batch.

The key contrast is this: **Continuous trading finds prices through a stream of tiny decisions. An auction finds a price through one big decision.**

Why Open and Close Are Special (and Risky)

It is tempting to think the opening price is simply "yesterday's close plus a small update." In reality, the open is a moment when:

- overnight news has accumulated,
- investors around the world have had time to react,
- and many portfolio trades are scheduled to occur.

So when the market opens, you do not get a gentle, continuous trickle of orders. You often get a **surge**.

The close has its own surge because:

- many funds and benchmarks use the closing price for valuation,
- index funds may need to trade near the close to track the index,
- and traders may want to reduce overnight risk.

In other words, the open and close are not "just another minute." They are **coordination points** for the entire market.

The Auction Clearing Price: A Plain-English View

An auction tries to choose a price that produces the **best match** between buyers and sellers in the batch.

A helpful mental picture is to imagine lining up all buy interest and all sell interest and asking: **At what price can we trade the most shares without leaving a large imbalance?**

More concretely:

- At a **lower** price, more buyers are willing to buy, but fewer sellers are willing to sell.
- At a **higher** price, more sellers are willing to sell, but fewer buyers are willing to buy.

The clearing price is where these two forces come closest to meeting, often with rules designed to:

- maximize executed volume,
- minimize leftover imbalance,
- and produce a price that is consistent with the surrounding market.

You do not need the full rulebook to understand the intuition: **batching creates stability because it uses more information at once.**

Why Auctions Can Be More Stable Than Continuous Trading

Auctions can reduce several sources of instability that are amplified in continuous trading.

Less sensitivity to split-second timing

In continuous trading, small differences in timing can determine queue position, and queue position can determine fills. That makes speed valuable and can encourage rapid cancel/replace behavior.

In an auction, because orders are collected over a window, the market's outcome depends less on microsecond arrival time and more on the

overall balance of supply and demand. This tends to reduce the importance of "being first in line" in the price discovery process.

Aggregation reduces air pockets

Recall the limit order book idea of depth: if the book is thin near the best prices, a market order can walk through levels and cause a jump.

An auction effectively **builds depth by aggregation**. Orders that would have been scattered across time get considered together, which often produces:

- a more meaningful executed volume at one price, and
- less tendency for the price to leap across gaps created by momentary cancellations.

A single reference price can coordinate behavior

In fast markets, uncertainty about the "right" price can cause liquidity providers to step back, widening spreads and reducing displayed size. Auctions help by producing a **single reference price** that market participants can coordinate around.

This coordination function becomes especially important after sharp moves, which brings us to a critical application.

Volatility Halts: Restarting the Market with an Auction

During extreme volatility, many venues use **volatility halts** (temporary pauses) designed to slow down disorderly trading. The core idea is not merely "stop trading." It is: **Stop the stream long enough to rebuild liquidity, then restart trading with an auction-like process that can re-establish a stable price.**

Why an auction for the restart?

- When trading resumes, many participants want to act at once (some to exit, some to enter, some to hedge).
- If the market reopened as a pure stream with thin depth, the first few orders could cause wild jumps.
- A reopening auction collects interest, finds a clearing price, and allows a larger amount of trading to occur at a single coordinated level.

This is one of the clearest examples of market design acknowledging a hard truth: **continuous trading is efficient most of the time, but not always robust under stress.**

Continuous vs. Auction: What Each Is Good At

It helps to summarize the tradeoff without romanticizing either mechanism:

Continuous Trading (Stream)	Auctions (Batch)
Fast, responsive, constant price updates	Coordinated price discovery at key moments
Time priority and queue position matter	Less dependent on split-second ordering
Works well when liquidity is steady	Helps when orders surge or liquidity is fragile
Can become jumpy when depth vanishes	Can reduce gaps by aggregating demand and supply

The Through-Line to Flash Crashes

This section connects directly to flash-crash dynamics:

- A flash crash is often a story of **continuous trading under stress**: liquidity pulls back, the stream becomes thin, and aggressive orders (or automated responses) can cause rapid price dislocations.
- Auctions are one of the market's main tools for **re-coordinating** after such dislocations—at the open, at the close, and after halts.

The deeper lesson is that "the market" is not one single mechanism running uniformly all day. It is a set of mechanisms chosen for different conditions. Continuous trading emphasizes immediacy and constant updates. Auctions emphasize coordination and stability when the flow of orders is most lopsided.

With the mechanics of the book, order aggressiveness, trading costs, matching rules, and auctions in place, we are now equipped to explore what happens when these pieces interact across many venues—and what can go wrong when liquidity fragments, disappears, or becomes hidden.

Chapter 3

A Fragmented World: Where Trading Happens

If you picture the stock market as a crowded room of shouting traders in lower Manhattan, you are picturing a ghost. Today, the 'market' is actually a fractured archipelago of over fifty disparate electronic islands-server farms scattered across New Jersey and beyond-connected by fiber-optic cables. This chapter peels back the curtain on this invisible geography to show you exactly where your trade goes when you click 'buy', and why the simple concept of a stock price is actually a technological miracle of synchronization.

3.1 The Modern Venue Landscape

In the early mental picture of the stock market, there is *one* place where trading happens: a famous exchange, a bell, a crowd, and a single "official" price. That picture is useful as a starting point—and it captures something important about how markets *used* to be organized—but it is no longer a good map of where modern trading actually occurs.

To understand dark pools, flash crashes, and sudden liquidity failures later in this book, we need a more realistic map. Modern markets are best imagined not as one building, but as a *network*: many different venues, many different rulebooks, and many different computers updating at nearly the same time. A single stock (say, Apple) can be traded in dozens of places within the same second. In calm times, this network behaves as if it were one market. In stressed times, the fact that it is a network—with weak links, delays, and differing incentives—matters a great deal.

This section introduces the three main venue families you need to know:

- **Lit public exchanges** (the "visible" markets most people think of),
- **Electronic Communication Networks (ECNs)** (electronic marketplaces that helped accelerate and multiply where trading could occur), and
- **Internalizers and dark pools** (private broker-dealer venues and other Alternative Trading Systems, or ATS, where trading can occur with less pre-trade transparency).

Venue Family #1: Lit Public Exchanges ("the visible market")

A **lit exchange** is a public marketplace where bids and offers are displayed ("lit up") for others to see. When you hear names like NYSE or Nasdaq, you are thinking of this category.

Lit exchanges have three characteristics that make them central:

- **Displayed quotes:** Participants post *limit orders* to buy or sell at specified prices. Those prices and sizes are published to the market (subject to the exchange's rules and market data products).
- **A matching engine with transparent rules:** The exchange runs a computerized matching engine that decides which order

trades first. The details vary, but the basic idea is consistent: price priority first, and then time priority among orders at the same price.

- **Public price discovery:** Because quotes are displayed, other market participants can react. In normal conditions, this public competition helps concentrate attention around a "best" bid and offer.

A useful way to think about a lit exchange is as the market's *public scoreboard.* It does not necessarily trade the *most* shares (that can vary by stock and time), but it plays an outsized role in forming the reference prices that everyone else watches.

Venue Family #2: ECNs (the electronic expansion of "where trading can happen")

Historically, exchanges were physically rooted: a particular place, a particular community of members, a particular process. As trading became electronic, new marketplaces emerged that were built from the start as software.

An **Electronic Communication Network (ECN)** is an electronic system that matches buyers and sellers, typically with speed and automation as its defining features. In practice, the term ECN is sometimes used loosely, and modern regulation and market structure have blended categories. For our purposes, you should remember the core intuition:

> An ECN is a trading venue that looks and behaves like an exchange (it matches orders electronically), but it arose from the shift to fast, networked trading and helped multiply the number of places where quotes and trades could occur.

Why do ECNs matter for understanding fragmentation?

- **They made "one stock, many places" normal.** Once trading is software, it can be hosted in multiple data centers, run by multiple operators, and compete on speed and fees.

- **They increased the importance of routing.** If there are multiple electronic venues, someone (usually your broker's algorithms) must decide where to send each piece of an order.
- **They intensified latency competition.** When markets are networks, microseconds start to matter. The difference between venues becomes not only *price* but also *time*.

For a casual investor, the key takeaway is not the precise legal definition; it is the practical consequence: electronic venues expanded the ecosystem, which made the market more competitive—and also more complex.

Venue Family #3: Internalizers and Dark Pools (private ATS and broker-dealer execution)

Now we reach the category that tends to surprise newcomers: a meaningful share of trading may happen *without* first showing a quote to the public market.

Two closely related concepts sit here:

Internalization (broker-dealer internalizers).

A broker-dealer may fill customer orders *from its own inventory* or by matching buyers and sellers *within its own systems*, rather than immediately sending the order to a public exchange. This is called **internalization**. If you imagine a large broker as a "shopping mall" with many customers entering at once, internalization is the mall pairing a buyer and seller inside, instead of sending both out to the town square.

Internalization can be motivated by:

- **Cost control:** avoiding certain exchange fees,
- **Speed:** filling an order quickly inside the broker's own infrastructure, and
- **Business incentives:** capturing the bid-ask spread or earning rebates/avoiding fees depending on the venue economics.

Dark pools (ATS with limited pre-trade transparency).

A **dark pool** is a type of **Alternative Trading System (ATS)** where trading interest is not displayed publicly in the same way as on lit exchanges. The defining feature is **reduced pre-trade transparency**. Trades still occur, and the market can learn about them after the fact through reporting rules—but the *quotes* that would have been visible on a lit exchange are typically not shown in advance.

Why would anyone want that?

- **To reduce signaling and price impact.** If a large institution needs to buy a lot of shares, broadcasting that intent can push the price up before the order is completed. Dark pools aim to reduce the "everyone sees you coming" problem.

- **To seek price improvement.** Some dark venues are designed to execute at prices slightly better than the public best bid/offer, under certain conditions.

A critical nuance for later chapters: *dark* does not mean *illegal* or *invisible to regulators*. It means that the venue is not displaying the same kind of public, continuous quote that a lit exchange displays. This trade-off—less public information in exchange for potentially less market impact—is one of the central policy debates of modern market structure.

How one stock ends up trading "in fifty places at once"

At this point, the natural question is: if there are many venues, why doesn't the market splinter into many unrelated prices?

In normal conditions, several forces keep prices roughly aligned:

- **Competition:** if one venue is posting a meaningfully worse price than another, order routers tend to avoid it.

- **Arbitrage:** fast traders and market makers actively buy where it is cheap and sell where it is expensive, pushing venues back into alignment.

- **Reference pricing:** many off-exchange executions are priced with reference to public quotes (for example, around the best bid and offer). This ties private execution back to the public "scoreboard."

But notice what those forces rely on:

- **Fast information flow** (quotes and trades must travel across the network),
- **Sufficient liquidity** (enough resting orders to absorb trades), and
- **Functional routing** (algorithms must be able to find and access liquidity).

When markets are calm, these are present and the network behaves as a single market. When markets are stressed, any of the three can weaken. That is where fragmentation stops being a background detail and becomes a driver of instability.

A mental map: the market as a hub, spokes, and an outer ring

Keep this simplified mental map in mind as we go forward:

- **Center (lit exchanges):** the public price-setting arena.
- **Middle layer (ECNs / electronic venues):** additional electronic marketplaces competing on speed, fees, and microstructure design.
- **Outer ring (internalizers / dark pools):** private execution, often referencing public prices but not showing the same public quotes ahead of time.

The important lesson is not that one layer is "good" and another is "bad." The lesson is that each layer has a different relationship to *transparency*, *speed*, and *price impact*. Those differences are manageable most days. They become consequential when liquidity thins and the market needs to coordinate quickly.

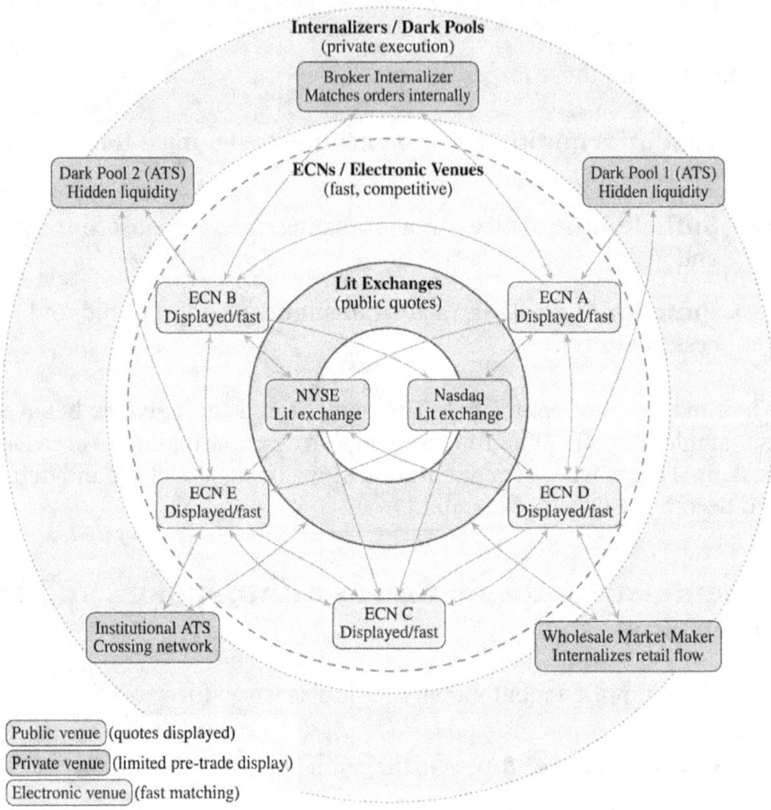

Why this taxonomy matters later

This venue map is not trivia; it is the stage on which liquidity crises play out.

In later chapters, when we discuss a sudden "air pocket" in liquidity or a flash crash, the key question will often be:

> *Which parts of the network stayed connected, and which*

parts fell out of sync?

Lit exchanges, ECNs, and private ATS/internalizers each respond differently under stress because they differ in transparency, incentives, and how orders are routed and matched. By learning the map first, you will be able to follow the story later when the market's network begins to strain—and when the comforting idea of "one market, one price" turns out to be an approximation rather than a guarantee.

3.2 Fragmentation and Complexity

In the previous section, we built a simple map of *where* trading happens: a center of lit exchanges, a surrounding layer of electronic venues, and an outer ring of internalizers and dark pools. That map explains why a single stock can trade in many places during the same minute.

Now we confront the deeper question: *so what?*

Fragmentation is not merely "many venues." Fragmentation means that what used to be one shared pool of buyers and sellers is now *split* into many smaller pools, each running on its own computers, with its own queue, and its own tiny clock. In ordinary conditions, the network behaves as if it were one market. In stressed conditions, that network can behave like many partially synchronized markets. That is when complexity becomes fragility.

The core problem: one price, many places

When people say, "Apple is trading at $X," they are describing a comforting illusion: a single, unified truth.

In reality, at any instant there are multiple truths:

- different venues showing slightly different best bids and offers,
- different queues (who is "first in line" at a price) at each venue,
- different latencies (how long it takes messages to travel to and from each venue),

- and different types of liquidity (displayed, hidden, conditional, internalized).

The market still *aims* to produce one reference price, but it must do so across a distributed system.

A good analogy is a chain of grocery stores that all change prices electronically. If every store updates at the same time, customers see one price. But if some stores update a few seconds later, you temporarily have a scattered set of prices. In markets, the time differences are not seconds—they can be microseconds to milliseconds—but the logic is the same. The market becomes a **synchronization problem**.

Synchronization: why markets have "location" even though they're digital

A non-obvious fact about modern markets is that they have geography.

Not geography in the sense of city landmarks, but in the sense of *data centers and fiber routes*. Trading venues are computers in specific locations. Many U.S. equity venues operate in New Jersey data centers, and the time it takes for a message to travel between them is finite. Even if that time is tiny, it is not zero.

The market wants a single best price. The infrastructure delivers many nearly-simultaneous prices.

Under calm conditions, high-speed competition keeps these differences small. Under stress, small differences can widen quickly because:

- quotes update rapidly and unevenly,
- some venues throttle, slow, or temporarily protect themselves,
- market makers reduce or cancel quotes to manage risk,
- and order routers must make decisions based on information that is already aging.

Synchronization is therefore not a philosophical issue; it is a mechanical one. It lives in the timing of messages and the capacity of systems.

Liquidity doesn't disappear all at once; it fractures

When the news says "liquidity vanished," it sounds like a single event. In a fragmented market, liquidity often vanishes *in pieces*.

To see why, recall what "liquidity" means in practice:

- You can buy or sell quickly
- *without* moving the price much
- because there are enough resting orders willing to trade near the current price.

Now imagine liquidity distributed across many venues. Each venue might have a small stack of resting orders at the best price and the next few prices. If a burst of selling hits the system, those small stacks can be depleted quickly *venue by venue*. Instead of one deep reservoir, you have many shallow puddles.

This is one of the most important intuitions for flash-crash dynamics:

Fragmentation can turn "deep liquidity" into "many thin slices of liquidity."

A single large trade that would have been absorbed by a centralized order book can, in a fragmented world, force routers to chase liquidity across venues, consuming the best prices in multiple places almost simultaneously.

Complexity for humans becomes automation for machines—and that creates new failure modes

Fragmentation makes markets too complex for humans to navigate directly. So machines navigate them:

- **Smart Order Routers (SORs)** decide where to send each order slice.
- **Market makers** run models that quote across many venues and constantly update or cancel.

- **Arbitrage strategies** keep prices aligned by trading the differences.

This automation is not an optional add-on. It is the glue that holds fragmented markets together.

But there is a catch: automation introduces *systemic coupling*. Many independent firms may run broadly similar logic under stress:

- If volatility rises, reduce quote size.
- If adverse selection risk rises, widen spreads.
- If inventory becomes unbalanced, cancel and re-post.

When many participants react in the same direction at the same time, liquidity can pull back *everywhere*, and it can do so quickly.

This is why "complexity" is not just "hard to understand." In market structure, complexity also means:

More interacting components, more feedback loops, and more opportunities for correlated retreat.

The fragility of the network: small disruptions can have outsized effects

A fragmented market is a network. Networks can fail in ways centralized systems do not.

Here are the main network fragilities to keep in mind:

Latency makes information stale

In a single centralized book, the best bid and offer are updated in one place. In a fragmented network, everyone is constantly asking:

Is that quote still there?

If a venue shows shares available at $100.00 and you route an order there, by the time your order arrives those shares may already have been taken by someone closer, faster, or routed earlier. Your order then "misses" and must be re-routed, often to a worse price. Under stress, this happens repeatedly across venues, amplifying price moves.

Queue priority becomes a competitive weapon

Even if two venues show the same price, the experience of trading can differ because of queue position:

- On Venue A, you might be first in line at $100.00.
- On Venue B, you might be 5,000 shares back in the queue at $100.00.

In fragmented markets, speed is often about *queue position* rather than raw execution time. Under stress, when the top of book is thin, being late by microseconds can mean trading at the next price level down.

Routing creates "chase" dynamics

When liquidity is scattered, routers may split an order and send pieces to multiple venues. If the market is moving, routers can wind up chasing a retreating best price:

- The router targets the best displayed price.
- The best displayed price disappears before the order arrives.
- The router re-targets the next best venue/price.
- Repeats, now in a faster-moving market.

This is not irrational behavior; it is a mechanical consequence of trying to trade in a distributed system while the system is changing.

Venue-level protections can desynchronize the ecosystem

Venues may implement mechanisms designed to maintain orderly trading (for example, volatility interruptions, limit up/limit down bands, or other controls). While these are often helpful, they can also create temporary discontinuities:

- One venue pauses or constrains trading.
- Another venue continues trading.
- Liquidity and price discovery shift abruptly to the venues still operating normally.

A centralized market has one set of brakes. A fragmented network has many brakes, applied at different times, with different triggers. During calm markets, this is barely noticeable. During fast markets, it can matter.

A concrete stress scenario: "Apple in two places"

To make synchronization feel real, consider an oversimplified but instructive example.

Assume Apple is trading around $200.00. Two venues are showing the best bid:

- Venue X: Bid $199.99 for 200 shares
- Venue Y: Bid $199.99 for 300 shares

A large sell wave arrives and multiple routers and market makers react at once:

- Venue X's 200-share bid is hit and disappears.
- Venue Y's 300-share bid is partially hit, but still exists.
- Some traders still *see* the old quote from Venue X for a moment due to message delays.
- Orders that route toward Venue X arrive to find no liquidity at $199.99 and execute lower (or re-route).
- Market makers, detecting the speed and imbalance, cancel additional bids on both venues.

From the outside, this can look like a sudden air pocket: the best displayed prices evaporate and the next available bids are meaningfully lower. Nothing mystical happened. The network did what networks do under load: it fell slightly out of sync, and the mismatch between what was visible and what was actually executable widened.

Why fragmentation can be stable *and* unstable

It is important to hold two truths at once:

- **Fragmentation can improve markets in normal times.** Competition among venues can reduce explicit trading costs, encourage innovation, and give different participants different ways to trade.
- **Fragmentation can worsen markets in abnormal times.** When the system is stressed, the same dispersion that fosters competition also increases the number of moving parts that can drift apart.

Think of it like modern air travel. Many airports and routes make travel cheaper and more flexible on ordinary days. But when a storm hits, delays cascade through the network. The network's normal efficiency becomes the network's vulnerability.

3.3 The Quest for Best Execution

The previous sections gave us two essential pieces of the puzzle.

First, we mapped the venue ecosystem: lit exchanges, electronic venues, and private execution (internalizers and dark pools). Second, we saw what fragmentation *does* to the market: it turns a single pool of liquidity into a network of smaller pools that can drift out of sync, especially under stress.

Now we face the practical question that every investor, even a casual one, is implicitly asking:

When I click "Buy" or "Sell," where does my order actually go—*and who decides?*

In modern markets, the answer is rarely "to the exchange." The more accurate answer is:

Your order goes to your broker's ***routing system****, and that system decides how to navigate the fragmented network to achieve* ***best execution****.*

The key piece of machinery doing this work is the **Smart Order Router (SOR)**. Think of a SOR as a high-speed GPS that constantly recalculates routes in a city where roads appear and disappear in milliseconds.

Best execution: a principle, not a single number

"Best execution" sounds like it should be simple: get the best price. But in real markets, execution quality is multi-dimensional.

A broker trying to execute an order must often balance several objectives at once:

- **Price:** can we get a better price than currently displayed?
- **Speed:** how quickly can we complete the trade?
- **Certainty of fill:** is the displayed liquidity real and accessible, or likely to vanish?
- **Market impact:** will our order move the price against us?
- **Total cost:** commissions, fees, rebates, and implicit costs from slippage.
- **Opportunity cost:** if we wait for a better price, do we risk missing the trade?

For a small retail order, market impact is usually minimal, and the central struggle is often between *price* and *speed/certainty*. For a large institutional order, market impact and information leakage can dominate everything.

So best execution is not a single point. It is a *trade-off problem* performed under uncertainty.

Why smart order routing exists at all

In a centralized market, routing is trivial: you send the order to the one book. In a fragmented market, routing becomes part of the market's basic functioning.

A modern broker is typically connected to:

- multiple lit exchanges,
- multiple electronic venues,
- one or more internalization mechanisms,
- and possibly one or more dark pools or other ATS.

Each of these destinations differs in:

- available liquidity at each price level,
- queue priority rules,
- fee schedules (including maker-taker or similar economics),
- likelihood of price improvement,
- and latency (how fast you can reach it and how fast you hear back).

If the market is a network, the SOR is the part that tries to make the network behave like one market from the customer's perspective.

The Smart Order Router (SOR): the broker's microsecond decision engine

A **Smart Order Router** is a set of algorithms that decides:

- **1) Whether to split an order** into smaller pieces,

- **2) Where to send each piece** (which venue),
- **3) In what sequence** (parallel versus one-after-another),
- **4) When to cancel and reroute** if liquidity disappears,
- **5) When to post versus take liquidity** (add a limit order or hit an existing quote),
- **6) Whether to seek hidden liquidity** (for example in dark pools),
- **7) How to respect constraints** (order type, limit price, time-in-force, and regulatory obligations).

A useful mental model is to imagine that the SOR is constantly answering three questions:

- **1) What is the best price we can access right now?** This may involve checking displayed quotes and estimating the probability that those quotes are still available by the time the order arrives.
- **2) What is the best price we can access without revealing too much?** For larger orders, the act of routing itself can leak information. Hitting multiple venues aggressively can signal urgency. Posting visible size can invite others to trade ahead.
- **3) What is the fastest reliable route to completion?** A slow route can be expensive in a moving market. But a fast route that crosses the spread repeatedly can also be expensive. SORs attempt to balance these costs.

A concrete example: how a single order becomes many child orders

Suppose you enter an order to **buy 1,000 shares** of a stock with a limit price of $50.00. At the moment you click, the fragmented market might look like this (simplified):

- Exchange A: offers 200 shares at $49.99

- Exchange B: offers 150 shares at $49.99
- Exchange C: offers 300 shares at $50.00
- Dark Pool D: potential hidden sellers around $49.99–$50.00 (unknown size)
- Internalizer E: may offer a small amount of price improvement (depending on rules and conditions)

A naive approach would be to send all 1,000 shares to one exchange and hope for the best. A SOR typically does something more surgical:

- **1) Send IOC child orders** for 200 and 150 shares to Exchanges A and B to capture the best visible price.
- **2) Ping dark pools** simultaneously with a small child order to test for hidden liquidity.
- **3) Decide whether to post or take liquidity** for remaining shares: post as a resting limit order or take liquidity to finish quickly.
- **4) Cancel and reroute as needed** if a quoted size vanishes before arrival.

To the investor, it feels like "one buy order." Mechanically, it can be dozens of messages: route, cancel, replace, and execute—all while the best prices are shifting.

This is one reason fragmentation can feel invisible in calm markets: SORs do the work of stitching the pieces together.

The SOR's conflicting incentives: speed, price improvement, and fees

A realistic description of routing must include an uncomfortable fact: the broker is not merely a neutral messenger. The broker is an agent navigating a web of incentives.

At a high level, a SOR may be pulled in different directions:

- **Speed:** send to the fastest venue (or the venue where fill probability is highest).
- **Price improvement:** seek executions slightly better than the displayed quote (often associated with certain off-exchange mechanisms).
- **Fee minimization (or rebate capture):** choose venues based on the economics of adding vs. taking liquidity.

These goals can align, but they can also conflict. For example:

- The venue with the best displayed price might be slower to access or have a long queue.
- The venue offering price improvement might provide uncertain fills.
- The cheapest venue from a fee perspective might not be the best from a fill-quality perspective in a fast market.

From the standpoint of market stability, this matters because routing decisions collectively shape where liquidity concentrates and how quickly it can evaporate. When stress hits, many routers may make similar choices at the same time, amplifying the rush toward (or away from) certain venues.

Hidden liquidity and the search problem

In a fragmented market, not all liquidity is displayed. Some liquidity is:

- **hidden by design** (dark pools),
- **conditional** (willing to trade only under certain conditions),
- or **internal** (available only inside a broker's system).

This creates what computer scientists would call a **search problem**: the router must decide how much time and how many attempts to spend looking for better liquidity that is not visible.

If the router searches too aggressively:

- it may delay execution,
- and it may miss the opportunity if the market moves.

If it searches too little:

- it may execute quickly but at a worse price than necessary,
- and it may concentrate flow on the most obvious venues, potentially worsening congestion.

This is the heart of best execution in a fragmented world: you are not just trading against other investors; you are trading in a system where the best opportunities may be partially hidden and constantly moving.

Why routing can fail under stress (and why it can worsen stress)

During calm markets, SORs often make fragmentation feel harmless. During fast markets, routing can become a source of instability.

Here are three common stress mechanisms:

- **1) Stale quotes and "misses":** When the market moves quickly, quotes can disappear faster than routers can hit them. A series of "misses" forces repeated rerouting, which increases message traffic; increases latency (systems get busier); and pushes executions to worse prices as top-of-book liquidity is repeatedly found to be gone.
- **2) Liquidity taking cascades:** If routers decide that waiting is too risky, they may switch from posting to taking liquidity (crossing spreads to guarantee a fill). If many routers do this simultaneously, it can consume the best bids/offers across venues; widen spreads; and accelerate short-term price moves.
- **3) Correlated retreat:** Many routing and market-making systems share similar risk controls. When volatility spikes, they may collectively reduce order size; widen spreads; or pull quotes. The market then experiences a sudden drop in accessible liquidity that is not caused by a single actor, but by many independent actors reacting similarly.

A practical takeaway: "best execution" is an engineering and governance challenge

For the reader, the main lesson is not that routers are good or bad. It is that in a fragmented market, **execution quality is produced by an ecosystem of algorithms and rules**. That ecosystem must:

- coordinate across venues,
- handle delays and stale information,
- and remain robust when the market becomes fast and thin.

This is why debates about market structure often revolve around routing and data. If you want one market to behave like one market, you need reliable information about the many markets—and you need a way to stitch them together.

The bridge to the next section: why the data feed becomes destiny

Everything a router does depends on what it believes the market looks like *right now*:

- Where is the best bid and offer?
- How much size is really there?
- Has it already traded?

But in a fragmented system, there is no single "now." There are multiple clocks, multiple message paths, and multiple views of the market.

That brings us to the next essential piece of infrastructure: the **Consolidated Tape** and the construction of the **National Best Bid and Offer (NBBO)**—the attempt to turn many disjointed streams into one reference reality, and the illusions that latency can create along the way.

3.4 The Consolidated Tape

In the previous section, we followed your order into the market's maze and saw why smart order routers (SORs) exist: they try to turn a fragmented network of venues into something that feels like *one* market.

But that raises a foundational question. A router cannot route intelligently unless it has a reliable picture of the market. And most investors—even many professionals—take for granted the picture on their screen: a last price, a best bid, a best offer, and a chart that appears to summarize "what is happening."

Where does that picture come from?

In U.S. equities, the attempt to create a single, stitched-together view of a fragmented market is called the **Consolidated Tape**. And the most important number it helps produce is the **National Best Bid and Offer (NBBO)**.

The Consolidated Tape is meant to answer two deceptively simple questions:

1. **What is the best available price to buy right now?** (the best offer)
2. **What is the best available price to sell right now?** (the best bid)

The complication is that "right now" is not a single moment in a distributed system.

Quotes vs. prints: what you *could* trade vs. what *did* trade

Before we discuss the tape, we need one clean distinction.

A quote is an invitation. A quote is a bid or offer: "I will buy 100 shares at $99.99" or "I will sell 100 shares at $100.01." Quotes are about *possibility*. They represent liquidity that might be there when you arrive.

A print is a fact. A print is a completed trade: shares actually exchanged hands at a specific price and size. Prints are about *history.* They are what your chart and "last price" are built from.

Both are vital. Quotes tell routers where liquidity appears to be. Prints tell everyone what recently happened.

In a calm market, quotes and prints line up neatly: displayed bids and offers trade, and the last price moves smoothly. In a fast market, that relationship can become messy:

- quotes can appear and vanish before you can hit them,
- prints can occur in venues you are not watching directly,
- and the timestamps you see may not reflect the true sequence of events across venues.

This is where the Consolidated Tape enters the story.

The Consolidated Tape: a "marketwide newswire"

The Consolidated Tape is best understood as a *newswire* that carries market events (quotes and trades) from many venues and attempts to publish them as one stream.

The goal is not poetry; it is practicality:

- Market participants need a *shared reference* for the best bid and offer.
- Brokers need a reference for *best execution* obligations.
- The public needs a coherent way to see prices without subscribing to every venue's private feed.

But there is an unavoidable constraint: the tape is built from messages that must travel.

A quote update generated inside one exchange's matching engine is like a camera flash at a stadium. You do not see it instantly from every seat. The message must:

1. be created at the venue,
2. travel across networks,
3. be processed and consolidated,
4. and then be delivered to your screen.

Even when this happens extremely fast, it still takes time. And in markets, time is not a rounding error.

NBBO: the "best" price is a calculation, not a location

The **National Best Bid and Offer (NBBO)** is the best displayed bid and the best displayed offer *across the entire market* (across the venues that contribute to the consolidated view).

Conceptually, NBBO is simple:

- collect the best bid from each venue,
- take the highest one as the national best bid,
- collect the best offer from each venue,
- take the lowest one as the national best offer.

In practice, NBBO is a moving target because:

- each venue updates at different times,
- messages arrive out of order,
- and the "best" quote might be gone by the time you try to trade against it.

This produces a crucial insight for understanding flash crashes and liquidity air pockets:

> **NBBO is a snapshot assembled from many cameras. The cameras are not perfectly synchronized.**

Most of the time, the mismatch is tiny and harmless. Under stress, it can become meaningful.

Latency: the gap between market reality and what you see

Latency is often described as a technical detail, but it creates a very human illusion: the feeling that the screen is reality.

In truth, the screen is a *delayed reconstruction*.

To see the mechanism, imagine a very fast sequence:

1. A large sell order hits Venue A and consumes the best bid.
2. Market makers cancel bids on Venues B and C in response.
3. A new best bid forms lower on Venue D.

Those events occur in the matching engines first. Only afterward do they become:

- quote updates on direct feeds,
- consolidated updates on the tape,
- and finally the numbers on a trader's screen.

During that short journey, two things can be true at once:

- the displayed NBBO still shows an older best bid,
- while the executable reality has already moved.

That is not fraud. It is physics and engineering.

The illusion that matters most: "I saw that price, so why didn't I get it?"

Many people first encounter market fragmentation through a frustrating experience:

The quote said $100.00. I placed the order. Why did I get $100.03?

In a fragmented, fast market, this can happen even with perfectly functioning systems:

- The $100.00 offer was real when it was displayed.
- It was taken or canceled before your order arrived.
- The tape (or your broker's view) updated a fraction of a second later.
- Your order executed against the next available liquidity.

This is why professional execution systems care about more than the displayed price. They care about:

- **fill probability** (how likely the quote is to still be there),
- **queue position** (are we early enough in line to get it),
- and **information freshness** (how old is the quote we are acting on).

In calm markets, those concerns fade into the background. In stressed markets, they dominate.

Why fragmentation makes the tape harder

If all trading happened in one place, the tape would be a simple report of that one place. Fragmentation forces the tape to stitch together:

- many venues,
- many message streams,
- many microstructure rules,
- and many different latencies.

More venues means more stitching. More stitching means more chances for slight mis-orderings, slight delays, and short-lived inconsistencies.

When liquidity is abundant, inconsistencies are quickly arbitraged away. When liquidity is thin and volatility is high, inconsistencies can persist long enough to matter:

- routers may route toward liquidity that is already gone,
- market makers may pull back when they cannot trust the visible picture,
- and feedback loops can accelerate price moves.

In other words, the tape is not just a reporting system. It is part of the market's coordination mechanism. Under stress, coordination becomes fragile.

A visual intuition: "Reality" vs. "The Tape"

The following diagram gives a clean mental model of the relationship between events happening at venues and the consolidated view seen by traders. The key feature is the gap: the tape is delayed and can briefly present a version of the market that is already history.

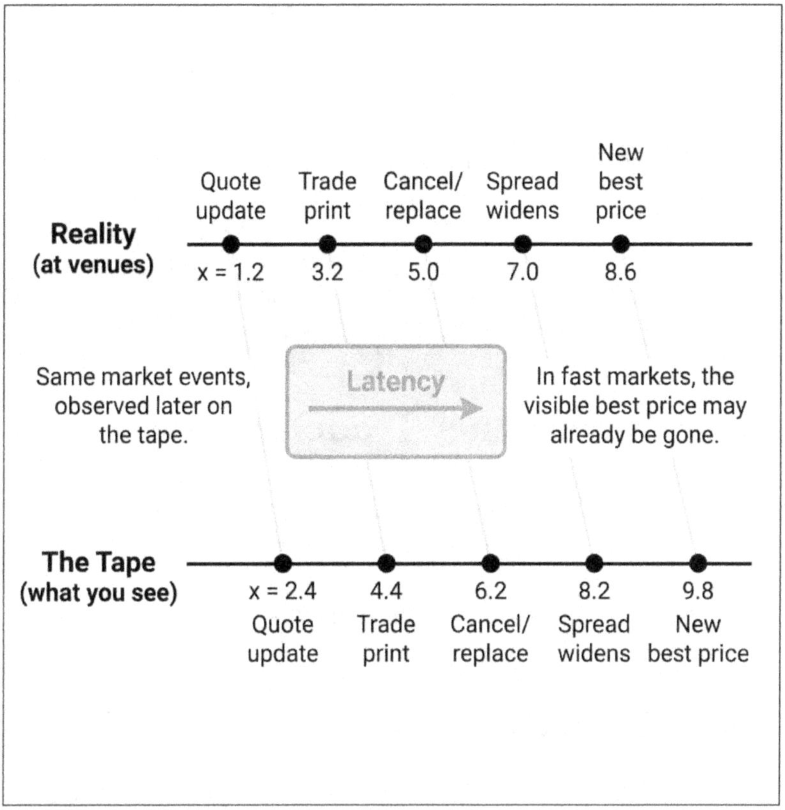

Why this matters for flash crashes and liquidity crises

In the calm regime, the tape works so well that you forget it exists. In the stressed regime, the tape can become a source of confusion and a contributor to instability.

The mechanism is not mysterious:

- When volatility jumps, quotes change faster.
- Faster quote changes make information stale more quickly.

- Stale information increases execution uncertainty.
- Increased uncertainty causes liquidity providers to widen spreads or pull back.
- Wider spreads and thinner books increase volatility further.

This is a feedback loop: **uncertainty about the true state of the market can reduce the willingness to provide liquidity**. And without liquidity, price moves become sharper and more discontinuous.

3.5 Transparency Trade-offs

We have now built the full mechanical picture of a modern equity market.

- Trading happens across many venues—lit exchanges, electronic venues, and private systems.
- Liquidity is therefore fragmented, which creates synchronization challenges and network fragility.
- Brokers rely on smart order routers to navigate that network in real time.
- The Consolidated Tape and NBBO attempt to stitch many venues into one reference "market," but latency means the stitched picture can lag behind reality.

Why did we build markets this way?

Does fragmentation create healthy competition, or does it undermine transparency and price discovery?

This section does not take a side. Instead, it lays out the trade-off clearly, because that trade-off is the foundation for understanding why dark pools exist and why debates over market structure are so persistent.

What "transparency" means in market structure

Transparency is often used as a moral word—as if more is always better. In markets, transparency is better understood as a design parameter. There are different kinds of transparency, and they help (or hurt) different goals.

Pre-trade transparency.

How much of the market's interest to buy and sell is visible *before* a trade occurs? Lit exchanges have high pre-trade transparency. Dark pools have low pre-trade transparency.

Post-trade transparency.

How quickly and accurately are completed trades reported to the public? Most modern markets have strong post-trade reporting requirements, but the details (timing, venue identifiers, special conditions) matter.

Transparency about incentives and routing.

Even if prices are visible, the market can be opaque if participants do not understand *why* orders go where they go (fees, rebates, internalization arrangements, and conflicts of interest).

When critics say "markets are opaque," they may mean any of these. When defenders say "markets are transparent enough," they may be referring to a different one. Much of the debate is confusion over definitions.

The case for fragmentation: competition, innovation, and resilience in normal times

The strongest argument *for* fragmentation is that competition among venues can benefit investors in ordinary conditions. The logic is intuitive: if there are multiple marketplaces, they must compete to attract order flow.

That competition can take several forms.

Lower explicit costs

Venues compete on:

- access fees,
- maker-taker (or other) pricing structures,
- technology costs passed through to participants,
- and the overall cost of trading (including the ability to obtain price improvement).

In a single-venue monopoly, there is less pressure to keep these costs low. With many venues, there is constant pressure to offer better economics.

Innovation in market design

Fragmentation has historically encouraged experimentation:

- new order types,
- new matching rules,
- new auction mechanisms,
- and new approaches to handling large orders.

Some innovations are beneficial. Some create complexity that later has to be reined in. But the engine of competition can produce genuine improvements.

Multiple ways to trade for multiple needs

Investors do not all want the same thing.

- A retail investor may want a fast fill and possibly small price improvement.
- A pension fund may want to buy a large position without broadcasting its intent.
- A market maker may want to quote continuously but manage risk across venues.

Multiple venue types can serve these different needs. A market with only lit, fully displayed execution might reduce some forms of opacity, but it could also increase information leakage and transaction costs for large traders.

Resilience (sometimes) through redundancy

In principle, multiple venues can provide redundancy. If one venue has an outage, trading can continue elsewhere.

This is real, but it is not a free lunch. Redundancy can become fragility if the system depends on tight synchronization across many nodes. The same network that provides alternative paths can also create more points of failure and more opportunities for drift.

The case against fragmentation: complexity, adverse selection, and weakened price discovery

The strongest argument *against* fragmentation is that it can degrade the market's ability to produce a clean, reliable public price and a level playing field for accessing liquidity.

Complexity is itself a cost

Fragmentation forces the market to spend resources on:

- routing infrastructure,
- high-speed connectivity,
- data feed processing,
- synchronization mechanisms,
- and compliance across many rulebooks.

These are not purely "wasteful" costs—they help the system function—but they are real economic burdens. And complexity tends to advantage participants who can afford the best technology and the most sophisticated optimization.

A simple way to say it:

In a fragmented market, part of "being a trader" becomes "being a network engineer."

The public price can become a reference point rather than the main event

If substantial trading occurs off-exchange (for example, through internalizers or dark venues), then the public lit market can become:

- the place where prices are formed (price discovery),
- while another set of venues captures a large share of executions.

This creates a tension sometimes summarized as "free riding": private venues may rely on public prices to set execution benchmarks while contributing less displayed liquidity to the public order book.

Whether this is truly harmful depends on magnitudes, rules, and the quality of post-trade reporting. But the concern is straightforward: if too much volume leaves the lit market, the lit market can become thinner, and thinner lit markets can be easier to move and more fragile under stress.

Adverse selection and the incentive to hide

In a high-speed environment, displayed liquidity can be "picked off" when information changes. If you post a visible quote and news hits, faster traders may trade against you before you can cancel.

As a result, sophisticated liquidity providers may:

- reduce displayed size,
- widen spreads,
- rely more on hidden/conditional orders,
- or shift activity to venues where they feel better protected.

This can become a self-reinforcing cycle: the more dangerous it feels to display liquidity, the less liquidity gets displayed.

Unequal information and unequal speed

The Consolidated Tape is designed to provide a shared public view, but we have already seen why the public view can lag behind venue reality. If some participants see changes sooner (through faster or richer feeds and faster processing), then "transparency" becomes layered:

- transparent for those with the best infrastructure,
- less transparent for everyone else.

From a policy perspective, this raises questions about fairness and market quality: should the market's reference picture be equally timely for everyone, or is it acceptable that some participants have a systematically fresher view?

The debate in one sentence: competition vs. coordination

We can compress the entire policy debate into a single tension:

Fragmentation increases competition among venues, but it makes coordination across venues harder.

Competition tends to reduce certain costs and drive innovation. Coordination is necessary for stable price discovery and reliable execution under stress.

In calm markets, competition dominates the story. In crisis markets, coordination dominates the story.

What regulators and exchanges are trying to optimize (and why it is hard)

Market structure policy is difficult because it attempts to optimize multiple objectives simultaneously:

- **Efficient price discovery:** prices should incorporate information quickly and accurately.
- **Fair access:** similarly situated participants should have comparable access to the market.
- **Low transaction costs:** explicit and implicit costs should be minimized.
- **Robustness under stress:** the market should not fail catastrophically during volatility.

- **Innovation and competition:** the system should improve over time rather than stagnate.

These goals can conflict. For example:

- More pre-trade transparency can improve public price discovery but increase information leakage for large investors.
- More venue competition can lower fees but increase data complexity and synchronization risk.
- Stronger protections against being picked off can encourage quoting but may slow down price adjustment.

So policy debates often sound circular because they are, in a sense, debates about which imperfection we prefer to live with.

A practical lens for readers: "Which problem are we trying to solve?"

When you hear arguments about dark pools, internalization, or the number of exchanges, it helps to ask one clarifying question:

Which problem is the proposal trying to solve, and what new problem might it create?

For example:

- A proposal that pushes more volume onto lit exchanges may strengthen displayed liquidity and the public quote, but it may increase market impact for institutions trying to trade large size.
- A proposal that encourages more off-exchange price improvement may benefit small orders, but it may reduce the incentives to display liquidity publicly.
- A proposal that changes fee structures may alter routing incentives, but it may also shift where liquidity appears and how stable it is during volatility.

This is why market structure is not a one-time engineering problem. It is an ongoing balancing act.

How this sets up the rest of the book

We can now state the big idea that will run through the chapters on dark pools and flash crashes:

Market fragmentation is a deliberate design that trades simplicity for competition.

In normal markets, the design can work remarkably well. In stressed markets, the same design can produce strange and sometimes dangerous behavior:

- liquidity that appears to be there but isn't,
- prices that move discontinuously,
- and cascades driven by synchronized algorithms responding to imperfect information.

Dark pools exist because transparency is not free: revealing intent can be costly. Flash crashes become possible because coordination is not guaranteed: stitching a network together takes time, and under stress the seams can show.

That is the transparency trade-off in its most useful form: not as a moral debate, but as a clear explanation of why the modern market is fast, competitive, complex—and occasionally fragile.

Chapter 4

Into the Dark: Understanding Dark Pools

Imagine a bustling stock exchange floor, filled with shouting traders and flashing screens where every buy and sell is public record. Now, imagine a soundproof, windowless room next door where billions of dollars change hands in total silence. This is the world of dark pools-not a criminal hideout, but a necessary sanctuary for the market's biggest whales. In this chapter, we turn on the lights to reveal how these private venues work, why they are essential for your pension fund, and the hidden dangers that lurk when trading happens in the dark.

4.1 What Dark Pools Actually Are

By the time most people hear the phrase *dark pool*, they have already been primed by movies, headlines, and internet lore to imagine something like an offshore casino: hooded figures, secret codes, and a market rigged in a back room.

The reality is more mundane—and, precisely because it is mundane, more important to understand.

A **dark pool** is best described as a **private trading venue** where participants can buy and sell financial instruments (most commonly stocks) **without displaying their orders to the public before the trade occurs**. That last clause is the whole point. In market-structure language, dark pools have **pre-trade opacity**.

Pre-trade opacity: what is "dark" about a dark pool?

When traders say an order is *lit*, they mean it is visible on a public order book: other market participants can see that someone is willing to buy at a certain price (a *bid*) or sell at a certain price (an *ask/offer*). When an order is *dark*, it means the order is not published in that public queue ahead of time.

So **"dark" refers to the lack of light (transparency) on the order book**, not necessarily to anything illegal or sinister. A dark pool is not "dark" because it is unregulated wilderness; it is "dark" because the *intentions* (who wants to trade, how much, and at what price) are hidden until an execution happens (or does not happen).

In practical terms, **a dark pool is like a private room adjacent to the main marketplace**. People can still trade, but they do not have to announce to the entire crowd what they are about to do.

A quick translation: public exchanges vs. private venues

To keep the vocabulary simple, it helps to sort trading venues into two buckets:

- **Lit markets (public exchanges):** Orders are displayed in a public limit order book (LOB). You can see bids and asks and how much quantity is waiting at each price. This is what most people intuitively imagine when they think "the stock market."
- **Dark pools (private venues):** Orders are *not* displayed pub-

licly before they trade. If you place an order, other participants generally cannot see it sitting there. A trade may occur if a matching order arrives, but the *rest of the world does not watch your order waiting in line.*

This is why dark pools are often called **off-exchange** venues. The phrase is easy to misunderstand. It does *not* automatically mean "outside the law"; it primarily means "not on a public exchange order book."

What dark pools are *not*

Because the term is loaded, it helps to clear away three common misconceptions.

Myth 1: A dark pool is a separate stock market with its own prices.

Most dark pools are not trying to invent a new price for Apple or Tesla. They are typically designed to *execute* at prices derived from the public market. (We will explain the most common mechanism—*reference pricing* and midpoint execution—in the next section.)

Myth 2: "Dark" means the trades are invisible forever.

The defining feature is **pre-trade** opacity, not necessarily **post-trade** secrecy. In many cases, once a trade occurs, it is reported to the broader market through standard reporting channels (often with a slight delay or with less detail about where it happened). The key difference is that the *order* was not advertised in advance.

Myth 3: Dark pools are only for "shadowy" actors.

Many users are mainstream institutions: mutual funds, pension funds, and asset managers that trade on behalf of ordinary savers. The motivation is often practical execution quality, not intrigue. The *controversy* around dark pools comes from how they interact with the public markets, not from the idea that every participant is a villain.

A plain-English definition you can keep in your head

Here is a definition that will stay useful as the book gets more technical:

> **A dark pool is a private trading venue that matches buyers and sellers without displaying their orders publicly before the trade.**

That is all you need for now: **private venue + hidden orders (before execution)**.

In the sections that follow, we will build from this foundation in the most natural order: first, *why* large traders might prefer not to reveal themselves in a public order book; then, *how* a trade can be priced if the orders are not displayed; and finally, *what can go wrong* when trading happens "in the dark."

4.2 The Institutional Motive: Hiding the Elephant

In the previous section, we stripped dark pools down to their simplest definition: **private trading venues with pre-trade opacity**. Now we can ask the natural next question:

If hiding orders sounds suspicious, why would a normal, reputable investor ever want *to hide?*

The answer is not espionage. It is **physics**—market physics.

Markets respond to large, visible demand the way a small swimming pool responds to an elephant stepping into it: the water level jumps, waves ripple outward, and anyone nearby gets soaked. In trading, that "splash" is called **market impact**. And for big investors, market impact is not a theoretical nuance. It is often the *largest single cost* of trading.

The elephant in the swimming pool: why size changes everything

Suppose a mutual fund needs to sell 10 million shares of a company. That number is not exotic. Large funds routinely hold positions measured in millions or tens of millions of shares, because they manage billions of dollars for retirement plans, university endowments, and everyday investors.

Now picture the same trade in a public, lit market:

- In a lit market, orders (or at least quotes and visible depth) are displayed.
- Other participants can see supply and demand building up at various prices.
- As the fund begins to sell, it consumes the highest bids first.
- If the selling continues, it must accept lower and lower bid prices to keep finding buyers.

Even if the fund tries to break the 10 million shares into smaller pieces, the market can infer what is happening. A steady stream of sell orders can be detected by humans, but more importantly, by algorithms designed to recognize patterns.

The end result is the classic nightmare of any large seller:

The more you try to sell, the worse the price you get.

This is not because anyone is "evil." It is because the market is an auction. When the crowd learns a large seller is in the room, the crowd adjusts.

The three-part trading cost that big investors obsess over

Retail investors often think of trading costs as commissions. Institutional investors think in a different decomposition. For them, the main costs are typically:

- **1. The spread:** the gap between the best visible buy price (bid) and sell price (ask). Crossing the spread is a direct, mechanical cost of immediacy.
- **2. Market impact:** the price movement caused by your own trading. If you are big enough, *you* are part of the weather.
- **3. Information leakage:** the indirect cost of other people learning what you are doing and trading ahead of, around, or away from you.

These are tightly linked. Information leakage often *creates* market impact: once others believe a large seller is active, they lower their bids (or stop bidding), which forces the seller to accept worse prices.

Dark pools are designed to reduce the second and third items—**market impact** and **information leakage**—by removing the public advertising step that makes those costs explode.

Why a visible large order moves the market (even before it executes)

It is tempting to think the market moves only when trades occur. In reality, markets move when *beliefs* change, and beliefs change when information appears.

A large visible order changes beliefs in at least four ways:

1) It signals urgency or private information. A huge sell program might mean "we must raise cash quickly" (urgency), or it might mean "we know something bad" (information). Outsiders do not know which, so they protect themselves.

2) It invites "front-running" in the broad, non-criminal sense. This term is often used for illegal behavior (a broker trading ahead of a client). But there is a broader, legal phenomenon: if traders *anticipate* that a large seller will push prices down, they sell first. The market drops *before* the fund is done.

3) It causes liquidity providers to pull back. Market makers and other liquidity providers post bids to earn the spread, but they are not obligated to stand in front of a truck. If they suspect a large seller is about to roll through, they reduce quoted size or widen spreads. Liquidity thins right when the fund needs it most.

4) It creates a "self-fulfilling" price path. Once the market believes a large seller is present, prices drift lower as bids step down. The seller then faces worse prices and must either slow down (risking not finishing) or speed up (making the impact worse). Either choice is costly.

This is why the elephant analogy matters: the splash is not mainly about *one* trade. It is about what the crowd does *in response* to the elephant being seen.

Dark pools as a practical solution: trading without broadcasting

Now return to the core feature from the previous section: **pre-trade opacity**.

In a dark pool, an institution can attempt to execute some of its large order *without* displaying a giant "I am selling" sign to the market. If the trade matches, it happens quietly; if it does not, it simply does not happen. Either way, the institution has reduced the chance that outsiders will detect the full size and direction of its intent.

Think of the dark pool as enabling two protective layers:

- **Size protection:** the market does not see the full depth of the institution's interest.

- **Timing protection:** the market is less able to infer a persistent pattern of buying or selling in real time.

This can be beneficial not just for the institution as a corporation, but for the end-investor—the teacher's pension plan, the 401(k), the charity endowment—because those investors bear the cost of poor execution.

A concrete story: selling 10 million shares in a lit market

To make the mechanism intuitive, imagine there are only a few visible bids on a public exchange:

Visible Bid Levels (Buyers)	Price	Shares
Best bid	$10.00	100,000
Next bid	$9.99	150,000
Next bid	$9.98	200,000
Next bid	$9.95	400,000

A seller with 10 million shares cannot finish at $10.00, because there are not 10 million shares waiting to buy at $10.00. The seller must "walk the book" (consume multiple price levels), which pushes the average sale price down.

And that table is optimistic, because it assumes bids remain in place. In practice, bids may disappear when the seller shows up, making the book even thinner.

Why institutions cannot simply "be patient"

A common reaction is: *Why not just sell very slowly, over weeks, on the public exchange?*

Sometimes they do. But patience is not always available:

- **Portfolio rebalancing deadlines:** index funds and ETFs rebalance on scheduled dates.
- **Client flows:** redemptions require cash; new inflows require buying.
- **Risk limits:** if a position becomes too large or too risky, it must be reduced.
- **Event risk:** earnings announcements, mergers, or macro shocks can force repositioning.

Institutions are not trading for entertainment; they are managing constraints. When constraints tighten, the ability to trade without moving price becomes central. Liquidity is not just "can I trade?" It is "can I trade *without* self-inflicted damage?"

The trade-off: secrecy reduces impact, but does not guarantee safety

Dark pools are attractive because they can reduce the visible splash. But it is important to keep expectations realistic:

- A dark pool does not create liquidity out of thin air. A buyer still must exist.
- A dark pool does not eliminate market impact entirely. Large trades can still move prices, especially if the market senses the imbalance through other channels.
- A dark pool substitutes one set of risks (being seen) for another set (not knowing who you are trading against, and whether they are better informed). We will confront that risk explicitly later when we discuss adverse selection and "toxic flow."

For now, hold onto the main motive:

Institutions use dark pools to reduce information leakage and market impact when trading sizes that are too large to reveal safely in public.

With that motive established, the next step is mechanical: if dark pools hide orders, *how do trades get priced*? If the venue is not displaying a public auction, where does the execution price come from?

That is where the dark pool's reliance on the lit market becomes unavoidable—and where the midpoint price enters the story.

4.3 Mechanics of the Dark: Trading in the Shadows

In the last section we established the motive: large institutions want to trade without broadcasting their intent, because visible size can move the market against them. That explains *why* dark pools exist.

Now we tackle the next question, the one most readers ask immediately:

> If nobody can see the orders, how does a dark pool know what price to trade at?

The short answer is that most dark pools do *not* discover prices the way a public exchange does. Instead, they **borrow** prices from the public (lit) markets. In market-structure terms, dark pools commonly rely on **reference pricing**.

Price discovery vs. price taking (a crucial distinction)

A public exchange is designed to do **price discovery**. When bids and offers are visible, the exchange continuously answers a live question:

> What is the best price someone is willing to pay right now, and the best price someone is willing to accept right now?

Those two numbers are the core of the modern electronic market:

- **Best Bid:** the highest visible buy price currently available.
- **Best Ask (Offer):** the lowest visible sell price currently available.

The difference between them is the **spread**. In many liquid stocks, the spread can be only a penny. But even a penny matters when you are trading millions of shares.

A dark pool, by contrast, is usually designed to be a **price taker**. It does not run a public auction with a visible queue. It typically says, in effect:

> We will execute your trade at a price derived from the lit market's best bid and best ask.

That is what makes the relationship between lit and dark so intertwined: the dark venue often depends on the lit venue to tell it what "fair" means *right now*.

Reference pricing: importing a public price into a private room

Reference pricing means the dark pool sets its execution price by referencing a widely observed public benchmark. The benchmark is usually tied to what is called the **NBBO**—the **National Best Bid and Offer**. Conceptually, the NBBO is the best bid and best offer available across the major public venues.

This matters because a dark pool needs a defensible answer to an awkward question:

> Why should either side believe the execution price was reasonable?

By pegging to a public reference (like the best bid/offer), the dark pool can say: "We did not invent a price in secret. We used the same public prices everyone else could see."

Midpoint execution: the most common intuition

The most famous reference-priced execution is the **midpoint**.

If the best bid is $10.00 and the best offer is $10.10, then the midpoint is:

$$\frac{10.00 + 10.10}{2} = 10.05.$$

Why is midpoint execution attractive? Because it **splits the spread**. Both sides improve relative to trading immediately on a lit exchange:

- A **buyer** who would have paid $10.10 on the exchange instead pays $10.05 (a 5-cent improvement versus the offer).

- A **seller** who would have received $10.00 on the exchange instead receives $10.05 (a 5-cent improvement versus the bid).

No magic is required. The value comes from avoiding the "pay the spread" cost of taking liquidity on a lit market—*provided* you can find a counterparty.

Midpoint intuition in one picture

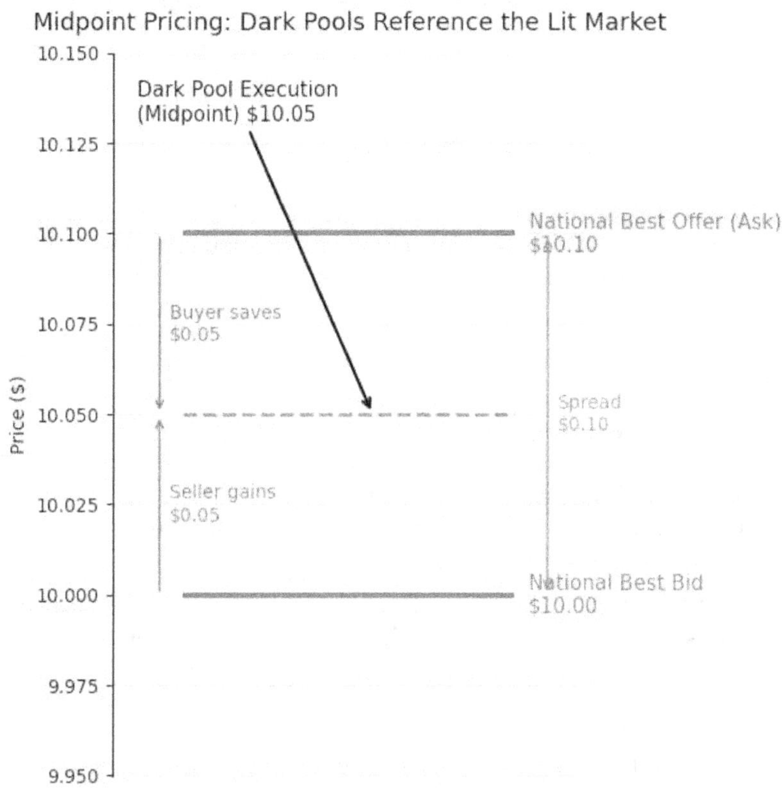

So what actually happens when you submit an order to a dark pool?

Although each venue has its own rulebook, the basic sequence is often:

- **You submit an order.** It might be a buy or a sell, and it may include constraints (size, minimum size to execute, time-in-force, and so on).

- **The order is not displayed publicly.** This is the "dark" feature: pre-trade opacity.
- **The venue checks the current reference prices.** Usually this means some form of best bid/offer from the lit markets.
- **The venue attempts to match you.** If an opposite-side order exists (or arrives), the dark pool can execute at the referenced price rule (commonly midpoint).
- **If no match exists, nothing happens.** Your order may rest in the dark pool (still hidden) or expire, depending on your settings and the venue's rules.

Two points are worth emphasizing because they prevent a lot of confusion later:

A dark pool is not guaranteed execution. A public exchange will execute your marketable order immediately (though perhaps at an unpleasant price) because there is visible liquidity to hit. A dark pool can only execute if a natural counterparty is present at the referenced price. If no one is there, your order may simply wait.

A dark pool execution is often "better" than the displayed bid/ask, but not better than the *true* price. Midpoint execution looks like a bargain relative to paying the ask or selling at the bid. But it is only a bargain if the midpoint is a fair reflection of the stock's value at that moment. If the lit market prices are stale, moving, or about to jump, the midpoint can be a trap. (That is the doorway into adverse selection, which we will address later.)

Why the lit market still matters (even when you trade in the dark)

At this stage, you can see the central tension in modern market structure:

- Dark pools exist to reduce market impact and information leakage for large traders.

- Yet many dark pool executions depend directly on lit market quotes for pricing.

In other words, the dark room uses the public room's clock to tell time.

This is not a flaw; it is the design. But it creates a dependency that becomes crucial when markets get stressed. If the lit market becomes jumpy—spreads widen, quotes flicker, liquidity disappears—then the reference price a dark pool relies on can become less stable, and the "safe" midpoint can become less meaningful.

The key takeaway before we move on

> **Dark pools typically do not discover prices; they execute using prices referenced from the public (lit) market, often at the midpoint between the best bid and best offer.**

That sets up the next, uncomfortable question. If the dark pool is offering hidden liquidity at an attractive price, who is on the other side of your trade—and why are they willing to give you that price improvement?

Sometimes the answer is benign (a natural buyer meets a natural seller). Sometimes it is not. That is where we meet the sharks.

4.4 The Risk of Adverse Selection: Swimming with Sharks

So far, dark pools have sounded almost too reasonable.

- They are private venues with **pre-trade opacity**.
- Institutions use them to avoid the **market impact** of being seen.
- They often execute at a **reference price** taken from the lit market, frequently the **midpoint**, which appears to benefit both sides.

That is the sales pitch. Now comes the catch.

The uncomfortable question: if midpoint is such a good deal, why does anyone give it to you?

When you trade on a lit exchange, you can see the auction: bids, asks, and at least some sense of the line you are stepping into. In a dark pool, the very feature you came for—*not being seen*—also means you cannot easily see *who* you are trading with, or *why* they are there.

This is where we meet a core concept in market microstructure:

Adverse selection is the risk that the party willing to trade with you is doing so because they know something you do not.

In plain English: you get filled *because you are the "good" side of the trade for them.*

A friendly pool can become a hunting ground

It helps to keep the whale story from the prior section in mind. Dark pools were built to help whales trade quietly. But a venue built for whales can attract sharks, because whales leave a trail of value:

- A large, patient institutional order can represent **predictable flow**.
- Predictable flow is valuable information.
- If someone can detect it faster than others, they can trade in front of it, around it, or against it.

The dark pool does not broadcast orders to the public, but it does *still* generate information to those inside the room: fills, partial fills, timing patterns, and other signals about what kind of counterparties are present.

This brings us to another term you will hear from practitioners:

Toxic flow is order flow that tends to be informed or opportunistic—the kind that makes liquidity providers regret trading.

A dark pool is attractive when it contains *natural* buyers and sellers (two institutions with genuine portfolio needs) meeting quietly. It becomes dangerous when it contains a high share of traders who are there primarily because they are *good at picking off other people's orders*.

The "fast fill" paradox: why a quick execution can be a warning sign

Retail investors often celebrate fast execution. Institutions in dark pools sometimes do the opposite: a fill that is *too fast* can be suspicious.

Here is the intuition.

Suppose you place a dark order to **buy** at the midpoint. If the stock's true value is stable, getting a midpoint fill is genuinely good: you avoided paying the full ask.

But what if the public price is about to rise? Then the midpoint you paid just now may look cheap in a moment. Who would be eager to sell to you at the midpoint if the price is about to go up?

Potentially, someone who suspects the price is *not* about to go up—or someone who has reason to believe it is about to go *down*. In other words, the very willingness of the counterparty to trade at midpoint may contain information.

Practitioners sometimes describe this as "regret":

If you trade and immediately regret it, you may have been adversely selected.

A concrete example: midpoint fill, then the floor drops

Keep the numbers simple. The lit market shows:

$$\text{Bid} = \$10.00, \quad \text{Ask} = \$10.10, \quad \text{Midpoint} = \$10.05.$$

You place a dark buy order and get filled at \$10.05. Great, right?

Now imagine that a split second later, new information hits the market (or a large sell program becomes visible elsewhere). The lit market reprices to:

$$\text{Bid} = \$9.70, \quad \text{Ask} = \$9.80, \quad \text{Midpoint} = \$9.75.$$

Your trade at $10.05 is suddenly above the new midpoint. You did not just "save half the spread." You bought right before a drop.

That is adverse selection in its simplest form: the counterparty sold to you at a price that was about to look too high.

Why dark pools can amplify adverse selection risk

Dark pools can increase adverse selection risk for structural reasons, even if no one is breaking rules.

1) You see less of the market's intent. In a lit order book, you may not know who is behind each order, but you can see the *shape* of supply and demand: depth, gaps, sudden cancellations, and pressure near the top of book. In the dark, that information is not visible.

2) The reference price can be "stale" or fragile. Dark pools often reference the lit best bid/offer. In calm conditions, that reference is a good approximation of a fair, competitive price. In fast conditions, the lit quotes can flicker, spreads can widen, and displayed liquidity can evaporate. The midpoint might still be computed, but it may be computed from a *less trustworthy* public snapshot.

3) The most opportunistic traders prefer hidden venues. If a strategy relies on speed and surprise, a dark venue can be attractive. The trader is not advertising their intent either. They are trying to interact with others at moments when the reference price has not yet caught up to reality.

4) Execution quality becomes path-dependent. In a dark pool, you often do not know whether you are getting filled because:

- the venue has healthy natural liquidity, or
- your order is being selectively hit when it is profitable for someone else to do so.

Two venues can both advertise "midpoint fills," yet produce very different outcomes for long-term institutional traders.

Where HFT fits in (carefully, without caricature)

High-frequency trading (HFT) is often blamed for everything from flash crashes to bad hair days. That is not helpful. Many HFT firms act as liquidity providers on lit exchanges, tightening spreads and increasing displayed depth in normal times.

However, HFT is relevant here because the *advantage* in many HFT strategies is:

- faster reaction to public price changes,
- faster inference about order flow,
- faster routing across fragmented venues.

In a fragmented market, information propagates through multiple pipes. Some participants are simply closer to the pipes.

In that environment, adverse selection can show up as a very specific pattern:

You get filled in the dark *right before* the lit market moves against you.

Again, this does not require a conspiracy. If one trader processes information faster, they will tend to trade when the current reference price is favorable to them and avoid trading when it is not. The slower party experiences this as "I only get filled when it's bad for me."

How professionals talk about this risk: "toxic" versus "benign" fills

Institutions often evaluate venues not by marketing terms but by observed outcomes. They ask questions like:

- After our dark-pool fills, does the price tend to move against us?

- Are fills clustered at moments of volatility (when reference prices are least stable)?
- Do we get partial fills that seem to "ping" us and then disappear?
- Does performance differ by time of day or around news events?

These questions reflect a practical goal: identify whether a venue is delivering **benign liquidity** (natural counterparties, genuine size matching) or **toxic liquidity** (opportunistic counterparties with better information or speed).

The central trade-off of trading in the dark

You can now state the trade-off cleanly:

Dark pools can reduce market impact by hiding your intent, but they can increase adverse selection because you may trade against better-informed or faster counterparties.

This is why dark pool usage is not simply "good" or "bad." It is conditional. In calm markets with balanced natural flow, midpoint dark trading can be an efficient way for large investors to reduce costs. In stressed markets or in venues with highly opportunistic participation, midpoint fills can become expensive in a different way: through regret.

A bridge to the next section

- Dark pools *use* lit markets for reference prices.
- Dark pools also *compete* with lit markets for volume.
- The quality of the lit price matters for everyone—including the traders in the dark.

This creates a feedback loop. If too much activity moves into private rooms, the public auction may become thinner and noisier, which makes the reference price less reliable, which makes dark execution riskier.

That is the "parasite paradox" we will examine next: the dark depends on the light, yet it can also drain it.

4.5 The Parasite Paradox: Lit and Dark Interaction

We can now put the full picture together.

- In Section 1, we defined dark pools as **private venues with pre-trade opacity**: orders are not displayed publicly.
- In Section 2, we saw why that privacy is valuable: it can reduce **information leakage** and **market impact** when institutions trade elephant-sized orders.
- In Section 3, we explained how dark pools often work mechanically: they **reference** prices from the lit market, frequently executing at the **midpoint** of the best bid and offer.
- In Section 4, we confronted the principal risk: dark trading can expose you to **adverse selection**—getting filled precisely when it is worst for you.

This final section zooms out. Instead of asking whether a given dark trade is good or bad for one investor, we ask a market-wide question:

> What happens to the *public* market if too much trading migrates into private rooms that use public prices but do not publicly contribute orders?

That tension is what critics call the **parasite paradox**. It is not a moral accusation; it is an ecosystem description.

The paradox in one sentence

A simplified statement of the paradox is:

> **Dark pools rely on lit markets for price discovery, but by attracting volume away from lit markets, they may weaken the very price discovery they depend on.**

If that sounds abstract, read it as an everyday analogy.

A lit market is like a town square where people publicly shout bids and offers. The crowd's shouting is noisy, but it produces a clear *consensus price*. A dark pool is like a set of private side rooms where people agree to transact at "the town square price" without participating in the shouting.

If too many people stop shouting in the square and move into side rooms, the square becomes quieter. But *quieter* is not always better. Sometimes quieter means *thin*. Thin means fragile.

Why lit markets matter: the public auction is a price engine

It is easy to treat the lit market as merely one venue among many. But the lit market plays a special role because it is the main place where **price discovery** happens in real time.

Price discovery requires at least three ingredients:

- **Competition:** many buyers and sellers simultaneously.
- **Visibility:** bids and offers that can be compared (even if only at the top of book).
- **Commitment:** displayed orders that are firm enough to trade against.

The lit market supplies these ingredients by forcing interaction in public. The best bid and offer are not just numbers; they are the outcome of a continual contest among participants.

That contest does important work for the whole financial system:

- it anchors valuations for portfolios,
- it supports index pricing,
- it provides a reference for derivatives,
- it supplies benchmarks for best execution analysis,

- and (crucially for our story) it provides the **reference price** dark pools often use.

How volume leaving the lit market can weaken the "price engine"

Now we examine the claim that dark pools "drain" volume. This can happen in a straightforward way:

- If two institutions execute a large trade in a dark pool, that volume does not appear as displayed liquidity on the lit exchange.
- The lit book therefore has fewer orders resting at various prices.
- With fewer resting orders, the visible depth becomes thinner.

Thinner visible depth has predictable consequences. When a new marketable order hits a thin book, it moves the price more. In microstructure terms, the price becomes more **impact-sensitive**. Spreads can widen, and quotes can become more jumpy.

This is not because dark pools are "bad." It is because **the lit market's job is to absorb trading pressure in public**. If you remove some of the absorbers, pressure produces bigger moves.

A simple feedback loop: from fragmentation to fragility

Here is the ecosystem logic, step by step:

Step 1: Lit markets create a reference price. Public bids and offers form the best bid/offer and the midpoint. This is the "clock" the whole market uses.

Step 2: Dark pools execute using the reference price. They offer midpoint and other reference-priced executions without displaying the underlying interest.

Step 3: Attractive executions pull volume off-exchange. If midpoint trading is cheaper than paying the spread on-exchange, order flow migrates—especially for large traders trying to avoid impact.

Step 4: Lit market depth erodes; spreads and volatility can rise. With less displayed competition and depth, it becomes easier for prices to move with relatively small trades, and liquidity providers may widen spreads as protection.

Step 5: Dark pools inherit a noisier reference price. If the lit market becomes thinner and more volatile, the reference price dark pools peg to becomes less stable, and dark executions become riskier.

Step 6: More participants seek darkness (or pull back entirely). If volatility rises and adverse selection risk grows, some traders prefer hidden execution even more—or they provide less liquidity everywhere. Both outcomes can further weaken the lit market.

This loop is the heart of the parasite paradox: the dark and lit markets are not independent competitors; they are a coupled system.

Why this matters most during stress

In calm conditions, the system can function smoothly:

- the lit market is deep enough to produce reliable quotes,
- dark pools execute at midpoint without much drama,
- and the overall market appears liquid and stable.

But the book you are reading is about what happens when markets suddenly go wrong. In stressed conditions, the coupling becomes more dangerous:

- The lit market can experience **spread explosions** and **liquidity pullbacks**.
- Reference prices can become fragile, updating rapidly or gapping.
- Dark pools may reduce activity (to avoid trading at unreliable references) or become more selective.
- Traders can lose confidence in both venues at once: lit feels expensive, dark feels risky.

When that happens, a market can feel like it is losing its shock absorbers. The public book thins. The private rooms become cautious. The ability to transfer risk smoothly deteriorates.

Even if a full "flash crash" does not occur, the mechanism is the same family: liquidity is not a constant; it is a behavior. In stressed moments, liquidity can vanish because liquidity providers decide the compensation (spread) is not worth the risk (adverse selection). Fragmentation can make that decision propagate faster across venues.

Is the "parasite" label fair? A balanced view

Calling dark pools "parasitic" is rhetorically powerful, but it can oversimplify. A more careful view recognizes two truths at once:

Truth 1: Dark pools can improve execution for large investors. Reducing market impact can benefit end-investors. Forcing every large trade to be fully visible could raise trading costs and ultimately harm pensioners and savers.

Truth 2: Price discovery is a public good inside markets. A robust lit market benefits everyone, including dark pools, because it generates trustworthy reference prices. If too much trading avoids public competition, the remaining displayed market can become less representative and more fragile.

So the real question is not "dark pools: good or evil?" It is:

> How much trading can be private before the public price engine becomes too weak to support the entire system?

Regulators, exchanges, brokers, and institutional investors all wrestle with versions of that question, because the "right" balance depends on market conditions, stock liquidity, and the evolving technology of routing and execution.

A practical takeaway: why market fragmentation matters to ordinary investors

Even if you never route an order to a dark pool yourself, the lit/dark interaction can affect you indirectly:

- It influences **spreads** (how much you pay to trade).
- It affects **volatility** (how stable prices feel).
- It shapes **execution quality** for mutual funds and ETFs you own.
- It can amplify **liquidity shocks** when conditions deteriorate.

In other words, market fragmentation is not a technical footnote. It is part of the plumbing that determines whether markets behave like orderly auctions or like unstable crowds.

Closing the chapter

Dark pools began in this chapter as something mysterious. They end as something more precise: a rational tool with a built-in tension.

> **Dark pools reduce the cost of being seen, but the market still needs a public place where prices are discovered in the open.**

That tension sets the stage for the next part of our journey. When liquidity becomes thin, and when too many participants try to hide at once, markets can shift from "efficient" to "brittle." And brittle markets are the ones that are vulnerable to sudden breaks.

Chapter 5

The Speed Race: Algorithms and High-Frequency Trading

Imagine a trading floor not filled with shouting men in colorful jackets, but with silent rows of humming black server cabinets. In this new world, a 'long-term investment' might last only a few seconds, and the difference between profit and loss is measured in the time it takes light to travel through a fiber-optic cable. We are leaving the era of human judgment and entering the speed race, where mathematical formulas battle each other for micro-pennies, thousands of times per second.

5.1 The Rise of Automation

Imagine you are responsible for trading on behalf of a large pension fund. You are not trying to "beat the market" in the movie-trader sense. Your job is more practical and, in some ways, more difficult: move an enormous position from one state to another (cash into stock, or stock into cash) while disturbing the market as little as possible.

That practical goal is the starting point for modern automation in trading.

In the earliest, more manual era, executing a large trade often meant calling a broker, who would work the order by hand—phoning around, negotiating with specialists on an exchange floor, and trying to find the other side. The process was slow, relationship-driven, and opaque. It also had a crucial advantage: a human could exercise discretion, pausing when the market felt "thin" and accelerating when it felt "liquid."

As markets became electronic, that discretion did not disappear. It became code.

The fundamental problem: size moves prices

The basic microstructure fact that motivates algorithmic execution is simple:

- **Liquidity is finite at each price.** Even in a very active stock, there are only so many shares available to buy at the current best ask, and only so many shares available to sell at the current best bid.
- **A large, urgent order consumes that liquidity.** A buy order that is too big will "walk the book"—it buys the cheapest shares first, then the next cheapest, and so on—pushing the transaction price upward. A large sell order does the opposite.
- **Your own trading becomes your enemy.** The more aggressively you trade, the more you may pay (if buying) or the less you may receive (if selling). This is called **market impact**.

So the question that changed trading is the one institutional traders face every day:

> How do you buy or sell a million shares without announcing it to the market and without moving the price against yourself?

Automation is, at its core, an answer to that question.

From a single "parent" order to many small "child" orders

If you walked onto a trading floor in the old days and said, "Sell 1,000,000 shares," you would immediately create a problem: everyone would infer you have urgent information or urgent needs. Other traders would step back, spreads would widen, and the price would likely fall before you finish.

Electronic markets made that inference easier, not harder. Screens update quickly; data is copied, redistributed, and analyzed by machines. A single giant order displayed in a public limit order book is like shining a flashlight into a dark room: everyone now knows where you are standing.

Modern execution therefore treats the big trade as a **parent order** that should not be shown directly. Instead, it is **sliced** into **child orders**—smaller pieces that are released gradually.

Conceptually, it looks like this:

- The investor decides the **total size** to trade (e.g., sell 1,000,000 shares).
- An execution program (an **algorithm**) determines **how fast** to trade and **in what form** (limit orders, marketable orders, routed to which venues).
- The program sends a sequence of small orders (e.g., 1,000 shares at a time, or 5,000 shares at a time), monitors fills, and adjusts as the market changes.

This slicing is not cosmetic. It changes what other participants can infer. If the market only sees 1,000-share orders appearing intermittently, it is harder to distinguish a large institution working an order from ordinary background flow.

Why automation was inevitable

The shift from manual execution to algorithms happened for structural reasons:

Speed and fragmentation.

Trading is no longer concentrated in one physical place. A single stock can trade simultaneously across many exchanges and alternative venues. That means:

- the "best price" can flicker between venues,
- displayed liquidity can appear on one exchange while hidden liquidity sits elsewhere,
- and routing decisions (where to send the next small order) must be made continuously.

A human cannot reliably watch dozens of venues tick-by-tick and react with consistent timing. Software can.

Consistency and discipline.

Institutional traders face the temptation to overreact: chase the price, panic when volatility rises, or accelerate at exactly the wrong moment. A well-designed execution algorithm enforces a plan: trade at a target pace, avoid signaling, and reduce impulsive behavior.

Measurement.

Once execution is coded, it can be measured: slippage, fill rates, adverse selection, and market impact can be tracked. That feedback loop (measure $\rightarrow$ improve) is much harder when execution is purely discretionary.

Execution algorithms: the digital workhorses

It helps to separate two ideas that casual readers often blend together:

- **An execution algorithm** is primarily about *how* to trade (slicing, timing, routing).
- **A predictive strategy** is about *what* to trade (forecasting returns or direction).

In this section, we are focused on execution. Execution algorithms are closer to logistics than to prophecy. They try to answer questions like:

- Should we trade quickly now, or wait?
- Should we post a limit order (patient, but may not fill) or send a marketable order (immediate, but may pay the spread)?
- Which venues look safest for minimizing information leakage?

To make those decisions, an algorithm watches basic market signals:

- current bid and ask (the spread),
- recent trade volume (how busy the market is),
- short-term volatility (how jumpy prices are),
- and fill quality (are our orders getting filled in a way that helps or hurts?).

Crucially, the algorithm does *not* need to be brilliant about the future to be valuable. It just needs to be disciplined about *not causing damage* while executing a large trade.

Iceberg orders: showing the tip, hiding the mass

One of the most intuitive execution tools is the **iceberg order** (also called a **reserve order**). The metaphor is accurate: only a small portion of the total order is displayed to the public market at any moment.

Suppose you want to sell 200,000 shares, but you only want to show 2,000 shares at a time. You might place an iceberg with:

$$\text{Total (hidden) size} = 200{,}000, \qquad \text{Displayed size} = 2{,}000.$$

To everyone watching the public book, it looks like there are only 2,000 shares for sale at that price. When those 2,000 sell, another 2,000 automatically "refresh" and appear, continuing until the hidden reserve is depleted or the order is canceled.

Icebergs aim to solve two problems simultaneously:

- **Reduce signaling risk:** revealing a million-share intention invites others to trade ahead of you or step away from providing liquidity.

- **Maintain execution presence:** you still want to participate in the market, not vanish entirely.

The key trade-off is subtle: hiding your full size may protect you from being targeted, but it can also reduce the visible liquidity others rely on, which can matter during stressed markets. This tension—between *visible* liquidity and *hidden* liquidity—is one of the recurring themes in flash-crash dynamics.

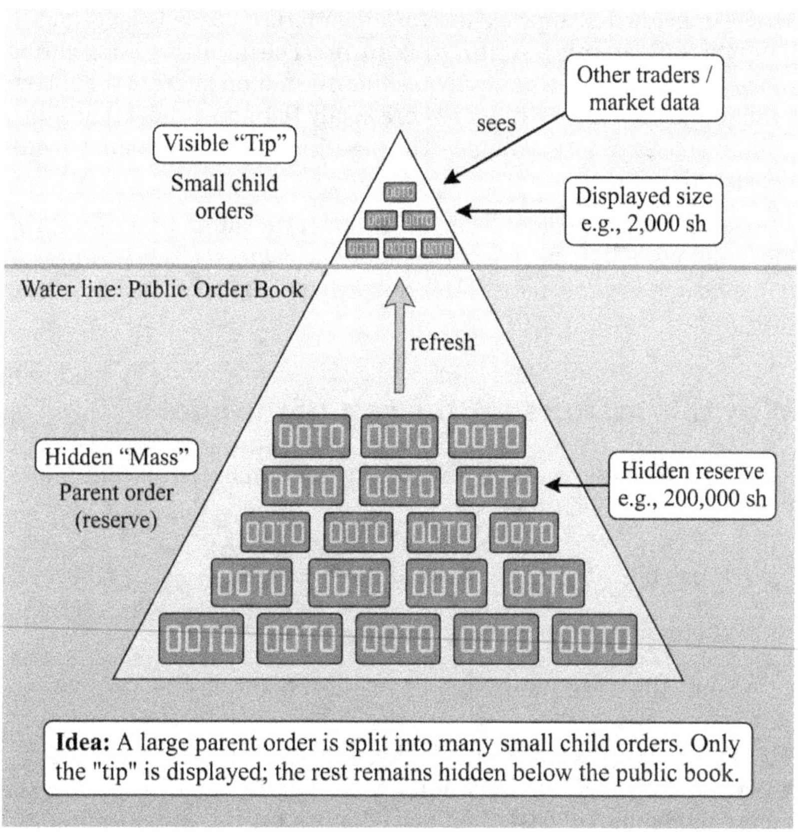

Rule-based execution: stealth with a speed limit

Slicing an order into pieces is only the first step. The next question is *when* to release each piece.

A simple rule-based approach might be:

- trade a fixed amount every minute,
- avoid trading when the spread widens beyond a threshold,
- pause if price moves sharply against the order (a sign you may be detected or the market is destabilizing).

More sophisticated approaches track the market's activity level and attempt to trade **in proportion to volume**. The intuition is straightforward: if the market is naturally trading 10 million shares today, your 1 million shares can be hidden more easily than on a quiet day with 1 million shares of total volume. The algorithm tries to "blend in" with the crowd.

This is why you will often hear institutional execution described in almost biological language: *leave a small footprint, avoid predators, do not splash in shallow water.* It is not poetry; it is practical microstructure.

Why this matters for the rest of the book

Automation changed trading by turning execution into a continuous, high-speed decision process:

- break big intentions into small visible actions,
- route those actions across many venues,
- and adjust the pace based on market conditions.

That system works remarkably well in normal times. But it also creates a new kind of fragility: when many participants use similar rules (or react to the same signals), their behavior can become synchronized. In calm markets, synchronization looks like efficiency. In stressed markets, it can look like sudden emptiness—liquidity that was present a moment ago simply vanishes.

The next step, therefore, is to distinguish ordinary automation from the specialized class of firms built around speed itself: high-frequency traders, whose edge is not patience or long-term information, but reacting first.

5.2 Defining High-Frequency Trading

We saw how modern markets learned to *hide size*. A large institution that wants to buy or sell without moving the price breaks a single intention (a *parent order*) into many small actions (the *child orders*). That shift matters because it changed the market's "texture": instead of a few large, obvious trades, we now see a constant drizzle of tiny updates—orders appearing, canceling, and reappearing across many venues.

High-Frequency Trading (HFT) is built to operate inside that drizzle.

What HFT is not: a faster version of long-term investing

Many people hear "high-frequency" and imagine a superhuman stock picker that predicts where prices will be tomorrow and then trades thousands of times to exploit that prediction.

That picture is usually misleading.

A traditional investor (a mutual fund, a pension fund, an individual saving for retirement) typically cares about:

- **fundamentals** (earnings, growth, interest rates),
- **horizons** measured in months or years,
- and **directional exposure** (being long or short because they believe price will rise or fall).

An HFT firm, in contrast, is often closer to a *traffic engineer* than a forecaster. Many HFT strategies are designed to:

- react to tiny, short-lived changes in supply and demand,
- trade *very* frequently with small profit per trade,
- and keep directional risk small by not holding inventory for long.

In other words, HFT is less about "knowing the future" and more about **reaching the present first**.

A practical definition: speed as a business model

High-Frequency Trading is not a single strategy. It is a **style of trading** defined by a set of operational characteristics:

- **Very low latency.** The firm invests heavily to reduce the delay between receiving information and sending an order.
- **High message rates.** HFTs submit, modify, and cancel orders at extremely high speed (many more messages than actual completed trades).
- **Short holding periods.** Positions are typically held for seconds, milliseconds, or less; overnight risk is often minimized.
- **Small edge per trade.** Many HFT strategies aim for fractions of a cent to a few cents per share, repeated at scale.
- **Automation end-to-end.** Decisions are made by software systems that process market data, manage risk, and route orders without human intervention in real time.

A useful mental model is this: if an institutional execution algorithm is trying to *quietly move a boulder* across the market, an HFT system is trying to *skate across the surface* of the market as smoothly and quickly as possible, collecting tiny gains for providing immediacy or for being first to react.

Latency: the key word you should not skip

The core concept behind HFT is **latency**.

Definition (plain English). Latency is the time it takes for information to travel to you, for you to process it, and for your response to reach the market.

Even if your trading logic is brilliant, it cannot help you if you learn the new price after everyone else has already traded on it.

Where latency comes from. Latency is not just "computer speed." It is the sum of several delays:

- **Transmission delay:** how long it takes for data to travel through fiber, microwave, or other networks.
- **Processing delay:** how long your systems take to decode market data, update internal models, and decide what to do.
- **Queueing delay:** how long your message waits before being handled by exchange gateways or internal systems.
- **Matching delay:** the time until your order reaches the exchange's matching engine and is processed relative to other incoming orders.

This is why HFT has an "engineering" flavor. Firms spend on:

- optimized software and hardware,
- specialized network connections,
- and sometimes physical proximity to exchange data centers ("co-location").

The details vary, but the economic point is stable: **when profits come from being first, milliseconds matter**. In some contexts, microseconds matter.

Why speed matters financially: two quick stories

Abstract talk of microseconds can feel detached from reality. Two short scenarios show why latency becomes money.

Story 1: the disappearing quote. You are a fast market-making system quoting:

$$\text{Bid } 100.00 \quad \text{Ask } 100.01$$

Suddenly, new information hits the market and the fair value jumps up. If you are slow to cancel your old ask at 100.01, someone else may buy from you at 100.01 just before you update. That is not a win; it is a loss disguised as a trade.

So speed here is defensive: **cancel quickly to avoid being picked off** when your quote becomes stale.

Story 2: the race to supply immediacy. An institutional execution algorithm starts buying aggressively (perhaps because its rules tell it to keep up with volume). Liquidity at the best ask is consumed. In the brief window before prices fully adjust across venues, fast traders may be able to:

- detect that the market is about to move,
- adjust their quotes first,
- and earn spreads by being the first providers of new liquidity at the updated price level.

In this story, speed is offensive: **react first, reprice first, and trade first**.

Both stories are about the same thing: the market is a moving target, and latency determines whether you hit the target or get hit by it.

HFT firms as the new "middle layer" of markets

To place HFT in the market ecosystem, compare three roles:

- **Investors:** want exposure. They ultimately want to own (or sell) an asset because of cash flows, risk, or portfolio needs.

- **Institutional executors:** want *good execution*. They are paid to convert big intentions into trades while minimizing impact and information leakage.
- **HFT firms:** often specialize in *immediacy and microstructure*. They profit from providing liquidity, managing spreads, and reacting quickly to changes in order flow and prices.

This is why it is fair to say that many HFT firms function as a digital replacement for older forms of intermediation. In earlier eras, a human specialist (or dealer) stood between buyers and sellers, using discretion to smooth trading. Today, much of that smoothing function is automated and distributed across many firms and venues.

However, the replacement is imperfect. A human specialist might keep providing quotes during stress because of obligations, relationships, or judgment. An HFT system is governed by rules and risk limits. If its models detect danger—or if volatility makes inventory too risky—it may simply stop quoting or widen spreads sharply. That behavior is rational for the firm, but it can feel like liquidity "evaporating" to everyone else.

A simple distinction: liquidity provider vs. liquidity demander

One of the cleanest ways to understand HFT is to ask a mechanical question:

*Are they mostly **posting** orders for others to trade against, or mostly **hitting** existing orders?*

Many HFT strategies are, at least part of the time, **liquidity providers**. They post bids and offers, earn the bid–ask spread when they buy at the bid and sell at the ask, and try to keep their inventory near zero.

Other HFT strategies are more **liquidity demanding**. They send marketable orders to exploit tiny, fleeting opportunities (including reacting to price changes across venues).

Real firms often do both depending on conditions, and the same firm can switch modes quickly. The important point is that HFT is tightly linked to the **microstructure plumbing** of markets: quotes, cancellations, spreads, and the speed at which all of those update.

Why this section matters for flash crashes

Flash-crash-style events are not caused by one villain pushing one button. They are more often the product of many fast systems responding to the same stress signals at once.

HFT is central to that story because:

- HFT firms are deeply involved in the *day-to-day supply* of displayed liquidity (quotes).
- Their willingness to supply that liquidity depends on models and limits that can change abruptly when volatility rises.
- Small delays and fragmented venues mean that during turmoil, different parts of the market can temporarily disagree about price, widening spreads and increasing uncertainty.

So, defining HFT is not about labeling traders as "good" or "bad." It is about understanding a crucial mechanism: in modern electronic markets, **speed is a form of capital**. Firms that invest in low latency can earn money by reacting first, but the same speed can amplify instability when many algorithms pull back simultaneously.

5.3 Market Making and Inventory

The previous section defined High-Frequency Trading (HFT) as a style of trading built around low latency, high message rates, and short holding periods. Now we can answer the natural next question:

> How do you make money trading at high speed without making a big bet on whether the market goes up or down?

One of the most common answers is **market making**. Market making is not glamorous, but it is foundational. In a fragmented electronic market, it is often the mechanism that turns a crowd of buyers and sellers into something that feels like a continuous "market" rather than a series of awkward negotiations.

The bid–ask spread: the market's built-in toll

To understand market making, you need one piece of vocabulary: the **bid–ask spread**.

- The **bid** is the best price currently available for someone who wants to *sell* immediately (because a buyer is willing to buy at that price).
- The **ask** (or **offer**) is the best price currently available for someone who wants to *buy* immediately (because a seller is willing to sell at that price).
- The **spread** is:

$$Spread = Ask - Bid.$$

If the bid is $100.00 and the ask is $100.01, then the spread is $0.01 (one cent). That penny is not a random annoyance. It is the market's way of pricing immediacy. If you want to trade *right now*, you usually pay the spread.

What a market maker actually does

A market maker tries to be available on both sides of the market at once:

- posting a **buy** limit order at (or near) the bid, and
- posting a **sell** limit order at (or near) the ask.

When a seller arrives and wants immediacy, they may hit the market maker's bid. When a buyer arrives and wants immediacy, they may lift the market maker's ask. If the market maker manages to buy at the bid and later sell at the ask, the spread is their gross revenue on that round trip.

This is the economic heart of market making:

> **Provide immediacy** to others, and try to earn the **spread** as compensation.

There is no requirement that the market maker predict the long-term direction of the stock. In fact, many market makers attempt to keep their net position near zero, precisely so that their profits come from the spread rather than from a directional bet.

A tiny profit, repeated at scale

The spread can look laughably small. A penny? Sometimes less?

But market making is a scale business. If you earn $0.01 per share (one cent) and you trade 2 million shares in a day on round trips, that is $20,000 in gross spread capture. If you can do it across many symbols, many venues, and many days, the economics become meaningful.

The catch is that the spread is not a gift. It is payment for taking on a specific risk that becomes acute during volatility: **inventory risk**.

Inventory risk: the "hot potato" problem

Inventory risk is easiest to understand with a simple example.

Suppose a market maker posts quotes:

Bid 100.00   Ask 100.01

and a seller hits the bid. The market maker buys shares at $100.00. For a moment, the market maker is **long** inventory.

If nothing else happens, the market maker would like to sell that inventory at $100.01 to a buyer, earning the spread.

But what if the price drops to $99.90 before the market maker can sell?

Then the market maker is holding stock that is now worth less. The single cent of spread they hoped to earn is overwhelmed by a ten-cent adverse move. This is why market makers often behave as if inventory is a hot potato: they want to hold it only briefly, and they want to pass it along quickly.

Why inventory becomes dangerous in fast markets. During calm periods, prices move slowly enough that buying at the bid and selling at the ask is often feasible. During volatile periods, the market can jump between price levels so quickly that:

- you buy at the old bid just before prices fall, or
- you sell at the old ask just before prices rise.

Either way, you are transacting at a stale price and getting "run over" by the next move.

This is not mainly a moral story about predation; it is a mechanical story about timing. When the world changes faster than your quotes update, you can lose money simply by being available.

Adverse selection: losing to better-informed (or faster) traders

Inventory risk has a close cousin: **adverse selection**. This is the risk that the person trading against you is doing so because they know (or have detected) that the price is about to move.

A market maker's nightmare trade is:

- you *buy* from a seller right before bad news pushes the price down, or
- you *sell* to a buyer right before good news pushes the price up.

From the market maker's perspective, it can feel like this: the only time you get hit is when it is dangerous to be hit. In reality, what is happening is selection—traders are more likely to demand immediacy when immediacy is especially valuable. In electronic markets, "valuable" often means "the price is about to change."

This is one reason speed matters for market makers. Low latency is partly offensive (compete for trades) but often defensive: cancel stale quotes quickly to reduce adverse selection.

How market makers manage inventory (without getting philosophical)

Market makers do not rely on hope. They rely on controls. The exact implementations differ, but the logic is remarkably consistent.

1) Re-centering quotes. If the market maker has accumulated too much inventory (say, too long), it may:

- lower its bid (be less eager to buy more), and
- lower its ask (be more eager to sell what it has).

This tilts the odds toward reducing inventory.

2) Tight limits and forced exits. Many systems set hard limits: maximum long position, maximum short position, and maximum loss. If limits are reached, the system may:

- widen quotes dramatically (trade less),
- or temporarily stop quoting (trade almost not at all),
- or aggressively unwind inventory (becoming a liquidity demander).

3) Hedging (when possible). Some market makers hedge exposure with related instruments—for example, using futures or ETFs to offset broad market moves. Hedging is not always perfect, but it can reduce the most dangerous type of inventory risk: sudden market-wide price shocks.

These controls are rational at the firm level. But they matter systemically because they are often triggered by the same conditions (volatility spikes, spreads widening, prices gapping). When many market makers pull back at once, the market can go from liquid to thin quickly.

Why liquidity "vanishes": a mechanical chain reaction

To a casual observer, a flash crash or mini-crash can look like a mystery: one moment, the screen shows tight spreads and plenty of quotes; the next moment, prices gap and the book looks empty.

Market making explains how that can happen without any conspiracy:

1. Volatility rises (prices start moving faster).
2. Inventory risk and adverse selection rise with it.
3. Market makers widen spreads and reduce displayed size to protect themselves.
4. If stress continues, some market makers stop quoting or quote at much worse prices.
5. With fewer bids close to the current price, a market sell order has to "walk the book" farther, causing a sharp drop.

Notice what is happening: the market maker is not deciding "the price should crash." The market maker is deciding "I cannot safely stand here with tight quotes." When enough participants make that decision simultaneously, liquidity thins, and prices can move violently as orders search for the next available counterparties.

The spread is earned—but it is earned by holding risk

At this point we can state the market-making bargain clearly:

- **Reward:** capture the bid–ask spread by buying at the bid and selling at the ask.
- **Risk:** hold inventory, even briefly, while prices can move against you.

When markets are calm, the bargain looks attractive, spreads look stable, and quotes look deep. When markets are stressed, the bargain becomes dangerous, spreads widen, and liquidity providers retreat.

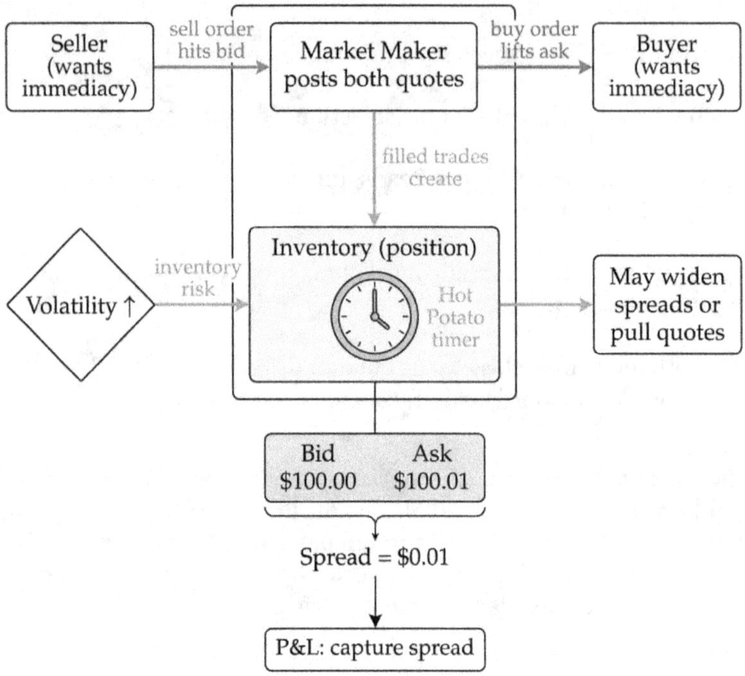

Connecting back to automation and forward to instability

Execution algorithms (from the first section) slice institutional orders into many small trades. HFT firms (from the second section) compete to react quickly to those trades and to the changing state of the order book. Market makers sit at the intersection: they often provide the quotes that sliced orders trade against.

That is why inventory is so important. When the market is calm, market makers can absorb order flow and keep trading smooth. When the market becomes scary, inventory becomes radioactive. The rational response is to reduce exposure—and when many market makers reduce exposure at once, the market can suddenly feel as if the floor has dropped out.

In the next section, we turn from the general economics of speed and inventory to one of the most controversial speed-based behaviors in fragmented markets: **latency arbitrage**, the exploitation of tiny time delays between venues.

5.4 Latency Arbitrage

Up to now, the story has been about *execution and intermediation*. Institutions slice large trades into child orders to avoid moving the price. High-frequency traders compete on low latency. Market makers try to earn the bid–ask spread while keeping inventory risk under control.

Those pieces set the stage for one of the most controversial activities in modern fragmented markets: **latency arbitrage**.

The phrase sounds technical, but the idea is simple:

> When the same asset trades in multiple places, a price change appears in one place first and elsewhere a moment later. Latency arbitrage is the attempt to profit in that brief gap.

To understand why this exists, we need one more structural fact about modern markets.

One stock, many venues, one unavoidable problem

In an ideal world, a stock would have one "official" price at each instant. In the real world, the same stock is quoted and traded across multiple exchanges and other venues. Even when everything is functioning well, these venues are *physically separate*, and information takes time to travel.

That time does not have to be long to matter. If you build a business around reacting in microseconds, then a delay of even a few milliseconds is an eternity.

So the key ingredient behind latency arbitrage is not greed or cleverness. It is **geometry**:

- venues are in different locations,
- signals move at finite speed,
- and markets update in discrete messages, not as a single synchronized heartbeat.

When prices change rapidly, those small delays become tradable.

The core scenario: stale quotes

Latency arbitrage is easiest to see through a concrete scenario. Imagine two venues quoting the same stock:

- **Exchange A (New York)** updates first.
- **Exchange B (Chicago)** updates slightly later.

Suppose the stock's true economic value jumps upward. Exchange A receives the buying pressure first, so the best ask on A rises. But for a brief moment, Exchange B is still showing the *old* ask.

That old ask is called **stale**.

If a fast trader can see the update on A and reach B before B updates its quotes, the fast trader can buy on B at the stale (too-cheap) ask and then, in effect, be holding stock that is immediately worth more in the updated market.

This is not "predicting" the future. It is harvesting a **time lag**.

Why this is called "arbitrage" (even though it is not free money)

In textbooks, arbitrage often means a risk-free profit: buy low in one place and simultaneously sell high in another, locking in a spread.

Latency arbitrage is messier. It is often *close* to that textbook idea, but not perfectly riskless because:

- the trader might fail to complete the second leg,
- the market might move again during the attempt,
- or the liquidity might disappear.

Still, it is called arbitrage because it is fundamentally about **price consistency across venues**. The trader is betting that the stale venue will soon "agree" with the updated venue, and is racing to trade in the instant before that agreement happens.

The speed race is physical, not just digital

It is tempting to imagine that this is simply about having a faster computer. But the more sobering truth is that latency is also about **distance**.

Signals cannot travel faster than the speed of light, and in real networks they travel slower than that. Even small differences in path length and technology matter:

- A **straight line** communication path is shorter than a route that zig-zags through network hubs.
- **Microwave** links can be closer to a straight line through the air.
- **Fiber** routes often follow rights-of-way and can be longer and more indirect.

This is how finance ends up investing in towers, dishes, and specialized routes. If your profits come from winning a race measured in milliseconds, then shaving even a small fraction of that time is economically meaningful.

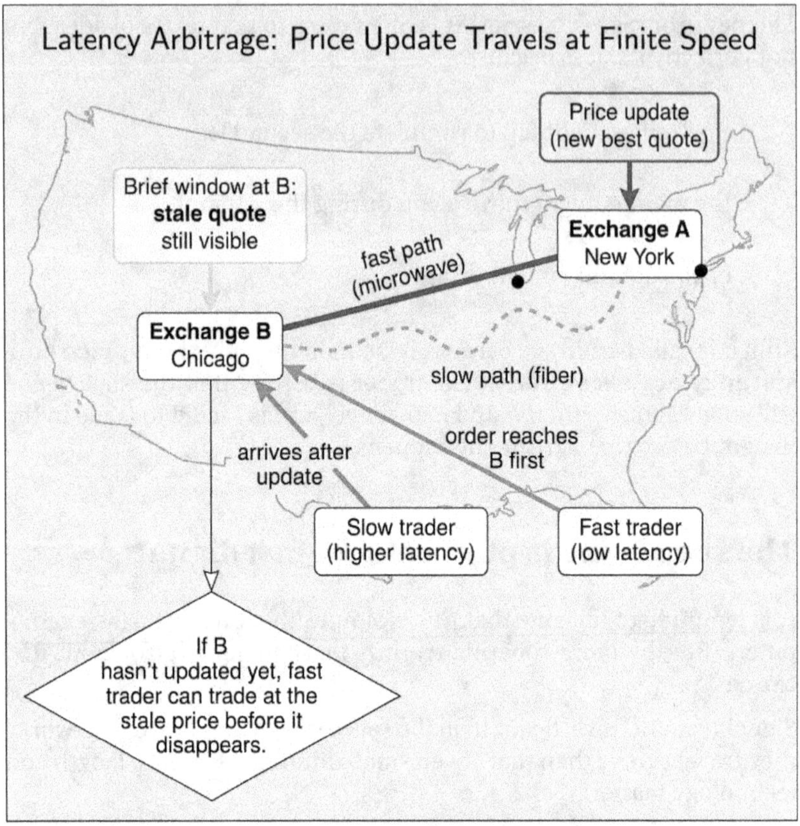

The "snipe" and why it feels unfair

In industry slang, a fast trader who hits a stale quote is sometimes said to **snipe** it: execute against it before it refreshes.

Why does this generate so much controversy?

Because from the perspective of the slower participant, the interaction can feel like this:

- "I posted a quote in good faith."
- "Before I even had time to update it, someone traded against me."

- "The only trades I get are the trades that hurt."

That last sentence is the intuition of **adverse selection** we discussed in market making, intensified by fragmentation. If the fastest traders can reliably pick off stale quotes, then posting tight quotes becomes less attractive. Market makers respond rationally by:

- widening spreads,
- quoting smaller sizes,
- or pulling quotes more quickly when markets move.

So even though latency arbitrage is pursued by a subset of firms, it can influence the market environment for everyone, because it affects how safe it feels to provide liquidity.

Why it persists: incentives created by fragmented, fast markets

Latency arbitrage is not primarily about a single clever trick. It is about incentives.

When:

- the same instrument trades in multiple venues,
- messages travel at finite speed,
- and the fastest participants can act before slower ones can update,

then a profit opportunity exists. Where an opportunity exists, someone will build a business to pursue it.

This is also why the "speed race" tends to escalate. If one firm invests in a faster link, the gap it creates can be monetized until competitors catch up. The prize is not a permanent monopoly; it is a temporary edge, renewed by constant engineering.

The connection to liquidity crises

Latency arbitrage matters in a book about flash crashes for one reason: it changes the **willingness to quote** during fast moves.

In calm markets, small cross-venue delays are mostly harmless background noise. In stressed markets, price changes propagate rapidly and unevenly across venues, and stale quotes become more common. That makes liquidity provision riskier. If market makers and other liquidity providers respond by widening spreads or pulling back, the order book can thin out precisely when it is needed most.

So latency arbitrage is not just a story about fast traders picking off slower traders. It is a story about how **finite-speed information** interacts with **fragmented venues** to shape liquidity.

5.5 Feedback Loops

So far, each part of the speed race has looked reasonable when viewed in isolation.

- Institutions slice big trades into small pieces to reduce market impact.
- High-frequency traders invest in low latency because reacting first is valuable.
- Market makers earn the spread, but protect themselves when inventory risk rises.
- Latency arbitrage exists because information reaches venues at different times.

None of these ingredients requires anyone to be irrational or malicious. And yet, modern markets sometimes behave as if they are brittle: a small shock becomes a sudden air pocket, spreads explode, and prices gap.

The missing concept is **interaction**. Markets are not one algorithm. They are *many* algorithms watching the same screens, reading the same signals, and reacting to each other. When those reactions reinforce one another, you get a **feedback loop**.

What a feedback loop means in trading (plain English)

A feedback loop occurs when

A price move → triggers trading behavior → causes more price movement

If the "more price movement" is in the *same direction* as the original move, the loop is **positive feedback**. Positive feedback amplifies.

In everyday life, positive feedback is what happens when a microphone picks up sound from a speaker and creates a screech: a small signal feeds itself until it becomes overwhelming. In markets, the screech is a rapid move and a sudden lack of liquidity.

Negative feedback, in contrast, stabilizes. A classic negative feedback mechanism in markets would be "price drops attract buyers," which can cushion declines. The risk in modern electronic markets is that, for short periods, stabilizers step back and amplifiers dominate.

Why automation makes feedback loops more likely

Humans can behave in herds, but they also hesitate, disagree, and get distracted. Algorithms behave differently:

- **They share inputs.** Many systems monitor the same variables: volatility, order book depth, spreads, last trade price, and recent returns.
- **They share rules.** Risk limits, volatility filters, and "pull back when things get scary" logic are common across firms.
- **They react quickly and consistently.** When a threshold is crossed, code executes with little delay and little ambiguity.

When many participants use similar triggers, a market can experience what engineers would call *synchronized switching*: many systems change state at once. In trading, that state change is often some version of "reduce exposure" or "stop providing liquidity."

The building blocks of an algorithmic spiral

To see how a spiral forms, we will construct it step by step from mechanisms you already know.

Step 1: a small initial push

It starts with something ordinary:

- a modest sell program begins,
- a news headline hits,
- a risk model at a fund reduces exposure,
- or a stop-loss level is reached by a group of traders.

On its own, this might be absorbed smoothly by market makers and other liquidity providers. The market might drift down a few ticks and recover.

Step 2: liquidity thins as market makers protect inventory

From the previous section, recall the market maker's bargain: earn the spread, but do not get stuck holding inventory when prices move fast.

When selling pressure rises, two things often happen at once:

- **Volatility increases.** Prices begin to move more quickly.
- **Adverse selection risk increases.** Traders hitting bids are more likely to be doing so because the price is falling.

A rational market maker response is to:

- widen spreads,
- reduce quoted size,
- cancel quotes more aggressively,
- or temporarily stop quoting at the best prices.

This is the first amplifying link: a moderate sell wave leads to less liquidity, which makes the next sell wave move the price more.

Step 3: execution algorithms keep up

Now bring back the institutions slicing orders.

Many execution algorithms are designed to trade with the market's activity. If volume rises or if a schedule says "you must finish by the close," the algorithm may increase its trading rate to avoid falling behind.

In a falling market, this can mean:

- more child sell orders arriving,
- hitting increasingly thin bids,
- producing a faster decline than anyone intended.

No single child order is large. But the *sequence* can be relentless, like a drumbeat.

Step 4: triggers fire in layers (trigger stacking)

Here is where feedback loops become particularly dangerous. Many systems contain thresholds such as:

- **Volatility filters:** "If volatility exceeds X, reduce quoting size."

- **Spread filters:** "If the spread widens beyond Y, stop posting at the top of book."
- **Loss limits:** "If P&L drops by Z, cut risk."
- **Momentum signals:** "If price falls quickly, sell to avoid bigger losses."
- **Inventory caps:** "If inventory becomes too long, stop buying and lower bids."

Trigger stacking occurs when one price move crosses multiple thresholds across many firms *at the same time*. The cascade is not just one system reacting. It is many systems simultaneously switching to defensive mode.

The sequence often looks like this:

1. Price drops modestly.
2. Spreads widen and depth thins.
3. The next trades cause a larger drop than expected because there is less depth.
4. The larger drop trips more volatility and loss thresholds.
5. More liquidity is pulled; more selling occurs.
6. The cycle repeats.

The key is that thresholds are *nonlinear*. A market can look stable for a while, then suddenly accelerate when it crosses a boundary that many systems share.

The "hot potato" goes market-wide

In the market making section, inventory was described as a hot potato: market makers do not want to hold it during fast moves.

Feedback loops can turn that local hot potato into a market-wide game.

In a fast decline:

- Market makers that buy from sellers accumulate inventory they do not want.
- They attempt to offload it quickly, often by lowering bids or by selling elsewhere.
- Other market makers see the same decline and reduce their own willingness to absorb more.

The result is not a stable transfer of inventory from impatient sellers to patient buyers. It is a sequence of increasingly impatient intermediaries trying to pass inventory to someone else. If end-investors (slower, discretionary buyers) do not step in quickly, the market can briefly feel as though *no one wants to be the final holder*.

When that happens, the bid side of the order book can become thin or even appear to vanish at nearby prices, and the price must fall until it finds a level where genuine buyers appear.

Why the limit order book makes spirals visible

Electronic markets make feedback loops visible through the **limit order book**. In stable conditions, the book typically has a "cushion" of bids below the current price and asks above it.

During a feedback loop:

- bids near the top are canceled or reduced,
- spreads widen,
- and the next market sell order has to search deeper for liquidity.

This creates what can look like a "gap" in the book: not because every buyer disappeared, but because the buyers that remain are now demanding a bigger discount to compensate for uncertainty and volatility.

A crucial misconception: "the machines caused it"

It is tempting to blame machines as if automation itself is the villain. That misses the point.

A more accurate statement is:

Automation can turn sensible individual rules into dangerous collective behavior when many participants share similar triggers and react at similar speeds.

Each participant is managing risk. Collectively, those risk reductions can remove liquidity when it is most needed.

This is also why feedback loops are hard to "see" in advance. The harmful pattern is not inside a single algorithm's code. It is in the *interaction* among many algorithms operating in the same environment.

From feedback loops to flash crashes

A flash crash is, in many cases, a feedback loop moving fast enough to outrun stabilizing forces. The stabilizers might include:

- discretionary traders stepping in to buy,
- slower market makers re-entering when prices look attractive,
- or mechanisms such as pauses and limits that slow the pace of trading.

When stabilizers arrive late, the market can overshoot—dropping farther than fundamentals justify—and then rebound sharply once liquidity returns. That whiplash is one of the signatures of a liquidity-driven event rather than a slow, information-driven revaluation.

What to remember

If you remember only a few ideas from this section, make them these:

1. **Feedback loops amplify.** A price move can trigger behavior that causes more of the same move.

2. **Liquidity is conditional.** It is abundant when risk feels manageable and scarce when risk feels unbounded.

3. **Trigger stacking creates cliffs.** Small changes can suddenly cross thresholds shared by many systems, leading to synchronized pullbacks.

These concepts will be the backbone for the later chapters on flash crashes and liquidity crises. Once you see markets as interacting automated systems—not just buyers and sellers—sudden breakdowns stop looking like mysteries and start looking like understandable (and, sometimes, preventable) chain reactions.

Chapter 6

When the Music Stops: Liquidity Crises

Imagine a crowded theater where everyone is enjoying the show. Suddenly, someone smells smoke. In a normal market, the exits are wide enough for people to leave gradually. But in a liquidity crisis, the doors mysteriously shrink to the size of mouseholes. This chapter explores what happens when the mechanism that allows us to buy and sell breaks down, turning a rational correction into a terrifying stampede where cash is king, prices become meaningless, and the "music" of the market comes to a screeching halt.

6.1 Signs of a Drought

Liquidity is one of those words that sounds academic until the day you need it—and suddenly it feels like oxygen. Most days, markets feel effortless: you click *buy* or *sell*, you get a fill, and the price barely twitches. That ease is not a law of nature. It is a condition—and like any condition, it can deteriorate.

A liquidity crisis rarely announces itself with a siren. It usually begins with subtle changes that look harmless in isolation: a spread that is a little wider than usual, an order book that looks a little emptier than it did yesterday, a price that starts jumping in "odd" increments instead of moving smoothly. These are the signs of a drought: the market still looks like a market, but the water level is falling.

This section teaches you how to recognize those early warning signs *before* a crash occurs. We will do it by separating two ideas that casual observers often confuse:

- **Trading volume** (how much trading happened), and
- **Market depth** (how much trading *could* happen without moving the price much).

Liquidity is not "how active" a market is

When headlines say, "Volume was huge today," many readers interpret that as, "The market was liquid today." Sometimes that is true. But it is not guaranteed, because volume is a *rear-view mirror* statistic. It tells you what happened *after* buyers and sellers already found each other.

Liquidity, by contrast, is about the market's *capacity*. It is the ability to trade *now* without paying a big penalty in price.

A simple way to think about it:

Volume is how many cars drove on the highway today.
Depth is how many lanes are open right now.

A highway can have impressive daily traffic (volume) and still be fragile if, at rush hour, only one lane is open (thin depth). One minor accident can then trigger a jam that looks disproportionate to the size of the initial problem.

Depth vs. Volume: the order book is the "water level"

Most modern markets are organized around a **limit order book**. At any moment you will typically see:

- **Bids:** standing orders to buy at specific prices.
- **Asks (offers):** standing orders to sell at specific prices.
- **Bid–ask spread:** the gap between the best bid and best ask.

Market depth describes how much size is waiting on those bid and ask levels—not just at the very best prices, but across multiple price steps. Deep markets have many "layers" of orders stacked up, ready to absorb trades. Thin markets have only a few.

Here is the crucial intuition: *price stability comes from inventory of willingness.* If there are many willing buyers at and near the current price, a wave of selling has to push through a lot of resting demand before price falls meaningfully. If there are only a few willing buyers, price can drop sharply even if nothing "fundamental" changed about the asset.

The easiest mental model is a water tank:

- The **current price** is the waterline you can see.
- **Depth** is how much water is *behind* that visible line—how much can be drawn out before the level falls.
- A **sell order** is opening a drain.

Two tanks can show the same waterline (same current price). But if one tank is almost empty, the level will drop fast the moment you open the drain.

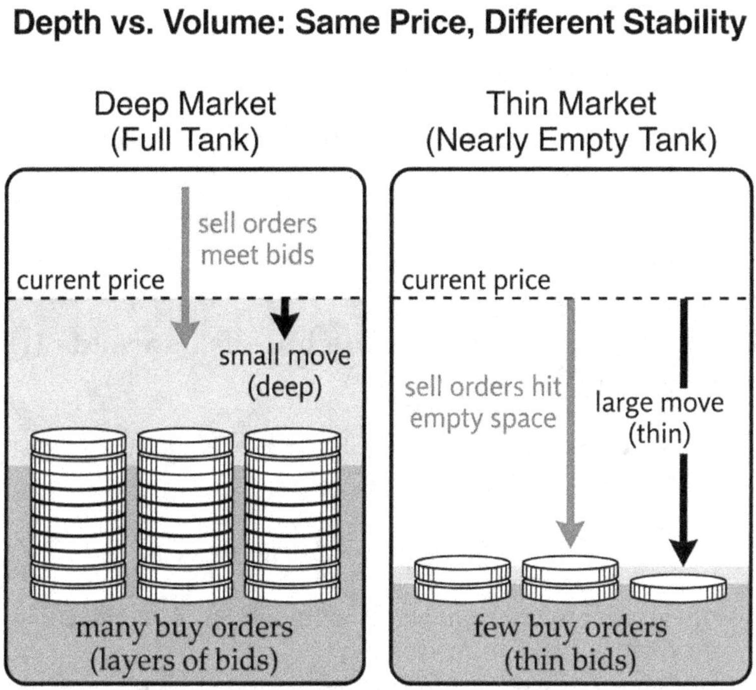

Same last price. Different depth.
Thin depth means price can gap down quickly.

A practical definition: "How much can I trade without moving the price?"

In a deep market, you can trade a meaningful amount and the price moves only a little. In a thin market, even moderate trades cause **slippage**—you get filled, but at progressively worse prices because you are chewing through the few orders that were available.

You do *not* need to see the full order book to understand the concept. Even with basic market data, you can watch for symptoms that often accompany thinning depth:

- spreads that widen,
- prices that jump in discrete steps (“gaps”),
- and executions that occur at worse prices than expected.

These are not merely annoyances. They are the market telling you that the cushion is shrinking.

Warning Sign #1: Widening bid–ask spreads (the “toll” goes up)

The **bid–ask spread** is the most visible price of liquidity. It is the toll you pay for immediacy:

- If you want to sell *right now*, you usually sell to the bid.
- If you want to buy *right now*, you usually buy from the ask.

In calm conditions, spreads tend to be narrow because market makers and other liquidity providers are comfortable posting quotes close to each other. In stressed conditions, spreads widen because posting a tight quote becomes dangerous. When prices are jumping, a liquidity provider worries about being the “last” buyer before a sudden drop (or the “last” seller before a sudden spike). To protect themselves, they quote wider.

What it looks like in real time. You might see a stock that usually has a one-cent spread suddenly trade with five, ten, or twenty cents between bid and ask. In a very liquid large-cap name, that is already a meaningful change in microstructure. In less liquid names (small caps, certain ETFs, off-the-run bonds), the widening can be far more dramatic.

Why it matters. A wider spread is not only a cost; it is also a signal that the market is starting to ration liquidity. In other words, the market is still functioning—but it is becoming *selective* about who gets to trade cheaply.

Warning Sign #2: Thinning order books (the shoreline recedes)

If spreads are the toll, **depth** is the road capacity. A market can show a reasonable spread and still be fragile if there is little size behind the best bid and ask.

The simplest version of thinning is: the top of book looks fine, but the levels behind it are empty. When selling pressure arrives, the best bid is consumed quickly and the next bids are far lower. The price does not smoothly "walk" down; it **gaps** down.

The receding tide analogy. Before some tsunamis, the water at the shoreline pulls back unusually far. To onlookers, it can look calm or even fascinating. The danger is not obvious until the wave arrives.

Thinning depth is the market's receding tide:

- The last traded price may look normal.
- The chart may look calm.
- But the hidden support—the standing willingness to buy—has quietly withdrawn.

When the wave of sell orders arrives, there is less water to absorb it.

Warning Sign #3: "Air pockets" and discontinuous prices

In a healthy, deep market, price changes often look continuous: trades occur across many nearby prices because the book has many layers. In a drying market, you begin to see **air pockets**—price levels with little or no resting liquidity.

Air pockets show up as:

- sudden jumps from one price to another,
- prints that appear "out of line" with the recent tape,
- and sharper intraday spikes in measured volatility.

This is not necessarily manipulation; it is often mechanics. If there are no meaningful bids between $100.00 and $99.50, then a market sell order that is only slightly larger than normal can cause the next trade to print at $99.50. The chart will later show a sharp step down, but the real cause was that the middle of the ladder was missing.

Warning Sign #4: High volume that feels "panicky" (volume as smoke, not comfort)

Volume can rise for healthy reasons (earnings news, index rebalancing, genuine disagreement about value). But in liquidity droughts, volume often rises for a different reason: **immediacy demand**. Many participants simultaneously decide, "I do not want to hold this risk for even one more minute."

That is when volume becomes smoke rather than comfort.

A key pattern to watch for is this combination:

Volume up + spreads wider + price jumps/gaps = liquidity likely deteriorating.

This combination matters because it suggests trading is happening *despite* poor liquidity conditions—not because the market is comfortably deep. In plain English: lots of people are trying to get out, and the market is charging them more to do it.

Warning Sign #5: Execution quality degrades (slippage becomes normal)

If you have ever placed a market order and been surprised by the fill price, you have experienced a small liquidity lesson.

During drought conditions, that surprise becomes common:

- A market order fills across multiple price levels.
- A limit order that "should" get filled does not (because quotes flicker or disappear).

- You see more partial fills, cancellations, and rapid quote updates.

For non-professional traders, the most practical takeaway is not to become obsessed with every micro-detail, but to treat repeated slippage as a *diagnostic*. If your fills are consistently worse than expected, the market is telling you something about its depth *right now*.

Putting the signs together: a simple "drought checklist"

No single metric predicts a crash. Liquidity crises are regime shifts, and regime shifts are recognized by *clusters* of symptoms.

Here is a compact checklist you can use to organize what you see:

- **1. Spreads:** Are bid–ask spreads widening relative to normal for this asset and time of day?
- **2. Depth:** Does price seem to move more than usual for the same apparent trade size?
- **3. Continuity:** Are there more gaps, jumps, or "air pockets" in the tape?
- **4. Volume context:** Is volume rising *alongside* worse trading conditions (wider spreads, jumpier price)?
- **5. Execution quality:** Are you seeing more slippage, partial fills, or missed fills?

If you see one item, be curious. If you see three at once, be cautious. If you see all five, treat the market as *thin* even if the headline volume looks impressive.

Why this matters for flash crashes and fragmentation

Market fragmentation (one asset trading across many venues, including lit exchanges and dark pools) can make liquidity look present when it is actually scattered. In calm times, that fragmentation can be efficient. In stressed times, it can amplify confusion: displayed quotes may represent only a small fraction of true available liquidity, and liquidity providers may pull back across venues at once.

That is why drought signs often precede sudden air pockets and rapid drops. A flash crash is not always about a sudden change in value. It is often about a sudden change in *tradability*.

The takeaway: learn to watch the waterline *and* the tank

The last traded price is the waterline. It is what everyone sees. But liquidity risk lives in the tank: the depth behind that price, and the willingness of others to take the other side when you need to trade.

When markets are healthy, you can ignore that plumbing and focus on stories, earnings, and macro narratives. When the plumbing starts to fail, the stories can wait. The drought signs—wider spreads, thinning depth, air pockets, panicky volume, and worsening execution—are the market quietly telling you: *the cushion is shrinking*.

6.2 The Rush to the Exits

In the previous section, we treated liquidity like a water supply: spreads are the toll, depth is the tank, and a healthy market has enough "stored willingness"—standing bids and offers—to absorb normal trading without dramatic price moves. A rush to the exits is what happens when that stored willingness vanishes at the exact moment everyone tries to use it.

A useful way to frame the problem is this: markets are not only places where prices are *discovered*; they are also machines that *match* impatient sellers with willing buyers. In calm conditions, that matching is routine. In a panic, the matching function can break down. Prices then fall not necessarily because the asset has suddenly become worthless, but because the market temporarily cannot find enough buyers at nearby prices.

A "run" is not just fear—it is a coordination problem

A classic bank run starts with a simple worry: "If other people withdraw first, the bank may not have enough cash for me." That fear becomes self-fulfilling. Even depositors who believe the bank is fundamentally fine may withdraw because they do not want to be *last*.

Market runs have the same logic. In a selloff, the question in traders' minds is often not "What is this worth over the next five years?" but:

> **If everyone sells now, will I be able to sell later without taking a catastrophic price?**

Once that question dominates, decisions converge. Traders who would normally provide liquidity (patient limit orders, bargain-hunting buys) become cautious. Traders who normally hold risk become urgent sellers. The market becomes **one-way**.

Two-way flow is what keeps prices "pinned"

In a functioning market, order flow is mixed:

- Some participants are buying (adding demand).
- Some are selling (adding supply).
- Many are doing both, at different price levels, for different time horizons.

This two-way flow creates a kind of natural stabilizer. If price falls a little, some buyers step in. If price rises a little, some sellers appear. Depth replenishes because participants are willing to post orders near the current price.

In a run, that stabilizer weakens. The book does not just get thinner; it also stops refilling. Sellers keep coming. Buyers hesitate. The same small shock that would have been absorbed yesterday now punches through multiple price levels.

Crowded trades: why everyone heads for the same door

The rush to the exits is amplified by **crowded positioning**. A trade is crowded when many investors, funds, and algorithms hold similar exposures and rely on similar assumptions about when they can exit.

Crowding can form for ordinary reasons:

- An asset becomes a popular "safe" holding (until it is not).
- A theme trade spreads (AI winners, energy momentum, low-volatility strategies).
- Many portfolios hedge in the same way (for example, selling index futures).
- Risk models encourage similar de-risking behavior at the same time.

Crowding matters because it changes the *shape* of selling pressure. Instead of a variety of opinions expressed gradually, you get synchronized action:

> **When the same exit is used by too many people, the exit becomes the risk.**

Why the usual buyers step aside: market makers are not obligated heroes

In movies, a panicked crowd is saved by someone who steps forward and calms the situation. In markets, that role is often imagined as the **market maker**. Many readers assume market makers must always be there, always buying when others sell.

In reality, modern market makers are businesses managing risk. Their normal function is to provide immediacy by quoting both sides: they buy at the bid and sell at the ask, repeatedly. They earn the spread (and sometimes rebates), but only if they can manage the risk of holding inventory.

During a fast selloff, that inventory risk explodes. If a market maker buys shares at $100 and the price falls to $98 seconds later, the spread they earned is trivial relative to the loss on inventory. The danger is not theoretical; it is mechanical. In a one-way market, the market maker can be repeatedly "hit" as price steps down.

So what do rational liquidity providers do when the risk of being run over increases?

- They **widen spreads** (charge more for liquidity).
- They **reduce quote size** (offer less depth).
- They **cancel and re-post** quotes more often (avoid being picked off).
- They sometimes **step away** entirely in certain venues or symbols.

This is not a moral failure; it is a feature of a system where liquidity provision is largely voluntary and risk-sensitive.

The vacuum effect: prices fall because there is no one on the other side

When most incoming orders are sells and few participants are willing to buy, the market experiences a **liquidity vacuum**. The word "vacuum" is important: it captures that the problem is not merely more supply than demand in an economic sense, but a disappearance of *nearby* demand in the order book.

In a vacuum:

- The best bid is consumed quickly.
- The next bid may be far lower (thin depth).
- The price does not glide; it **gaps**.
- Traders watching the tape interpret the gaps as danger and rush to sell too.

This creates a short, brutal feedback loop:

Selling -> Thin book -> Price gaps down -> More selling.

Notice what is missing: there is no stabilizing wave of buyers stepping in at small dips, because the dip is no longer small and the market no longer looks safe to trade.

Why "just place a limit order" is not a magic solution

A common piece of advice is: "Avoid market orders; use limit orders." That is generally sensible in thin conditions because market orders demand immediacy at any price. But in a rush to the exits, limit orders have their own problem: they can become *spectators*.

If price is falling rapidly, a buy limit order at $99 may never fill because:

- quotes can flicker (orders appear and disappear),
- trade-through dynamics and fragmentation can route executions elsewhere,
- the market can gap from $100 to $98 without trading meaningfully at $99,
- the limit buyer may cancel in fear before being filled.

The deeper lesson is not about the superiority of one order type. It is that in a run, **control and certainty both degrade**. Market orders give certainty of execution but poor price control. Limit orders give price control but uncertain execution. In stable markets you can often have both; in unstable markets you are forced to choose.

Stop orders and cascades: how "protective" triggers become accelerants

Many investors use stop-loss orders to limit downside: "If it falls to $X, sell." The intention is protective. The effect during a rush to the exits can be destabilizing.

Why? Because stops often convert into market sells when triggered. In a fast drop:

- Price falls into a cluster of stop levels.
- Stops trigger and become additional sell orders.
- Those sells push price down further.
- More stops trigger.

This is a **stop cascade**. It is one reason a selloff can feel like it suddenly "accelerates" after crossing certain levels that many traders were watching.

Why prices overshoot: the difference between value and tradability

In calm conditions, you can imagine a fairly tight link between price and valuation stories: cash flows, interest rates, growth expectations. In a run, a different variable dominates: **tradability**.

When tradability collapses, prices can overshoot what many would consider fair value because the marginal transaction is not being set by a patient investor. It is being set by whoever is forced, frightened, or programmed to sell *now*, matched against whoever is still willing to buy *at all.*

This distinction is critical for understanding flash-crash-like behavior:

> **In a liquidity run, the market is not primarily asking, "What is it worth?" It is asking, "Who can absorb this right now?"**

A timeline of a rush to the exits (a story you can recognize)

To make the mechanics concrete, consider a typical progression:

- 1. **Early stress:** spreads widen and depth thins (the drought signs).
- 2. **Initial shock:** a news event, a large sell program, or a cross-market move hits.
- 3. **Liquidity providers retreat:** quote sizes shrink; cancellations increase; fewer bids remain.
- 4. **Gaps appear:** price drops through air pockets; prints look discontinuous.
- 5. **Cascades ignite:** stops trigger; risk models de-lever; margin constraints tighten.
- 6. **Capitulation (sometimes):** eventually, either new buyers appear at much lower prices, or trading pauses/halts, or a large participant provides liquidity.

Notice how the narrative is less about a single villain and more about a system that becomes brittle when everyone attempts the same action at once.

Key takeaway: runs are "physics," not just psychology

Fear matters, but the defining feature of a rush to the exits is mechanical:

- too many sells arrive at once,
- too few buys are willing to rest nearby,
- liquidity providers protect themselves by stepping back,
- and the order book cannot absorb the flow without a large price concession.

6.3 Leverage and Forced Selling

Leverage turns a preference ("I want to sell") into an obligation ("I *must* sell"). Once selling becomes mandatory, the market can detach from fundamentals because the goal of the seller is no longer to get a fair price—it is to raise cash immediately, satisfy a constraint, and survive.

That **something** is **leverage**.

Leverage in plain English: buying with borrowed money

Leverage means using debt to increase exposure. The simplest example is buying $100,000 worth of stock with only $50,000 of your own cash and borrowing the other $50,000.

If the stock rises 10%, you make $10,000 on a $50,000 equity investment—a 20% return before interest costs. Leverage *amplifies gains*.

But it also amplifies losses. If the stock falls 10%, you lose $10,000—a 20% loss of your equity. At some point, the lender starts worrying about whether your remaining equity is enough to protect the loan. That is where margin enters.

Margin: the lender's safety buffer

When you borrow to hold a position, your broker (or prime broker) requires **margin**: a minimum amount of equity you must maintain relative to the position.

At a high level, there are two important ideas:

- **Initial margin:** how much equity you must post to open the trade.
- **Maintenance margin:** the minimum equity you must keep as prices move.

You do not need to memorize the regulatory details to understand the mechanics. The core point is this:

> **When prices fall, your equity shrinks. If it shrinks too far, you lose the right to choose your timing.**

The margin call: the moment choice disappears

A **margin call** happens when your equity falls below the required level. The broker then demands that you fix the deficiency, typically by some deadline:

- **Add cash or collateral** (increase equity), *or*
- **Reduce the position** (sell assets to shrink the loan exposure).

In calm markets, a margin call can be manageable: you wire in funds, sell a small piece, and move on. In stressed markets, it can be a trap, because the very act of selling to meet margin can push prices lower, causing other leveraged players to receive margin calls as well.

This is the key transition from a discretionary selloff to a forced liquidation:

> **Forced sellers do not wait for a better price. They sell because the constraint is binding *now*.**

Why forced selling can overwhelm fundamentals

Imagine a stock is worth, in your best long-term estimate, $100. If it trades down to $95, you might consider it a bargain. If it trades to $90, you might buy more. That is how fundamentals *should* stabilize prices.

Now add leverage. A fund might agree the stock is worth $100 but still be forced to sell at $90 because:

- their broker raised margin requirements (common in volatile periods),
- their investors are redeeming (they need cash),

- their risk model limits were hit (they must reduce exposure),
- correlated positions elsewhere are losing money (they need collateral).

In other words, the fund is not expressing a valuation opinion; it is meeting a financing requirement. The market price becomes, temporarily, a **financing price**—the price at which enough cash can be raised quickly to satisfy constraints.

The mechanical feedback loop: selling creates the reason to sell

Here is the most important idea in this section:

In leveraged markets, price declines can create forced selling, and forced selling can create further price declines.

This is not a metaphor. It is a mechanical feedback loop driven by balance sheets and rules.

We can describe the loop with a simple chain of events:

1. The price drops.
2. Equity cushions shrink.
3. Margin calls are triggered.
4. Automatic or urgent sell orders hit a thinning market.
5. The additional selling pushes prices down further.

The loop can accelerate because each step makes the next step more likely.

The "Margin Call Death Spiral" (central feedback loop)

The diagram below summarizes the vicious circle. It is the same story whether the leverage is in retail margin accounts, hedge funds, volatility strategies, or levered ETFs: when financing meets falling prices, selling can become self-feeding.

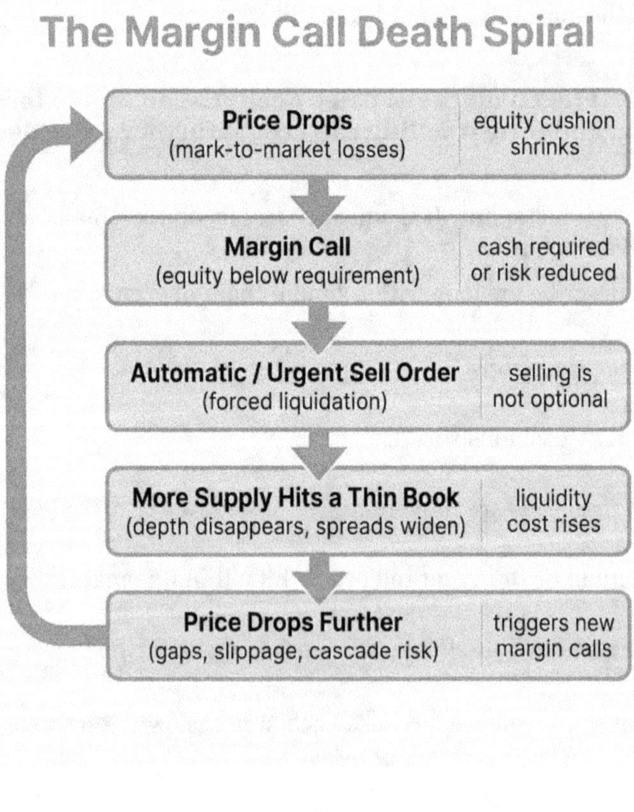

A concrete numerical example (small numbers, big intuition)

Consider a trader who buys $100,000 of an ETF using $50,000 of their own cash and $50,000 borrowed.

- If the ETF falls 10%, the position becomes $90,000.
- The loan is still about $50,000.
- The trader's equity becomes $40,000.

That is a 20% hit to the trader's equity from a 10% move in the asset.

Now imagine volatility rises and the broker increases the required margin. Even if the trader *believes* the ETF is fundamentally fine, the broker is managing *credit risk*. If the trader cannot add cash quickly, the broker reduces risk the simplest way: sell part (or all) of the position.

Two key implications follow:

1. **Leverage compresses time.** What could have been a patient decision becomes a deadline problem.
2. **Leverage couples participants.** One trader's forced sale can push price down and force another trader to sell.

Why this gets worse in exactly the conditions you most want it to improve

During stress, three things often happen simultaneously:

- **Prices fall** (reducing equity).
- **Liquidity worsens** (selling moves price more).
- **Financing tightens** (higher margin requirements, lower risk limits).

Notice the unpleasant alignment: the market demands more collateral at the same time that collateral is shrinking. This is why leveraged crises feel nonlinear. The system is not simply "moving against you"; the rules of engagement are changing mid-game.

Forced selling is contagious even without a "bad" asset

One of the most confusing features of crises is that high-quality assets can fall sharply. Leverage helps explain this. If a leveraged fund suffers losses in one area, it may sell unrelated assets simply to raise cash.

This is not irrational behavior; it is survival behavior. The fund is managing cash and collateral and credit lines. When those constraints bind, "best" assets are sometimes sold first because they are easiest to sell—at least at the beginning. As stress deepens, even those become hard to sell without large price concessions.

What to watch for (as a reader of markets, not a professional)

You usually cannot see leverage directly. But you can often infer its presence from market behavior:

- **Selloffs that accelerate late in the day** (deadlines and risk checks matter).
- **Sharp moves across many unrelated assets** (cash-raising behavior).
- **Repeated gap-downs after small bounces** (forced sellers use strength to liquidate).
- **Persistent widening spreads and thin depth** (liquidity providers protecting themselves from the cascade).

These clues do not tell you what the "true" value is. They tell you something else that can be more urgent in the short run: whether the market is being driven by *constraints* rather than *opinions*.

The takeaway: leverage turns the exit into a trapdoor

A rush to the exits can start with fear, uncertainty, or bad news. Leverage is what turns that rush into a **spiral**. Once margin calls and forced liquidation dominate, the market can fall far below what most participants consider reasonable—not because everyone suddenly revised their valuation, but because the system demanded cash faster than liquidity could provide it.

6.4 Contagion Effects

Up to this point, the story has been local. First, liquidity quietly deteriorates (spreads widen, depth thins). Then a rush to the exits begins (one-way selling meets hesitant buying). Then leverage turns selling from a choice into a requirement (margin calls and forced liquidation).

Now we add the twist that makes modern crises feel so bewildering: the damage rarely stays in the original market. It spreads.

This section explains **contagion**: how stress in one asset class, sector, or trading venue can spill over into others that seem unrelated. The headline might start with wheat futures, a regional bank bond, or a single volatility product—and end with broad equity indexes moving as if the entire economy changed overnight.

The key idea is simple:

Markets are connected by balance sheets and by algorithms. When one corner catches fire, the plumbing carries heat elsewhere.

Two channels of contagion: cash needs and mechanical linkages

Contagion usually travels through two broad channels. They often operate together, which is why the spread can be fast.

Channel 1: Funding and cash ("sell what you can")

When a trader or fund loses money in one place, it often needs cash immediately:

- to meet margin calls,
- to reduce leverage,
- to satisfy investor redemptions,
- or to post additional collateral to keep positions open.

Here is the unintuitive part: the asset that gets sold to raise cash is not always the asset that caused the loss.

If a hedge fund takes a sharp loss in wheat futures, it might sell Apple stock—not because it suddenly dislikes Apple, but because Apple is liquid enough to generate cash quickly. This is a crisis version of a household selling the easiest thing first:

In a cash crunch, you don't sell your hardest-to-sell asset. You sell your easiest-to-sell asset.

This is one reason high-quality, highly liquid assets can drop sharply during stressed periods: they become the funding source.

Channel 2: Arbitrage and hedging ("when one price moves, another must follow")

The second channel is more mechanical. In modern markets, many strategies explicitly link prices:

- index arbitrage (futures vs. baskets of stocks),
- ETF arbitrage (ETF shares vs. underlying holdings),
- options hedging (delta/gamma hedging),
- statistical arbitrage and cross-asset signals,
- relative-value trades (spreads between similar instruments).

These strategies are designed to keep prices aligned. In calm times, that alignment is stabilizing and efficient. In stressed times, the same linkages can transmit shocks quickly because they generate *required trades* across markets.

When an algorithm sees one leg move, it trades the other leg. When many algorithms do that at once, "one market's problem" becomes "everyone's order flow."

A realistic story: how one corner drags the rest

Consider a simplified chain reaction that does not require any villain, just normal institutional behavior.

Step 1: A shock hits Market A. Suppose wheat futures fall sharply due to a surprise policy decision or a sudden inventory report. Funds that are long wheat take losses.

Step 2: Margin requirements rise and cash is demanded. Because volatility rises, clearinghouses and brokers often demand more collateral. This is rational from a credit-risk perspective, but it forces funds to obtain cash quickly.

Step 3: The fund sells liquid holdings in Market B. The fund may not be able to exit wheat without severe slippage (thin depth, wide spreads). Instead, it sells something else: large-cap equities, index futures, or Treasury futures. Those markets are deep enough to absorb size—until too many participants do the same thing at the same time.

Step 4: Market B moves, triggering hedges and risk models. As equities drop, portfolio risk rises, volatility estimates jump, and systematic strategies reduce exposure. Option dealers hedge dynamically; risk-parity portfolios rebalance; vol-control funds de-risk. These actions create more selling.

Step 5: Liquidity providers retreat across venues. Now the drought signs appear broadly: spreads widen, depth thins, air pockets form. What began as a wheat problem has become a general liquidity problem.

This is contagion as a *balance-sheet wave*. It does not need the second market to share fundamentals with the first. It shares something more immediate: the need for cash and the need to manage risk.

Why diversification sometimes fails when you need it most

Many casual investors rely on diversification as a safety net: different assets should not all fall together. That logic often holds in normal environments. Contagion is the regime in which correlations rise sharply, sometimes toward one.

The reason is not that the world suddenly becomes simpler. It is that constraints become binding:

- A diversified portfolio is still financed through a single balance sheet.
- That balance sheet faces a single margin requirement and a single cash constraint.
- When the constraint binds, the portfolio is sold as a unit, even if its parts are unrelated.

In other words, diversification can reduce *fundamental* risk but not necessarily *funding* risk.

The role of indexes and ETFs: how modern wrappers transmit stress

Indexes and ETFs are not inherently dangerous. They are useful technology. But they create powerful conduits for contagion because they bundle assets together and make them tradable as a single instrument.

Two common transmission mechanisms are:

- **Index futures:** selling the futures can rapidly pull down the index level, and arbitrage links then pull down the underlying stocks.
- **ETFs:** heavy selling of ETF shares can force trading in the underlying basket (directly or indirectly through arbitrage activity), spreading pressure across many names.

In calm markets, these links help keep prices consistent. In stressed markets, they can distribute pressure broadly, even to constituents that had no news.

Derivatives hedging: when protection demands selling

Derivatives can also create contagion through hedging flows. The intuition is straightforward: if you buy insurance, someone sold you that insurance and may need to hedge.

For example:

- If many investors buy put options for protection, dealers who sold those puts may hedge by selling the underlying as it falls (depending on their net exposures).
- If volatility rises sharply, hedging can become more intense and more frequent.

This is not a moral critique of derivatives. It is an observation about mechanics: hedges are trades, and trades are order flow. When many market participants hedge in similar ways, the hedge itself can become a driver of cross-asset moves.

Contagion across time: why "temporary" stress becomes a persistent regime

Contagion is not only about prices moving together in a single afternoon. It can also change behavior over days and weeks.

After a shock:

- lenders may tighten credit terms,
- brokers may increase margin requirements,
- risk managers may lower limits,

- and investors may redeem from funds that experienced drawdowns.

These reactions can keep forced selling alive even after the original news is digested. The crisis becomes self-sustaining not because the original problem persists, but because **the system becomes more fragile**: less leverage is permitted, and liquidity provision is priced more expensively.

How to recognize contagion in real time (simple clues)

You do not need a professional terminal to notice contagion. You can often infer it from patterns that are hard to explain with a single narrative:

- **Unrelated assets moving together:** commodities, equities, and credit all sell off at once.
- **"Good news" not helping:** fundamentally strong assets fall anyway because they are sold for cash.
- **Rallies that fade quickly:** forced sellers use bounces to liquidate.
- **Liquidity symptoms spreading:** widening spreads and jumpy price action appear across multiple markets, not just one.

These patterns suggest the driver is not an asset-specific revaluation. It is a system-wide constraint event.

The takeaway: the market is a web, and stress travels along the strands

Contagion is the reason crises feel bigger than their origin story. A local shock becomes a global event because modern finance is tightly coupled:

- by funding and collateral,

- by arbitrage relationships,
- by hedging rules,
- and by shared risk management behavior.

Once you see the system as a web, the seemingly strange headlines make more sense: "Why did stocks fall because wheat fell?" Because the loss in wheat demanded cash, and cash was raised by selling stocks; because hedges and arbitrage translated one move into another; because thin liquidity amplified every step.

6.5 Liquidity vs. Solvency

We began this chapter by learning to spot a liquidity drought: spreads widen, depth thins, and the market starts to feel "hollow" even if volume is high. We then watched that drought turn into a rush to the exits, where one-way selling meets a retreating bid. Next, we added leverage, which converts voluntary selling into forced liquidation through margin calls. Finally, we saw contagion: how losses and hedges transmit stress across markets that appear unrelated.

There is one final distinction that ties these episodes together and prevents a common, expensive misunderstanding:

> **Liquidity is about timing. Solvency is about arithmetic.**

If you confuse them, you can panic at the wrong time, or trust the wrong fix. If you separate them, you can better understand why some crises pass with support and patience, while others end in default and restructuring.

Definitions in plain English

Liquidity: "I have value, but I can't turn it into cash quickly"

A person or institution is **illiquid** when they have assets, but not enough *cash-like* assets to meet immediate obligations. The problem is not necessarily that they are poor. The problem is that their wealth is locked up.

A household example:

- You own a house worth $500,000.
- You have $2,000 in your checking account.
- A $10,000 emergency bill arrives tomorrow.

You are not "broke" in a lifetime sense—your net worth may be positive—but you may be forced into an ugly decision: borrow at a high rate, sell something quickly at a discount, or miss the payment. That is liquidity stress.

Solvency: "Even if I sold everything, I still couldn't pay what I owe"

A person or institution is **insolvent** when their *liabilities exceed their assets*. This is not a timing problem. It is a balance-sheet problem.

A household example:

- You own assets worth $500,000.
- You owe $650,000.

Even with time and a fair sale, you cannot make everyone whole. Insolvency usually ends with restructuring, bankruptcy, or a bailout that forces someone else to absorb the loss.

Why crises blur the line

In real markets, liquidity and solvency interact, which is why they are often confused.

During a selloff:

- Assets may trade at fire-sale prices because liquidity evaporates.
- Mark-to-market losses can reduce measured equity.

- Margin requirements can rise at the worst possible moment.

This creates a dangerous illusion: an institution can *look* insolvent at distressed market prices even if, in a calmer environment with time to sell, it might be solvent. Conversely, an institution can *claim* a liquidity problem when it is actually insolvent and using time-buying language to avoid admitting losses.

So we need a disciplined way to think.

A simple balance-sheet framework

$$\textbf{Assets} - \textbf{Liabilities} = \textbf{Equity (net worth)}$$

Now add one more crucial idea: not all assets are equal in a crisis.

- **Liquid assets** (cash, Treasury bills, reserves) can be used immediately to pay obligations.
- **Illiquid assets** (loans, complex securities, thinly traded positions) may have value but cannot be sold quickly without a steep discount.

Liquidity crises are often about the *composition* of assets, not just the total.

How liquidity problems become solvency problems (the bridge)

A pure liquidity problem can sometimes be solved: provide temporary funding, wait for markets to normalize, avoid forced fire sales.

But liquidity problems can also *create* insolvency through a mechanism we have already studied: forced selling and feedback loops.

Here is the bridge in plain terms:

- 1. An institution holds assets that are fundamentally valuable but not easily sold.

- 2. Short-term creditors demand cash or more collateral (margin calls, funding withdrawals).
- 3. The institution sells assets quickly into a thin market.
- 4. Fire-sale prices lock in real losses.
- 5. Those losses reduce equity, potentially pushing the institution into insolvency.

This is why policy makers and risk managers obsess over liquidity. It is not merely about convenience. It is about preventing temporary stress from hardening into permanent damage.

What "the market" is really saying during a panic

In calm periods, market prices are often treated as reasonably informative estimates of value. In panic periods, prices also reflect **immediacy premia and liquidity discounts**.

In a drought:

- the bid–ask spread is a fee for immediacy,
- depth is scarce, so large trades move price,
- and leveraged players sell because they must, not because they believe.

So a steep price drop can mean at least three different things:

- 1. **Fundamental deterioration:** expected cash flows truly fell.
- 2. **Liquidity discount:** tradability collapsed temporarily.
- 3. **Constraint-driven selling:** leverage and funding forced liquidation.

Only the first is a clear signal of solvency deterioration. The second and third may reverse once liquidity and funding stabilize—but they can still be lethal if they trigger default before stabilization occurs.

Why central banks care: "lender of last resort" logic

In many systems, the central bank (and sometimes the government) plays a special role during severe liquidity crises: providing **liquidity backstops**. The idea is not to make bad businesses good. It is to keep a functioning system from collapsing due to a cash bottleneck.

A classic principle (in modern paraphrase) is:

> **Lend against good collateral to solvent institutions facing temporary liquidity stress.**

The intuition is practical:

- If the institution is solvent but illiquid, temporary lending can prevent a fire sale and a cascade.
- If the institution is insolvent, lending can become a subsidy that delays recognition of losses and shifts them to the lender (or taxpayer).

This is why crises often involve intense debate about whether a troubled institution is merely illiquid or truly insolvent. The policy response depends on the diagnosis.

A checklist for separating liquidity stress from solvency stress

No outsider can perfectly diagnose institutions in real time, especially during panic. But the distinction becomes clearer if you ask the right questions.

Questions that point to liquidity stress

- Are the assets plausibly valuable over time, but temporarily hard to finance or sell?
- Is the key problem short-term obligations (daily margin, overnight funding, near-term maturities)?

- Do prices look "gappy" and disorderly, with spreads exploding and depth disappearing across venues?
- Does the situation improve quickly when credible funding is provided (or when forced selling ends)?

Questions that point to solvency stress

- Even at reasonable (non-fire-sale) valuations, do liabilities still exceed assets?
- Are there durable losses in cash flows (defaults, fraud, permanent impairment)?
- Is the institution reliant on rolling over debt indefinitely with no credible path to repayment?
- Does additional liquidity fail to restore confidence because the underlying balance sheet is broken?

Think of liquidity as "can you make Tuesday's payment?" and solvency as "does the whole math work out?"

Why this distinction matters to market behavior

This chapter's events can now be reframed:

- **Signs of a drought** warned that the market's *trading capacity* was shrinking.
- **The rush to the exits** showed how two-way markets can become one-way when liquidity providers retreat.
- **Leverage and forced selling** explained how financing rules can create mandatory selling and price overshoots.
- **Contagion** demonstrated that balance-sheet constraints spread stress across assets.

In many episodes, the initial problem is liquidity. The tragedy is when liquidity stress is allowed to trigger insolvency through uncontrolled cascades.

The takeaway: treat "can't sell" and "can't pay" as different emergencies

Liquidity crises are about the ability to trade and fund positions without severe price concessions. Solvency crises are about ultimate ability to pay.

> **Illiquidity is a shortage of cash today. Insolvency is a shortage of value, period.**

When the music stops, both can appear at once. But if you can keep them conceptually separate, you can better understand why markets sometimes snap back after terrifying air pockets—and why, in other cases, the damage is permanent and the losses must be allocated through default, restructuring, or recapitalization.

Chapter 7

Anatomy of a Flash Crash

It happens faster than a coffee break. Billions of dollars vanish and reappear in minutes, leaving human traders staring at their screens in disbelief. This chapter dissects the lifecycle of a flash crash, moving from the initial accidental trigger to the catastrophic withdrawal of electronic liquidity, and finally, the chaotic scramble that restores order.

7.1 Defining a Flash Event

Markets fall all the time. Some declines are slow and painful; others are sudden and shocking. To understand *flash crashes*, we need a clean way to separate an ordinary market decline—the kind driven by changing beliefs about the economy—from a high-speed breakdown driven by the market's *plumbing*.

This chapter has been building a simple foundation: modern markets are not one place but many (exchanges, off-exchange venues, and internalizers), connected by routing rules and algorithms. Prices are not discovered by a single auctioneer; they are stitched together, millisecond by millisecond, by machines that constantly update quotes, cancel orders, and protect themselves from risk. A flash event is what it looks like when that stitching briefly fails.

A working definition: a price glitch, not a verdict

A **flash event** (or **flash crash**) is a rapid, extreme price move—usually downward—followed by a fast rebound, where the speed and shape of the move are out of proportion to any new information about fundamental value.

Think of it like this:

- A **normal decline** is the market *deciding* an asset is worth less (or at least that the future is riskier).
- A **flash crash** is the market *temporarily forgetting* what the asset is worth because liquidity briefly disappears.

That distinction matters because the best response is different. If the market is repricing value, you evaluate the news and your exposure. If the market's mechanism is malfunctioning, the problem is *execution and liquidity*—how trades are getting done (or not done)—not the long-run economic story.

The three hallmarks of a flash crash

Flash events come in different sizes and in different assets, but they tend to share three hallmarks. These hallmarks are practical: a casual reader can use them to diagnose what they are seeing in a chart or headline.

1) Impossible speed

A normal bear market is measured in *weeks, months, or quarters*. Even a sharp selloff driven by scary news typically takes time to spread as investors read, react, and reposition portfolios.

A flash crash is measured in *seconds to minutes*. The move is so fast that, on a human timescale, it feels discontinuous: the price seems to jump rather than slide. This speed is the first clue that the driver is not careful thought but automated interaction:

- quotes are being cancelled faster than new ones are posted,
- market orders are hitting an increasingly empty book,
- risk controls and volatility filters are switching behavior from *provide liquidity* to *avoid being run over*.

In other words, the defining feature is not merely that the market fell—it is that the market fell *faster than humans can collectively change their minds*.

2) A profound disconnect from economic reality

Normal declines are unpleasant, but they tend to remain within the realm of plausible valuation. If the economy worsens, earnings expectations drop; if interest rates rise, discount rates rise; if risk rises, investors demand a higher return. The price adjustment may be dramatic, but it is *explainable*.

A flash crash, by contrast, often prints prices that look absurd even as they happen: a highly liquid index future suddenly down several percent in moments, or a large-cap stock trading briefly at a price that implies instant catastrophe. The key is not that the price is *low*; it is that the price is *out of context*.

A simple way to feel this intuitively:

> If the only thing that changed was the *mechanism of trading* (quotes pulled, spreads widened, order book thinned), could you get this price without anyone learning anything new about the company or the economy?

If the answer is yes, you are in flash-crash territory.

3) The signature V-shaped recovery

The most distinctive fingerprint is the rebound. Normal bear markets may include rallies, but they rarely erase a large drop immediately. Bad news does not usually get *un-bad* in 90 seconds.

Flash crashes often show a **V shape**:

fast drop → brief dislocation → fast recovery.

Why does the price snap back? Because once the temporary liquidity vacuum eases, the market's error becomes obvious. Traders (human and algorithmic) step in to buy something that is clearly mispriced relative to related markets, recent prices, or fundamental anchors. The rebound is not kindness; it is opportunism and arbitrage restoring consistency.

Visual anchor: normal decline vs. flash crash

The chart below is not meant to match any single historical episode. Instead, it is a *conceptual* comparison designed to train your eye. Note the gradual slope of a normal bear market versus the near-vertical drop and immediate recovery of a flash crash.

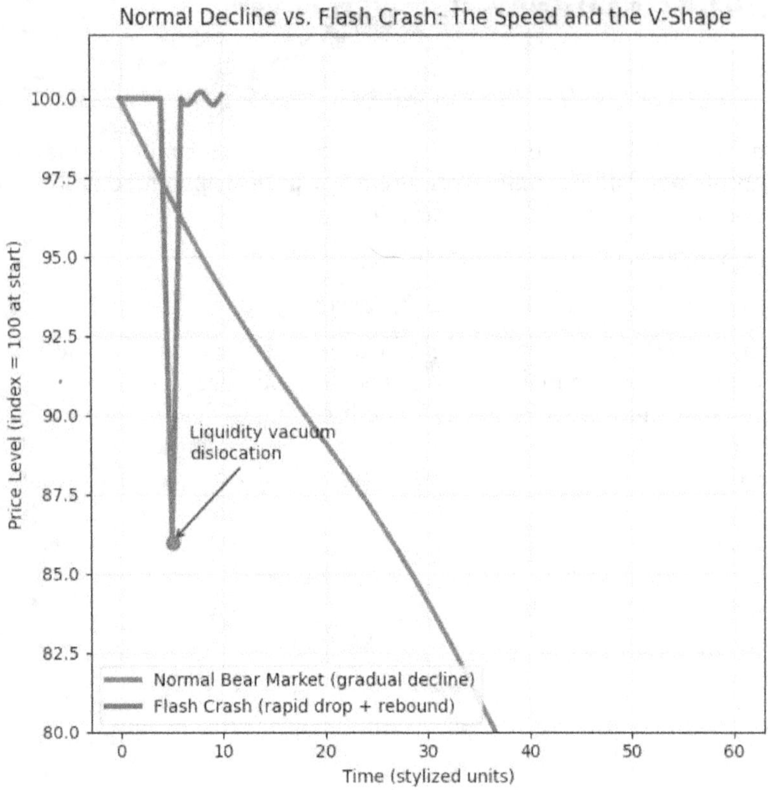

What a flash event is *not*

Because flash crashes are dramatic, it is easy to overinterpret them. A disciplined reader should learn what *not* to conclude from a sudden drop.

- **Not a recession signal.** Recessions and earnings collapses develop over months; flash crashes develop over seconds.
- **Not necessarily "smart money selling."** In flash events, the selling pressure may come from mechanical triggers (market orders, stop orders, hedging programs) interacting with an order

book that is thinning.

- **Not proof an asset is "really worth" the trough price.** A trade print during a liquidity vacuum reflects the scarcity of bids at that instant, not a considered valuation by the market as a whole.

This does *not* mean fundamentals are irrelevant. Sometimes bad news and microstructure interact: a legitimate fear can raise volatility, and higher volatility can cause liquidity providers to back away. But the hallmark of a flash crash is that the *mechanism* amplifies the move far beyond what the news alone would plausibly justify.

A plain-English way to diagnose the difference

When you see a sudden plunge, ask three questions in order. They are intentionally simple, and together they map to the three hallmarks.

- **How fast did it happen?** If the move unfolded in seconds or a couple of minutes, suspect microstructure.
- **What new information arrived at that exact moment?** If there is no clear, widely shared piece of news big enough to justify the size of the move, suspect microstructure.
- **Did it snap back quickly?** A rapid rebound suggests the drop was a dislocation rather than a durable repricing of value.

If you answer *fast, no clear news*, and *yes, quick rebound*, you are likely looking at a flash event.

Why this distinction is the key to the rest of the chapter

This chapter's remaining sections will explain *how* a flash crash forms. We will start with **the spark**: the seemingly small trigger that begins the move. Then we move to **the cascade**: the crucial moment when liquidity providers retreat, spreads widen, and the order book hollows out. Finally we examine **the rebound**: the return of rational pricing once arbitrage and human judgment re-engage.

For now, keep one mental model in focus:

> A normal decline is a change in *beliefs*. A flash crash is a temporary failure of *liquidity*.

Everything that follows is an unpacking of that single idea.

7.2 The Spark

In the previous section we defined a flash event by its *shape* and *tempo*: an impossible-speed drop, a price that briefly disconnects from economic reality, and a V-shaped snapback. That definition tells you what a flash crash *looks like*. Now we ask the next, very natural question:

> What *starts* it?

The surprising answer is that the initial trigger is often small, mundane, and almost embarrassing in hindsight. A flash crash does not require an economic earthquake. It can begin with something closer to a stumble—a minor shock that would be harmless in a deep, stable market, but becomes dangerous when it hits a fragile microstructure.

A key idea: the spark is rarely the bomb

To keep the logic straight, separate two roles:

1. **The spark:** the first push that knocks prices off balance.
2. **The cascade:** the mechanism that turns that push into a freefall.

The spark is the match; the cascade is the fuel and airflow that lets a small flame become a firestorm.

This distinction matters because people instinctively look for a dramatic explanation. When they see a chart that drops like a cliff, they assume there must have been dramatic news. But in flash events, the headline explanation is often a *thin wrapper* around a deeper mechanical story: once liquidity providers start stepping back, even a small initial shove can move prices a lot.

Three common types of sparks

Sparks come in many forms, but most fall into three broad categories:

1. a **human error** (the classic "fat finger"),
2. an **information hiccup** (confusing or ambiguous news),
3. a **large, clumsy order** (legitimate trading done in an unstable way).

These sparks differ in surface details, but they share one feature: they create a sudden imbalance between willing sellers and willing buyers *at that moment*. The imbalance does not need to be huge. It only needs to arrive when the market is most sensitive.

Spark #1: the "fat finger" and other input errors

A **fat-finger error** is exactly what it sounds like: someone intends to type one thing and enters another. But the modern version is broader than a mistyped number. It can include:

- selecting the wrong ticker symbol,
- choosing the wrong order type (e.g., market order instead of limit order),
- entering the right trade in the wrong direction (sell instead of buy),
- setting a decimal wrong (1,000 shares becomes 100,000),
- accidentally duplicating an order (sending it twice).

Why can this matter in an age of sophisticated systems? Because the market reacts to *prints and pressure*, not intentions. An erroneous sell order still sells. It still consumes bids in the order book. And it still creates a pattern that other algorithms may interpret as meaningful selling.

Why a simple mistake can ripple outward.

In a calm market, a wrong-way trade is usually absorbed with limited damage:

- there are plenty of bids near the current price,
- market makers replenish liquidity as it is consumed,
- other participants step in if the price becomes attractive.

But in a fragile moment—perhaps spreads are already wider than usual, or liquidity is thinner because volatility has been rising—the same mistake can punch a hole in the order book. That hole is not the crash; it is the opening that allows the crash to form in the next stage.

Spark #2: the ambiguous headline (information that is real, but unclear)

Another common spark is not a lie, but a **moment of confusion**. Information arrives that is:

- incomplete,
- misread,
- mis-timed,
- or framed in a way that algorithms cannot contextualize.

For a casual reader, this can feel strange: *Shouldn't markets process information efficiently?* Yes—over minutes, hours, and days. But in the first few seconds, markets are not an idealized classroom. They are a complex network of participants with different data feeds, different parsing systems, and different rules about when to trade.

Why confusion matters more than content.

In a flash event, what matters is not that the news is "bad enough." What matters is that the news creates a short-lived coordination problem:

- Some traders interpret the information as urgent and sell immediately.
- Others hesitate because the information is unclear, or because they are waiting for confirmation.
- Liquidity providers widen spreads or pull quotes because uncertainty has increased.

That hesitation is important. When many potential buyers pause at the same time—even briefly—the market becomes easier to push downward. The price drop itself then becomes a new "signal" that can trigger additional selling by rules-based strategies.

Spark #3: the large, clumsy sell order (the honest trade that lands badly)

Not every spark is a mistake. Sometimes the spark is simply a big institution trying to sell, hedge, or rebalance. The intent may be perfectly reasonable:

- a mutual fund meeting investor redemptions,
- an options dealer hedging exposure,
- a risk model demanding a lower equity weight,
- an execution desk unwinding a position.

The problem is *how* the order is executed.

Market impact in plain English.

A limit order book is like a stack of willing buyers at different prices. The highest bid is the best price available now, but it is not infinite. If you sell more than the best bid can absorb, you "walk down the book," selling to the next bid, then the next, and so on. This creates a mechanical drop even if no one learned anything new about value.

In normal conditions, liquidity replenishes as you trade. But in stressed conditions, replenishment slows. If a large sell program continues to push into a thinning book, prices can start to fall *because the book is being emptied faster than it refills.*

Why "clumsy" matters more than "large."

Large institutions typically try to avoid this by slicing orders and using algorithms designed to minimize impact. But an order can still be "clumsy" if:

- it is too aggressive (high participation rate),
- it is too concentrated in time,
- it is routed in a way that unintentionally hits the most fragile venues,
- it is executed with insufficient safeguards (e.g., few limit-price protections).

A large, careful execution can be absorbed. A large, rushed execution can become a spark.

When sparks become dangerous: the "dry forest" conditions

Sparks happen every day. Markets see erroneous orders, confusing headlines, and large trades constantly. Most do *not* cause a flash crash. So what determines whether a spark fizzles or ignites?

The answer is: **the state of liquidity and risk tolerance at the moment the spark hits.**

A flash crash is more likely when several fragility conditions are present at once:

- **Thin displayed liquidity:** fewer visible limit orders sitting in the book.

- **Wider spreads:** it already costs more to trade immediately, signaling caution by liquidity providers.
- **Elevated short-term volatility:** recent price moves are large enough to trigger defensive behavior.
- **Crowded positioning or one-way flow:** many strategies are leaning in the same direction, increasing the chance of synchronized selling.
- **Fragmented execution paths:** orders are routed across multiple venues, and liquidity may vanish in one place faster than another.

These are the dry leaves and wind. In such conditions, a spark that would normally be a footnote can become the first step toward a vertical drop.

A simple timeline: from spark to instability

To keep the narrative clear, here is a stylized timeline that bridges this section to the next one:

1. **A spark arrives.** A mistake, a confusing signal, or a large trade creates sudden sell pressure.
2. **The book thins.** Nearby bids are consumed; spreads widen; replenishment slows.
3. **Participants become defensive.** Liquidity providers reduce exposure, cancel quotes, or widen further.
4. **The market becomes brittle.** Each new sell order moves price more than it "should."

At this point, the system is primed. The spark has done its job: it has pushed the market from a stable regime (where liquidity is continuously offered) into an unstable regime (where liquidity is conditional and can be withdrawn).

What to remember before we move on

The most important takeaway is not a list of possible triggers. It is the principle behind them:

> In a flash crash, the spark is often ordinary. The catastrophe comes from the market's reaction—especially how quickly liquidity disappears when volatility rises.

That reaction is the subject of the next section. We will open the hood and examine **the cascade**: the moment when automated risk controls and market-making logic turn a small disturbance into a liquidity vacuum and a near-vertical fall.

7.3 The Cascade

In the last section, we saw that the *spark* is often unimpressive: a mistake, a confusing headline, or a large but poorly executed order. The spark matters mainly because it pushes the market into a more fragile state. The flash crash itself is born in the next phase: **the cascade**.

A cascade is the moment when a market stops behaving like a deep pool of liquidity and starts behaving like a trapdoor.

From "lots of buyers" to "no bids": what a liquidity vacuum really means

Liquidity sounds abstract, but in a limit order book it is visible and concrete. At any instant, the market is supported by a stack of buy orders (bids) at many price levels:

- the **best bid** is the highest price someone is currently willing to pay,
- below it are more bids at slightly lower prices,
- collectively, these bids are the **floor** that catches selling pressure.

A **liquidity vacuum** occurs when that floor suddenly thins out or disappears. The key word is *suddenly.* In normal trading, bids get consumed but also get replenished. In a flash crash cascade, bids get consumed and then *stop being replenished*—or worse, they are actively pulled away.

When that happens, selling pressure does not meet a normal cushion. It meets empty space.

Why would liquidity providers withdraw? Risk controls, not malice

Many people imagine market makers as entities that always stand ready to buy and sell. In reality, modern liquidity provision is often algorithmic and risk-managed. The algorithm is not designed to be a hero; it is designed to survive.

A simplified picture of an electronic market maker is:

- quote a bid and an ask (provide liquidity),
- earn the spread (tiny, but frequent),
- keep inventory (the shares/contracts held) within tight limits,
- reduce activity when the environment becomes dangerous.

When volatility spikes, two things happen at once:

1. **Adverse selection risk rises.** If prices are moving fast, a market maker worries that the people hitting its quotes know something it does not. The market maker fears buying right before a further drop.
2. **Inventory risk rises.** If a market maker buys during a fast decline, it can accumulate inventory that is losing value every millisecond.

So the algorithm does what it was built to do: it becomes conservative. Conservatism shows up as:

- **widening spreads** (quoting less aggressively),
- **reducing displayed size** (quoting fewer shares/contracts),
- **cancelling quotes** (temporarily stepping away),
- **switching off** certain strategies entirely when volatility or order-flow toxicity crosses thresholds.

Importantly, these behaviors can be rational for each individual liquidity provider and still be disastrous for the market as a whole. The cascade is a *coordination failure*: many independent risk controls react in the same direction at the same time.

The hollowing of the order book: how a small imbalance becomes a cliff

To understand the vertical drop in a flash crash, you need one mental image: the book is not one thick wall of demand. It is a stack of thin layers. If the top layers disappear, the next tradable price might be far below the last trade.

Here is a plain-English sequence of the cascade:

1. The spark creates a burst of selling (or a sudden absence of buyers).
2. The best bids are hit and removed.
3. Liquidity providers, seeing volatility and one-way flow, **cancel** or **back away**.
4. The remaining bids are now fewer and farther apart.
5. New sell orders arrive (often automatically), and they "walk down" the thinning stack.
6. Each trade prints at a worse price, which increases measured volatility and triggers more defensive behavior.

This is why flash crashes feel like a *freefall*. The market is not steadily negotiating a lower value; it is rapidly searching downward for any remaining bids.

Stop orders: the accelerant that sells into the void

The cascade is amplified by orders whose job is to *sell when things get bad.* The most familiar example is a **stop-loss order**.

A stop-loss is emotionally appealing: it promises discipline. But mechanically, it can behave like a delayed market order:

- the stop price is a **trigger**, not a guarantee,
- when triggered, it often becomes a **market order** (or a very aggressive limit order),
- it must execute even if the book is thin.

In a normal market, a triggered stop sells into a reasonably populated book. In a liquidity vacuum, a triggered stop sells into an emptying book. That is the recipe for a vertical move.

The cascade therefore has a feedback loop: price drops -> stops trigger -> more market sells -> price drops further. This is a **stop cascade**: many risk-management decisions, made independently, become synchronized selling pressure.

Spread explosions: the market's warning light

Even if you never look at a full order book, you can often see a cascade forming by watching the **spread** (the difference between the best bid and the best ask).

In calm markets, spreads are typically tight because:

- competition among liquidity providers forces quotes close together,
- risk is low enough that market makers are comfortable being aggressive.

During a cascade, spreads can widen dramatically because liquidity providers demand more compensation for risk or refuse to quote at all. A widening spread is the market's way of saying: *"Immediate trading is dangerous right now."*

For the casual trader, this is one of the most practical microstructure lessons in the book: in stress, the cost of immediacy rises sharply, and forced immediacy (market orders, stop orders, urgent hedges) can become extremely expensive.

Fragmentation makes the vacuum harder to see (and easier to trigger)

Modern markets are fragmented. The "best price" is an aggregation across venues, but the *depth* behind that best price may be scattered, hidden, or fleeting:

- some liquidity is displayed on exchanges,
- some is internalized by broker-dealers,
- some is in dark pools or hidden order types,
- much of it is cancelable within milliseconds.

In a cascade, liquidity does not withdraw uniformly. One venue may go thin first, routing may shift to another, and price discovery can momentarily become messy. Fragmentation does not *cause* every flash crash, but it can amplify confusion:

- participants see inconsistent signals across venues,
- routing decisions chase "the best price" into pockets of low depth,
- temporary dislocations can appear as different venues empty at different times.

The result is a market that can look solid at the surface (a best bid still exists) while being hollow underneath (little depth to absorb selling).

The "Order Book Hollow" visualization

The diagram below captures the central mechanism: bids are the floor. When risk controls trigger widespread quote cancellation, the floor collapses, and price falls until it finds the next layer of real demand.

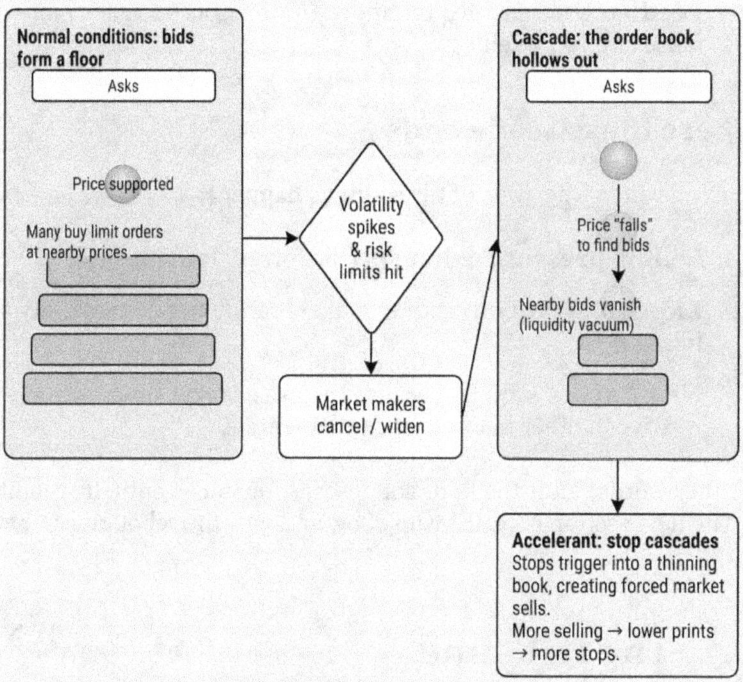

A compact mental model of the cascade

You can summarize the cascade in one sentence:

A flash crash is what happens when automated risk controls cause many liquidity providers to withdraw at the same time, so market sells (often triggered mechanically) hit a suddenly hollow order book and drive price downward in a near-vertical search for bids.

That sentence contains the whole mechanism:

- **Withdrawal** creates the vacuum (the missing bids).

- **Forced selling** exploits the vacuum (stops and urgent hedges).
- **Feedback** accelerates the move (lower prices trigger more defense and more selling).

Where the cascade ends

A cascade ends when one of three things happens:

1. **Selling pressure exhausts** (the forced flow finishes).
2. **Liquidity returns** (market makers re-quote once volatility stabilizes).
3. **New buyers step in** because the price is now obviously wrong relative to other markets or fundamentals.

In other words: after the floor collapses, someone eventually rebuilds it. The next section explains who does, and why the rebound can be so fast.

7.4 The Rebound

The previous section explained the cascade: quotes are pulled, spreads explode, and the limit order book hollows out. Prices then do what gravity does when the floor disappears—they fall until they find something solid.

But flash events are not defined only by the drop. They are defined by the *snapback*. If the cascade is the moment the market's plumbing fails, the rebound is the moment the system *self-corrects*. Rationality returns not as a moral victory, but as a profitable opportunity: when prices become obviously wrong, someone gets paid to fix them.

What "rationality returns" actually means

In a flash crash, the market is not confused about the long-run future of the economy. It is temporarily confused about *how to trade safely right now*. The rebound happens when participants regain confidence that:

- the price they see is not a trap,
- the next trade will not be dramatically worse,
- and the order book will not vanish the instant they provide liquidity.

So "rationality" here is not about philosophy. It is about microstructure: *Rationality returns when liquidity becomes* credible *again.*

That credibility comes from a mix of human decision-making and algorithms designed to detect mispricing.

The bargain that is too good to ignore

The rebound begins when the dislocation becomes large enough that it overwhelms fear.

During a cascade, many traders step away because they cannot tell whether the price drop is:

- a genuine information shock (something truly bad happened), or
- a microstructure shock (the market is momentarily malfunctioning).

As the price falls further, a different calculation emerges:

- If this is real bad news, the asset might be worth less *eventually*, but it is unlikely to be worth *this much less* in the next 30 seconds.
- If this is microstructure, the price is temporarily wrong, and the correction could be fast.

At some point, the expected payoff from buying becomes attractive even under uncertainty. That is the economic engine of the rebound.

Who buys first? The three "returning" buyer types

Different market participants re-enter at different times. Think of the rebound as a relay race in which several groups take turns providing the stabilizing force.

1) Cross-market arbitrageurs: "this price can't be right"

Arbitrageurs are traders who compare related prices and act when they diverge.

In a flash event, the strongest signal that a price is wrong is often *relative*:

- an ETF diverges sharply from its underlying basket,
- a stock diverges from its index or from highly correlated peers,
- a futures contract diverges from the cash index it tracks,
- the same instrument trades at inconsistent prices across venues.

Arbitrage is powerful because it does not require a deep opinion about a company's value. It requires only the belief that *internal consistency will be restored.* If a blue-chip stock is momentarily priced as if it were in bankruptcy while everything around it is not, that inconsistency becomes a trading signal.

Arbitrage buying is often aggressive, because the opportunity may last seconds. Ironically, the same speed that made the crash frightening makes the rebound possible: prices can correct quickly once enough capital decides the mispricing is obvious.

2) Market makers returning: from "defensive" to "competitive"

Liquidity providers do not disappear forever. They step back when volatility and adverse selection risk become too high. They return when the environment becomes tradeable again.

What changes?

- **Volatility stabilizes:** the next tick is less likely to be a disaster.
- **Inventory risk becomes manageable:** buying no longer feels like catching a falling knife.
- **Competition resumes:** once one market maker starts quoting again, others respond to avoid losing flow.

This is where spreads often tighten quickly. Tight spreads are not merely a comfort to traders; they are an indicator that liquidity is returning. As spreads tighten, more participants are willing to place limit orders. As more limit orders appear, the order book thickens. As the book thickens, price impact shrinks. The rebound becomes mechanically easier.

This is the mirror image of the cascade, but in reverse:

stabilization $\to$ quotes return $\to$ depth rebuilds $\to$ price impact shrinks.

3) Human discretionary traders: the "sanity check"

Even in highly automated markets, humans matter. They matter especially when the situation is ambiguous.

Discretionary traders (portfolio managers, prop traders, execution heads) often do two things during a flash event:

- **they pause:** to avoid being forced into the worst possible execution,
- **then they commit:** once they judge the move to be microstructure-driven rather than information-driven.

Humans are slower than machines, but they can incorporate context that is hard to encode:

- "There is no credible news."

- "Other markets are not confirming this move."
- "This looks like a liquidity air pocket, not a fundamental repricing."

When humans return, they often bring *size*. Their buying can reinforce and extend the rebound started by arbitrageurs and returning market makers.

Why the rebound is often V-shaped, not gradual

A common question is: why doesn't the price recover slowly, the way it fell slowly in a normal decline?

Because the drop in a flash crash is not a slow change in valuation. It is a temporary *execution imbalance.*

Once the imbalance is corrected, there is no reason for price to hover at the wrong level. If the asset traded far below reasonable reference points, then the first wave of buying does two things simultaneously:

- it lifts price back toward normal levels,
- it signals to others that the market is functioning again.

That second effect matters. In a panic, people fear that they will be the only buyer and will immediately regret it. When price starts to recover, it reduces that fear. In microstructure terms, it restores confidence that bids will not evaporate.

The result is a rebound that can be as fast as the fall.

The rebound is not always "fair" to every trader

It is tempting to tell the rebound story as if the market simply corrects itself and everyone is made whole. Real trading is messier.

Two traders can experience the same flash crash very differently:

- A trader with a stop-loss that converts to a market order might sell near the worst point.

- A trader with a patient limit bid might buy at a bargain and profit when prices normalize.

This is one reason flash crashes create anger and controversy. The market may "recover" in the chart, but some participants have already been executed at extreme prices.

The educational point is not moral; it is mechanical: *During a liquidity vacuum, order type becomes destiny.* Market orders and triggered stops demand immediacy at the exact moment immediacy is most expensive. Limit orders demand patience and may not execute, but they can avoid the worst prints.

A practical way to recognize the rebound in real time

For a non-professional reader, the rebound is easiest to recognize by watching three microstructure signals:

- **Spreads stop widening and begin tightening.** This indicates liquidity providers are returning.
- **Price stops printing new lows rapidly.** The downward momentum loses its mechanical fuel.
- **Related markets re-align.** ETFs and futures converge back toward their usual relationships; venue-to-venue prices become consistent.

None of these signals is perfect, but together they tell the story: the market is rebuilding the floor.

A bridge to the final diagnosis: information shock or microstructure shock?

The rebound completes the anatomy of a flash crash:

- the spark nudges the system,

- the cascade creates a liquidity vacuum,
- the rebound occurs when mispricing becomes a tradeable opportunity and liquidity becomes credible again.

Now we are ready for the final step of the chapter: **diagnosis**. After any violent move, the central question is not "How far did it fall?" but: *Was this a verdict about value (information), or a failure of trading mechanics (microstructure)?*

The next section gives you a simple framework for answering that question.

7.5 Information vs. Microstructure

We can now tell the full story of a flash event in three acts:

- **The spark** nudges the market off balance.
- **The cascade** turns that nudge into a liquidity vacuum as automated liquidity withdraws and forced selling accelerates.
- **The rebound** snaps price back when arbitrage and returning liquidity providers restore a credible order book.

This final section answers the practical question a reader should ask every time a chart suddenly falls apart:

> Was that a real repricing of value (information), or a temporary failure of trading mechanics (microstructure)?

The goal is not to turn you into a detective with perfect certainty. The goal is to give you a *diagnostic mindset*: a few simple tests that, together, separate most true information shocks from most microstructure shocks.

Two kinds of shocks that look similar on a chart

A price drop can be caused by many things, but for our purposes there are two big categories.

Information shock: the market learns something real

An **information shock** is a move driven by new beliefs about fundamentals:

- earnings or guidance surprises,
- macroeconomic news (inflation, jobs data, central bank actions),
- geopolitical events,
- credit events or balance-sheet revelations,
- regulatory decisions.

In an information shock, price is trying to find a *new equilibrium*. The market is not malfunctioning; it is doing what it is supposed to do—updating the price to reflect a changed world.

Microstructure shock: the market's trading mechanism malfunctions

A **microstructure shock** is a move driven primarily by how trading is organized and automated:

- sudden withdrawal of market-making quotes,
- stop cascades and forced market selling,
- spread explosions and thin books,
- fragmentation effects (liquidity disappearing in one venue before another),
- routing and execution feedback loops.

In a microstructure shock, price is not finding a new value; it is temporarily exploring the consequences of *missing liquidity*. The market briefly stops being a smoothly functioning auction and becomes a sequence of stressed executions.

The "plausibility test": does the move match any believable story?

Start with a simple sanity check. Ask:

> Is there news large enough to justify this move *right now*?

This question has two parts:

- **Magnitude plausibility:** could the news plausibly reduce value by this much?
- **Timing plausibility:** would the market reasonably incorporate that information this quickly?

If the answer is "yes" to both, information shock becomes more likely. If the answer is "no," microstructure becomes more likely.

Be careful: the absence of an obvious headline does not prove microstructure. Sometimes information travels unevenly. But in many flash events the key clue is the mismatch between:

- a violent, instantaneous price collapse, and
- a lack of proportionate, specific, widely acknowledged new facts.

The "shape test": does the chart show a V or a staircase?

Information shocks and microstructure shocks often have different *geometry*.

Information shocks tend to reprice, then consolidate

When a fundamental story changes, price often moves and then *stays moved*. You may see:

- a gap down at the open on earnings,
- a sharp intraday move after a policy announcement,
- a continuing drift over hours or days as portfolios rebalance.

The key is persistence. The new price is debated, but it is not immediately rejected.

Microstructure shocks tend to dislocate, then snap back

A microstructure-driven crash often has the signature **V**:

- a near-vertical decline,
- a brief period of chaos,
- a fast partial or full recovery.

The rebound is not necessarily perfect, but the speed matters. When prices snap back quickly, it suggests the market itself viewed the trough prints as anomalous.

The "cross-market consistency test": do related prices disagree?

During genuine information shocks, different markets may move by different amounts, but they tend to move *in the same direction* and remain roughly consistent.

During microstructure shocks, consistency can break down because the plumbing is stressed. Watch for:

- an ETF price diverging sharply from its net asset value (or from the moves in its major constituents),
- a futures contract behaving oddly relative to the cash index,

- the same stock printing extreme prices on one venue while other venues remain closer to normal,
- unusual gaps between bid/ask across venues (a fragmentation symptom).

In plain language: if the "ecosystem" of related prices stops agreeing, suspect microstructure. Arbitrage is the glue that normally keeps these prices aligned; when the glue temporarily fails, dislocations appear.

The "microstructure checklist": signals that the plumbing is the culprit

If you could see the market at high resolution during a flash event, you would often observe telltale mechanical symptoms. Even without professional tools, you can understand the logic behind them.

Spreads suddenly widen

Widening spreads are a sign that liquidity providers are defensive. If spreads explode during the drop and then tighten during the rebound, that pattern is highly suggestive of a liquidity vacuum rather than a change in value.

Depth disappears (the book goes thin)

In a flash crash, the problem is not only that people are selling—it is that there are fewer bids to absorb selling. Thin depth means each market sell has outsized impact.

Stop cascades and forced selling dominate

A rapid series of downward prints often triggers:

- stop-loss orders,
- margin-related liquidations,

- risk-parity or volatility-targeting de-risking,
- hedging adjustments.

These flows are not opinions; they are *rules*. Rules can synchronize. Synchronized rules can create cascades.

Trading halts, limit-up/limit-down events, or interruptions

While not present in every episode, interruptions often occur when markets detect disorderly conditions. They are not themselves the cause; they are evidence that the system is struggling to maintain orderly execution.

A practical decision framework (without pretending to be perfect)

Here is a disciplined way to combine the tests above. Think of it as scoring, not certainty.

Step 1: Identify the time scale.

- Seconds to a few minutes: lean microstructure.
- Hours to days: lean information.

Step 2: Search for proportional news.

- Clear, specific, widely disseminated news that matches the magnitude: lean information.
- Vague or absent news: lean microstructure.

Step 3: Check the recovery behavior.

- Fast, sharp rebound (the V): lean microstructure.
- Little rebound, or a new stable lower range: lean information.

Step 4: Ask whether related markets stayed coherent.

- Strong dislocations between linked instruments/venues: lean microstructure.
- Broad coherence across linked prices: lean information.

If three out of four point in the same direction, you usually have a reliable diagnosis.

Why the diagnosis matters: what each explanation implies

The difference between information and microstructure is not academic. It changes what the event *means* and what risks it reveals.

If it is information-driven

An information-driven drop implies:

- the asset may truly be worth less (at least under prevailing beliefs),
- volatility may remain elevated because the news continues to be processed,
- **buying the dip** is not automatically rational; it depends on your view of fundamentals and risk.

If it is microstructure-driven

A microstructure-driven drop implies:

- the market temporarily mispriced the asset due to missing liquidity,
- execution risk is the main danger (getting filled at extreme prices),

- order type and trading venue behavior matter enormously in stress,
- the event is a warning about fragility: liquidity can vanish when it is needed most.

In other words, a microstructure flash crash is a structural failure, not an economic verdict.

The chapter's final takeaway

If you remember only one lesson from this chapter, make it this:

> A flash crash is not primarily a story about fear; it is a story about **liquidity that was conditional** and **automation that withdrew it**.

Normal declines are the market digesting reality. Flash crashes are the market briefly losing its ability to trade smoothly. The chart may look similar in the moment—red candles, panic, falling prices—but the underlying cause is different. And once you learn to separate information shocks from microstructure shocks, market turmoil becomes less mysterious: you stop asking only "What happened?" and start asking the more useful question, "Which part of the system failed?"

Chapter 8

Stories from the Edge: Historic Case Studies

On May 6, 2010, the U.S. stock market lost nearly a trillion dollars in minutes, only to find it again before lunch. This chapter moves beyond theory to examine the wreckage of history's most startling market failures. By stepping through the timeline of the Flash Crash and witnessing ETFs trading for pennies, we uncover the universal patterns-and the chaos-that emerge when the machines pull the plug on liquidity.

8.1 The 2010 Flash Crash

On May 6, 2010, U.S. equity markets experienced a sudden, violent drop and an almost equally sudden rebound—a modern market panic compressed into minutes. This event is often called the *Flash Crash*, and within it traders remember the *"Crash of 2:45"*: a sharp plunge that culminated around 2:45 p.m. Eastern Time, when prices and liquidity briefly stopped behaving like the orderly markets most investors imagine. The key idea that connects this story to the earlier foundations of this book is simple: **prices are not facts; they are outcomes of a trading process**. When the process is stressed—

especially in a fragmented, algorithm-driven market—prices can gap, wobble, and even become nonsensical for short intervals. This section reconstructs the episode in a timeline mindset: step-by-step, minute-by-minute, showing how one large automated sell program met a market already on edge, and how high-speed strategies amplified the shock into a liquidity vacuum.

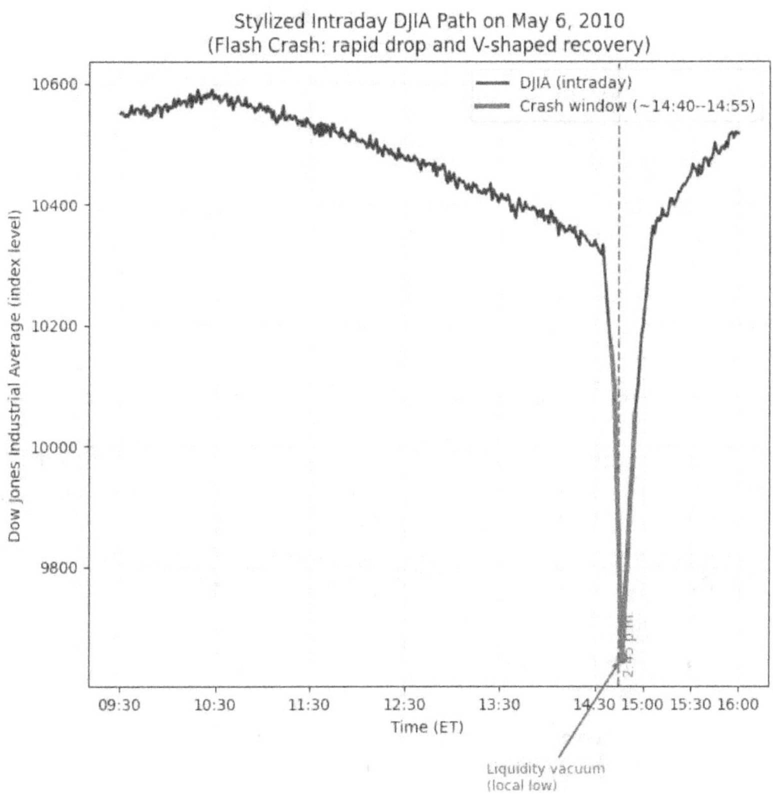

Why a Minute-by-Minute Reconstruction Matters

Most investors learn markets through *end-of-day* charts and neat historical returns. The Flash Crash cannot be understood that way. It is a story about **microstructure**: the mechanics of how orders become trades inside a fragmented electronic ecosystem.

In normal conditions, a large seller can transact by meeting many buyers across many prices with modest impact. During the Flash Crash, the critical failure was not "there were no buyers in the world." It was that, for a short period, **the market's willingness to display buy orders at reasonable prices evaporated**. When that happens, the price you see becomes less like a thermometer reading and more like the last number produced by a stressed machine.

A timeline mindset forces a crucial discipline:

- **What happened first?** (the trigger)
- **What feedback loop took over?** (the cascade)
- **What changed to end it?** (the recovery)

Setting the Stage: A Fragile Afternoon

By early afternoon on May 6, 2010, markets were already unsettled. Think of the order book as a crowd of potential counterparties. On calm days, the crowd is thick: if you need to sell, there are plenty of buyers near the current price. On tense days, the crowd thins: buyers step back, demand more "discount" before they commit, and the market becomes more sensitive to any large order.

Two practical features of modern markets matter here:

1. **Automation** – Large trades are commonly executed by algorithms that slice an order into many smaller pieces.
2. **Fragmentation and speed** – Liquidity is spread across exchanges and venues. Fast traders can react to the same signal in milliseconds.

In a fragile market, these are not neutral details. They determine whether a big order is absorbed smoothly or becomes the first domino.

The Trigger: A Large Automated Sell Program

The Flash Crash narrative begins with a large sell program in equity index futures (most famously the E-mini S&P 500 futures). Futures matter because they are a central "engine room" for price discovery: they trade quickly, in size, and they influence equity prices through arbitrage.

The important point is not a villainous intention; it is a **mechanical mismatch**:

- A **large** amount needed to be sold.
- The selling was executed by an **algorithm** that followed rules.
- The market's **capacity** to absorb the flow was shrinking.

A useful metaphor is pouring water into a drain. If the drain is wide open, the water disappears. If the drain is partially clogged, the same faucet setting floods the sink. The faucet (the sell algorithm) can be "reasonable" in normal times and still be destructive in stressed conditions if it does not adapt.

Minute-by-Minute: From Pressure to Panic

No reconstruction can be perfectly universal because different instruments and venues moved at slightly different times. But the *pattern* is consistent across accounts and post-event analyses: steady pressure becomes a rapid cascade, and then a swift repair.

Below is the event in a simplified timeline. The goal is intuition: how a selling program turns into a market-wide liquidity event.

2:32–2:38 p.m.: Selling Pressure Becomes Noticeable

What you would have seen:

- Index futures begin to slide more quickly than earlier in the day.

- Bid-ask spreads in related products widen.
- Depth (visible size in the order book) thins.

What is happening mechanically: the sell algorithm is feeding the market a persistent stream of sell orders. Liquidity providers (including high-speed market makers) respond in the way they are designed to respond: they quote less aggressively. In plain terms: *"If conditions are getting weird, I will either widen my prices or show smaller size."*

This is not cowardice; it is risk control. A market maker that keeps bidding strongly while prices fall can be run over by informed or fast traders. In a stressed tape, being "brave" can be indistinguishable from being "slow."

2:38–2:41 p.m.: The Feedback Loop Starts

What you would have seen:

- Faster, sharper downticks.
- A feeling that the market is "air-pocketing" between prints.

The key idea: hot potato trading. In normal times, a market maker buys from a seller and then gradually sells to longer-term buyers. In the Flash Crash, many fast participants did not want to hold inventory. Instead, contracts changed hands rapidly among fast traders: buy, then quickly sell; buy, then quickly sell. Volume can look healthy while *true risk-bearing liquidity* is disappearing.

High trading volume does not guarantee high liquidity.

Liquidity is about **willingness to hold risk at a stable price**. Hot-potato volume is the opposite: frantic passing of risk with little balance-sheet commitment.

2:41–2:44 p.m.: Liquidity Withdrawal and Spread Explosion

What you would have seen:

- Quotes become less reliable; bids step down quickly.
- Some market makers cancel quotes faster than they post new ones.

This is where the order book matters. Imagine a ladder of buy orders beneath the current price. In calm markets, the ladder has many rungs: you can fall one rung and still find another buyer right below. In a liquidity withdrawal, rungs disappear. When the market trades down, it can *skip* prices because there is simply no one standing there to buy.

At this point, fragmentation becomes a multiplier. Each venue sees a piece of the flow and reacts defensively. A small disturbance in one place becomes a broad retreat everywhere, because automated systems are all reading the same stress signals.

2:44–2:46 p.m.: The "Crash of 2:45"

What you would have seen:

- A near-vertical drop in many instruments.
- Sudden prints at extreme prices in some stocks and ETFs.
- Confusion: prices that look "obviously wrong" but still trade.

This moment is best understood as a **liquidity vacuum**. When bids disappear, even modest sell orders can hit much lower levels, not because the world revalued companies in 30 seconds, but because the trading mechanism temporarily lost its stabilizers.

A simple way to picture it is to separate two concepts that are usually fused in our minds:

- **Value** (a slow-moving belief about what something is worth)
- **Price** (the immediate outcome of who is willing to trade right now)

During 2:45 p.m., *price* briefly stopped being a good messenger for *value*. It became a report on a microstructure failure: bids pulled back, spreads widened, and transactions "walked down" thin books.

2:46–2:50 p.m.: Stabilizers Engage, and the Market Finds a Floor

Even the most chaotic electronic markets contain stabilizing forces. In the Flash Crash, several mechanisms and behaviors contributed to halting the free fall:

1. **Automatic pauses and protections** — Certain venues slowed, paused, or rejected trades under extreme conditions (the specific rules have evolved since 2010, but the idea is consistent: markets have circuit-breaker-like behaviors).

2. **Re-entry of liquidity providers** — Once prices overshoot and volatility signals stabilize, some market makers cautiously return. For them, extreme dislocations can become attractive opportunities *if* they believe the market is regaining order.

3. **Arbitrage and cross-market repair** — As futures, ETFs, and stocks diverge, arbitrage strategies begin pulling them back into alignment. This "repair crew" only works when trading is functioning well enough for participants to execute without being trapped.

The rebound is therefore not mysterious. It is what happens when the selling pressure slows and the mechanisms that connect markets restart. The same wiring that spreads stress can also transmit the recovery.

2:50–3:10 p.m.: V-Shaped Recovery, Lingering Damage

What you would have seen:

- Many index measures rebound sharply.
- Some individual names remain dislocated longer than the index.
- Post-trade reviews begin immediately: "What just happened?"

This is a crucial lesson for casual observers: an index can recover while many individual securities experienced absurd prints. The market can look "fine" again in aggregate, even though some participants were filled at terrible prices moments earlier. The Flash Crash was not just a chart event; it was an execution event.

The Amplifier: Why High-Speed "Hot Potato" Trading Can Drain Liquidity

It is tempting to blame speed itself. Speed is not inherently harmful. The deeper issue is **how strategies behave under stress**.

In calm markets, high-frequency market makers can:

- tighten spreads,
- add depth,
- and absorb short bursts of imbalance.

In stressed markets, the same firms can quickly switch regimes:

- quote less,
- cancel more,
- and reduce inventory limits.

This regime-switching can be rational for each firm and still disastrous collectively. If everyone is built to step back at the same time, the market experiences a coordinated retreat without any explicit coordination. The result looks like a panic because it *is* a panic—implemented through code.

A simple causal chain captures the amplification:

Large sell flow $\longrightarrow$ volatility rises $\longrightarrow$ market makers widen/cancel $\longrightarrow$ depth falls $\longrightarrow$ prices gap $\longrightarrow$ more stress signals $\longrightarrow$ further withdraw

This is the central "edge-of-market" lesson: **liquidity is conditional**. It is abundant right up until the moment it is not.

What the Flash Crash Teaches (Without Getting Ahead of Later Sections)

We will later examine ETF dislocations, broken prints, and the role of market fragmentation in more depth. For now, keep three grounded takeaways from the 2010 Flash Crash:

1. **A single large automated order can be a trigger, not because it is evil, but because it is relentless.** When an execution algorithm does not sufficiently adapt to changing liquidity, it can behave like a fixed-speed engine driving into a narrowing tunnel.

2. **High volume can coexist with low liquidity.** Hot-potato trading can inflate volume statistics while true risk-bearing capacity disappears. In a crisis, the question is not "How many contracts traded?" but "Who was willing to hold them?"

3. **A modern crash is a process, not a headline.** The "2:45" plunge was the visible cliff. The real event was the sequence: pressure, regime-switching, withdrawal, cascade, and then repair.

The Flash Crash is therefore not a historical curiosity. It is a compact demonstration of the book's core theme: when markets fragment and automate, the *plumbing* matters. In the next sections, we will follow that plumbing into specific failure modes—especially how linked instruments (like ETFs and their underlying stocks) can temporarily detach when the arbitrage link goes slack.

8.2 ETF Dislocations: When the Link Snaps

The Flash Crash timeline introduced a hard lesson: in a fast liquidity event, the market can briefly stop behaving like a smooth auction and start behaving like a series of gaps. Now we take the next logical step. If *one* market can go thin, what happens to products whose job is to *track* that market?

Exchange Traded Funds (ETFs) are designed to trade like stocks while *representing* a basket of assets (often stocks, sometimes bonds, commodities, or a mix). Most days, that design works so well that many investors forget there is any mechanism holding the ETF price near the value of its holdings. The Flash Crash reminded the world that the mechanism is not magic. It is a set of traders and algorithms doing a particular job, under particular rules, with particular limits. When those traders step back—even briefly—the link can snap.

This section explains how ETFs can momentarily decouple from the value of the assets they own, why those decouplings can produce absurd prints (including trades at pennies), and why the event is best understood as a failure of **the arbitrage link** during a liquidity vacuum.

Two Prices That Usually Agree (Until They Don't)

To understand an ETF dislocation, you need to keep two prices in your head at the same time:

- **The ETF's market price** – the price you see trading on an exchange, second-by-second, just like any stock.
- **The basket's value** – the combined value of the underlying holdings, often summarized as Net Asset Value (NAV) and, for many ETFs, also approximated intraday by an iNAV (an indicative value updated throughout the day).

In an ideal world, these two numbers are nearly the same. When they drift apart, specialized participants step in to close the gap. That activity is called **arbitrage**, and it is the invisible hand that keeps the ETF tethered to its holdings.

A useful mental model is an elastic band:

- The ETF price can move a little away from the basket value (the band stretches).
- Arbitrage pulls it back (the band snaps it toward fair value).
- In extreme stress, the band can effectively *stop working* for a few minutes (it goes slack or breaks).

Who Holds the Elastic Band? Authorized Participants and the Create/Redeem Mechanism

ETFs are not kept in line by goodwill. They are kept in line by a specific plumbing system involving **Authorized Participants (APs)** and a process known as **creation and redemption**.

Creation (when the ETF is too expensive)

If an ETF trades *above* the value of its holdings, an AP can:

- buy the underlying stocks in the correct proportions (the "basket"),
- deliver that basket to the ETF sponsor,
- receive newly created ETF shares,
- sell those ETF shares in the market at the higher price.

This increases the supply of ETF shares and tends to push the ETF price down toward the basket.

Redemption (when the ETF is too cheap)

If an ETF trades *below* the value of its holdings, an AP can:

- buy ETF shares in the market at the discounted price,
- redeem them with the ETF sponsor,
- receive the underlying basket,
- sell the basket at (roughly) its higher value.

This reduces the supply of ETF shares and tends to push the ETF price up toward the basket.

In calm markets, this works quickly enough that most investors experience ETFs as "tracking machines." But the mechanism depends on two assumptions that are often unspoken:

- the AP can trade the underlying basket without unacceptable risk, and
- the AP can reliably price the basket (i.e., the quotes and prints in the underlying are meaningful).

During a liquidity crisis, both assumptions can fail.

The Arbitrage Link Concept: Why It Can Turn Off

In the Flash Crash section, we saw a market-wide pattern: volatility rises, quotes widen, and depth disappears as liquidity providers reduce risk. ETF arbitrage is not immune to that pattern; it is built on top of it.

ETF arbitrage is a trading strategy. Like any strategy, it has risk limits. When the market becomes too fast or too uncertain, arbitrageurs may stop providing the service that normally keeps prices aligned.

Why would arbitrageurs step back precisely when mispricings are largest? Because in a crash, the apparent profit can be overwhelmed by execution risk.

Execution risk: the basket is hard to trade

An ETF is one symbol. The basket might be 100, 500, or 1,000 symbols. In calm times, the AP can hedge and trade across them smoothly. In stressed times:

- many constituents may have widening spreads,
- some may be gapping or trading sporadically,
- and the cost of getting in and out (slippage) becomes unpredictable.

If you cannot trust your ability to trade the basket, you cannot confidently arbitrage the ETF.

Pricing risk: the basket value becomes uncertain

In a crisis, the last traded price of a constituent stock might be stale (from seconds ago, which matters at high speed), or it might reflect an odd-lot print that occurred in a thin book. An iNAV is only as good as the underlying data feeding it. If underlying prices become unreliable, the ETF's "true" value becomes fuzzy—exactly when you need precision.

Balance sheet and inventory constraints

Arbitrage requires temporarily holding positions: long ETF/short basket, or vice versa. During a volatility spike, risk models and capital limits tighten. Even if a trade looks attractive, it may be disallowed or downsized by internal controls.

Put simply: during the worst minutes of a crash, the market asks arbitrageurs to do the hardest version of their job at the moment their tools are least effective.

How Absurd Prints Happen: From Decoupling to "A Penny"

When people hear that a stock traded for a penny, they often assume a computer error. More often, it is a market-mechanics story: a trade executed at the best available displayed price in an order book that has gone hollow.

ETF dislocations can create these moments because the ETF and the constituents can go thin *at the same time*. Here is a simplified pathway to an absurd print:

- **Stress rises** (rapid price moves, widening spreads, heavy selling).
- **Market makers step back** (less displayed size, wider quotes, more cancellations).
- **Underlying constituents become hard to price** (stale quotes, sporadic prints).

- **Arbitrage slows or turns off** (the elastic band loses tension).
- **The ETF becomes its own market** for a few minutes (price determined by the orders present *in the ETF* rather than by the basket).
- **A market order hits a thin book** and walks down to extreme levels, generating a shocking print.

Notice what is *not* required: fraud, a broken exchange, or a conspiracy. You can get extreme outcomes from ordinary rules applied to extraordinary conditions.

A Concrete Example (Simplified): The Book Goes Thin

Consider an ETF that normally trades at $100 and tracks a broad equity basket. In a calm market, the order book might look like this conceptually:

Side	Displayed interest near $100	Implication
Bids	Many orders at $99.99, $99.98, $99.97, ...	Selling pressure is absorbed gradually
Asks	Many orders at $100.01, $100.02, $100.03, ...	Buying pressure is absorbed gradually

In a crash minute, the same ETF can look like this:

Side	Displayed interest	Implication
Bids	A few small bids near $99, then almost nothing until $80	A sell order can "fall through" prices
Asks	Wide, jumpy offers; sellers are defensive	The next tradable price may be far away

If someone sends a *market sell order* ("sell now, whatever the price"), the exchange matches it against the best bids available. If bids are missing between $99 and $80, the trade can print near $80. If bids are missing even further down, you can print far below any reasonable estimate of the basket's value.

This is the same liquidity vacuum idea we saw in the Flash Crash—but now applied to a product that investors often treat as "safe" and "diversified."

Why ETFs Can Move More Than Their Holdings (Temporarily)

A natural question is: *If the ETF is just a wrapper around stocks, how can it fall more than the stocks inside it?*

In quiet times, it generally cannot, because arbitrage keeps it aligned. In stressed times, three effects can make the ETF appear to "overreact":

- **The ETF becomes the fastest exit door.** Selling an ETF is one click. Selling 500 individual stocks is 500 clicks (or a complex program). In a panic, investors and algorithms often choose the instrument that is easiest to trade quickly. That concentrates selling in the ETF.

- **The ETF trades continuously while some constituents effectively pause.** Even without formal halts, individual stocks can become illiquid or trade sporadically. If the underlying is not updating smoothly, the ETF can gap because its own order book is being hit while the basket is partially "frozen."

- **Hedging flows feed back into the underlying.** When professionals sell the ETF, they may hedge by buying or selling futures, other ETFs, or subsets of constituents. Those hedges can transmit stress across markets in complex ways, especially when multiple strategies respond to the same signals.

The important nuance: the ETF is not betraying its mission. The linkage mechanism is simply overwhelmed for a moment. The wrapper keeps trading, but the tether is slack.

The Human Interpretation Trap: "The ETF Must Be Broken"

When an ETF prints an absurdly low price, it looks like the fund "lost value." For long-term investors, that interpretation is usually wrong. What happened is closer to this:

- The **trading venue** experienced a temporary failure of displayed liquidity.
- The ETF price briefly reflected **order book scarcity**, not a thoughtful revaluation of the underlying assets.
- The arbitrage mechanism that normally enforces alignment was **paused by risk controls** and market frictions.

In other words, the ETF is not a promise that you can always sell at "fair value" in the worst minute of the year. It is a structure that tends to deliver fair pricing when the underlying market is functioning.

Practical Takeaways: How to Think (and Trade) During Dislocations

This book is not an instruction manual for day trading, but it would be irresponsible to describe ETF dislocations without translating them into simple behavioral rules. The following are not guarantees; they are common-sense ways to reduce exposure to the worst microstructure moments:

- **Prefer limit orders over market orders in fast markets.** A market order is a request for immediacy, not a request for a reasonable price. In a thin book, immediacy can be catastrophically expensive.
- **Do not assume "diversified" means "immune to gap risk."** Diversification reduces fundamental risk over time. It does not eliminate the short-term mechanics of liquidity withdrawal.

- **Remember the two-price model: ETF price vs basket value.** When headlines scream, ask: is this a genuine revaluation of the basket, or a temporary breakdown in the arbitrage link?
- **Liquidity is a service, not a constant.** The service is provided by participants with models and limits. When the environment exceeds those limits, the service degrades.

Where This Fits in the Larger Crash Story

The Flash Crash showed the *timeline* of a liquidity event: trigger, withdrawal, cascade, recovery. ETF dislocations show a related but distinct lesson: **market linkage is conditional**. ETFs, futures, and stocks are usually tied together by arbitrage relationships that act like mechanical couplers. In a crisis, those couplers can slip.

In the next case studies, we will broaden the lens further. If linkages can fail within equities (ETF to stocks), they can also transmit stress *across* asset classes (futures to bonds, bonds to FX). The common thread is not the instrument. It is the cascade pattern: when volatility spikes, liquidity providers reduce risk, and the mechanisms that normally keep markets aligned temporarily lose their grip.

8.3 Cross-Market Contagion

The Flash Crash showed how a modern equity market can lose its footing in minutes when liquidity providers withdraw and algorithms amplify the move. The ETF dislocation story added an important refinement: even when the underlying assets have not "changed value" in any fundamental sense, *the links that normally keep prices aligned can slip*. Now we widen the lens again.

A common misconception is that flash events are an "equity problem"—a quirk of stock exchanges, equity HFT, or the particular rules of listed markets. In reality, the same cascade mechanics can appear in markets that look completely different on the surface. Treasury bonds trade in dealer-centric networks and interdealer platforms; foreign exchange

(FX) trades across a global web of banks, electronic communication networks, and single-dealer platforms. The conventions differ, the jargon differs, and the venues differ. Yet the same core vulnerability remains:

When participants who usually absorb risk suddenly stop doing so, prices can gap and liquidity can vanish—even in the most important, most liquid markets in the world.

This section explains cross-market contagion: how a liquidity disruption in one instrument or venue can spill into others, why the pattern repeats across asset classes, and what the 2014 Treasury "flash rally" and FX flash events teach us about the common anatomy of modern instability.

A Unifying Framework: The Common Cascade Pattern

Before diving into Treasuries and FX, we need a single framework that ties the prior sections together. Think in four stages, which you have already seen in equities and ETFs:

- **Trigger:** An imbalance arrives (news, a large order, risk-off repositioning, a hedging wave).
- **Liquidity withdrawal:** Market makers, dealers, and algorithms widen spreads or reduce size.
- **Price cascade:** Thin books and defensive quoting cause gapping moves; stop orders and hedges can add fuel.
- **Repair:** Volatility slows, arbitrage/relative-value traders re-enter, and prices partially mean-revert.

The details of *who* withdraws and *how* orders route are market-specific. The shape of the crisis is not.

Treasuries: The Paradox of "Safest and Most Fragile"

U.S. Treasury securities are often described as the most liquid market on earth. They are the benchmark for "risk-free" rates, the foundation for pricing mortgages and corporate bonds, and the collateral plumbing for much of the financial system. That reputation makes Treasury flash events feel paradoxical: how can the deepest pool develop a whirlpool?

The answer is that liquidity is not just size; it is **continuous two-sided willingness to trade**. Treasury liquidity is highly concentrated in a small set of active dealers and electronic market makers, many of whom run sophisticated risk controls. In calm conditions, that concentration makes Treasuries efficient. In stressed conditions, it can make the market *brittle* if multiple liquidity providers step back at once.

Case Study Pattern: The 2014 Treasury Flash Rally

On October 15, 2014, the U.S. Treasury market experienced a sudden, dramatic move—often summarized as a "flash rally" in yields (prices up, yields down)—followed by a partial reversal. The purpose of highlighting this episode is not to relitigate every cause debated in post-event reports; it is to show that the same microstructure story can occur in a market that is not exchange-traded in the equity sense.

What "flash" looks like in bonds

In equities, a flash crash is often visualized as a steep drop in an index. In Treasuries, the most common headline metric is the yield on the 10-year note. A flash rally is a rapid fall in yields (a rapid rise in prices). The mechanics, however, are similar:

- order flow becomes one-sided,
- displayed depth thins,
- small additional orders produce outsized price changes,

- and once the market stabilizes, prices retrace part of the move.

Why a rally can be as destabilizing as a crash

Many readers instinctively associate instability with selling. In Treasuries, a sudden rally can be destabilizing for the same reason a sudden selloff is destabilizing elsewhere: it forces liquidity providers to manage inventory and hedges rapidly.

If dealers and electronic market makers are suddenly hit with aggressive buying (or if they buy because of a flight-to-quality surge), they can become inventory-constrained. Once a dealer's risk limit is approached, the dealer's behavior changes abruptly:

- quotes widen,
- the offered size shrinks,
- and the dealer may step out until the market calms.

This is the bond-market version of the regime-switching we saw during the Flash Crash: not a gradual reduction in liquidity, but a *cliff* driven by risk controls.

FX Flash Events: When a 24-Hour Market Gaps

Foreign exchange is often described as a continuous, global market. It does not have a single centralized exchange for most pairs, and it trades around the clock. That leads many observers to assume it cannot experience the kind of abrupt gaps seen in equities. Yet FX has had multiple flash episodes in major and minor pairs.

To understand how FX can "flash," you need to replace the idea of a single market with the reality of **a network of venues and liquidity streams**. In FX, the displayed price is often a composite:

- quotes from banks to clients,
- quotes on electronic communication networks,

- and quotes on interdealer platforms.

In calm times, these streams are tightly aligned by arbitrage and competition. In stress, they can fracture. A trader may see a quote on a screen that exists only in one stream, for a small size, for a fraction of a second.

Why time-of-day matters in FX

Unlike U.S. equities, FX does not have a single opening bell. But it does have **liquidity regimes** that follow the global clock. There are hours when London and New York overlap (deep liquidity), and hours when fewer major centers are active (thinner liquidity). Flash FX events frequently occur in thinner hours because:

- fewer dealers are streaming tight prices,
- risk limits may be tighter around uncertain periods,
- and a single burst of order flow can sweep through a shallow book.

In other words, "24-hour market" does not mean "24-hour depth."

How Contagion Jumps Between Markets

Cross-market contagion is not mystical. It travels along specific, well-used channels. Here are the most important ones for a non-professional reader to recognize.

Channel 1: Shared risk management (the same hands on multiple levers)

Large institutions manage risk across portfolios, not instrument-by-instrument. When volatility spikes in one area, they may reduce exposures across many areas simultaneously. This is especially true for:

- leveraged strategies (where margin demands rise as volatility rises),
- volatility-targeting or risk-parity-style allocations (where exposure is scaled down when volatility rises),
- and systematic funds that respond to the same signals across asset classes.

The outcome can look like "contagion" even when there is no direct economic link, because the same players are pulling back everywhere at once.

Channel 2: Hedging chains (one trade creates another)

Modern markets are connected by hedges:

- An equity selloff can trigger buying of Treasuries (flight to quality).
- A Treasury rally changes interest rate differentials, which can move FX.
- FX moves affect multinational earnings expectations, feeding back into equities.

These are not slow, academic relationships. They are encoded into trading systems. When the first move becomes sharp, the hedges can become urgent, turning linear relationships into nonlinear cascades.

Channel 3: Relative-value and arbitrage linkages (the couplers can slip)

The ETF section introduced the idea that linkages can fail when arbitrageurs step back. The same principle applies across asset classes:

- futures vs cash markets,

- on-the-run vs off-the-run Treasuries,
- spot FX vs FX futures,
- and rates products linked through swaps and basis trades.

When a relative-value trade is forced to unwind (because financing tightens or risk limits bind), it can create sudden pressure in multiple instruments at once.

Channel 4: Market-making capacity (liquidity providers share constraints)

Liquidity is often supplied by a smaller set of firms than the public realizes. Even when the firms differ by market, their constraints can be correlated:

- similar volatility filters,
- similar inventory limits,
- similar reliance on short-term funding or internal capital allocations.

If many liquidity providers reduce risk simultaneously, multiple markets can "go thin" together. That is the systemic version of the Flash Crash dynamic.

A Plain-English Diagnostic: Is This a Fundamental Move or a Liquidity Move?

In real time, it is difficult to tell whether a dramatic price move reflects new information or a temporary breakdown in trading conditions. But the framework from earlier sections extends well across markets.

Here are clues that you may be watching a **liquidity-driven** move:

- **Speed:** the move unfolds faster than news can plausibly be digested.

- **Gaps and air pockets:** prices jump through levels rather than trade through them.
- **Cross-venue inconsistency:** different platforms show meaningfully different prices.
- **Rapid partial reversal:** once the shock passes, prices retrace a large fraction quickly.

None of these prove there is no information component. They suggest that microstructure is doing much of the work.

Why This Matters for the Rest of the Chapter

A modern liquidity crisis is often a *network event*, not a single-market event.

The Flash Crash gave you the timeline mindset inside equities. ETF dislocations showed how the linking mechanism can fail even when the underlying value is not fundamentally changing. Treasuries and FX add the final piece: **the pattern is portable**. It can appear wherever electronic liquidity is conditional and risk controls can trigger synchronized retreat.

The next section will zoom in on the most psychologically jarring symptom of these episodes: *broken prices*. We will separate **quotes** (what the screen advertises) from **prints** (what actually traded) and explain how crisis microstructure can generate transaction prices that look impossible until you see the order book mechanics underneath.

8.4 Broken Prices: The Illusion on the Screen

The previous sections built a sequence of ideas. The 2010 Flash Crash showed how liquidity can vanish quickly and how fast strategies can turn a one-way order flow into a cascade. The ETF dislocation section showed that even when instruments are mechanically linked (ETF to basket), the link depends on arbitrageurs who may step back. Cross-market contagion widened the lens further: the same cascade mechanics can appear in Treasuries and FX because the underlying vulnerability is not the asset class, but the conditional nature of liquidity.

Now we confront the most unsettling symptom of all: **broken prices**. These are moments when the number on the screen looks like a tradable fact—$0.01, $100,000, down 90% in seconds—but the market's ability to transact at sensible prices has fractured. In a crisis, the screen can show *a price*, but not necessarily *a usable price*.

This section explains the discrepancy between quotes and prints, why absurd transaction prices can occur without a "software bug," and how placeholder quotes ("stub quotes") and thin order books can turn the market into a hall of mirrors.

The Two Meanings of "Price" That People Confuse

In everyday language, "the price" sounds singular and objective. In electronic markets, it is more accurate to think of prices as *layers*:

1. **Displayed quotes (the invitation)**: bids and offers that advertise willingness to trade at certain prices for certain sizes.
2. **Executable liquidity (the reality)**: how much you can trade *right now* without pushing the market far away.
3. **Last trade / prints (the footprint)**: the prices at which trades actually occurred, which can be extreme if the order book is thin.

Most of the time, these layers line up. The best bid/offer are close to the last trade, and depth is thick enough that trading a moderate size does not move the price much. During a liquidity vacuum, the layers separate:

- Quotes may exist but be tiny and fleeting.
- Depth may be missing at nearby levels.
- The next actual trade may occur far away from where the market "was" seconds earlier.

That separation is the essence of broken prices.

Quotes vs. Prints: The Market's "Brochure" vs. Its "Receipt"

A practical way to internalize the difference is this:

> **Quotes are the market's brochure. Prints are the receipt.** A brochure tells you what is being offered in principle; a receipt tells you what you actually managed to buy or sell.

In calm times, the brochure is trustworthy. In crisis times, the brochure can be misleading because it often reflects *the best available price for a very small quantity*—and sometimes that "best" is not stable.

Why prints can look absurd

Suppose a stock normally trades at $40 with thousands of shares available near the inside market. If panic hits and liquidity providers pull their bids, the order book might temporarily contain:

- a few shares bid at $39.50,
- then almost nothing until $30,
- then a small "stub" bid at $0.01.

If a market sell order arrives and there is not enough buy interest between $39.50 and $30, it will trade down. If there is still not enough interest, it can keep walking until it hits that $0.01 bid. The trade prints at a penny. The receipt is real. The market was not "valuing the company at a penny" in any meaningful sense. The market was revealing that **the book was empty**.

In that sense, absurd prints are often not a valuation signal; they are a **liquidity diagnostic**.

The Limit Order Book in a Crisis: When the Floorboards Disappear

To see why broken prices happen, we need to revisit the limit order book (LOB) in plain terms.

Normal market: many rungs on the ladder

In normal conditions:

- there are many bids below the current price at increments of a cent (or the tick size),
- and many offers above it,
- with meaningful size at each level.

If a seller hits the bids, the price might move a few cents or a few ticks, because the next rung is close and sturdy.

Crash market: missing rungs and a long fall

In stressed conditions:

- bids are canceled or reduced,
- spreads widen,
- and the book develops *gaps*—price levels with no standing orders.

A market order does not negotiate; it consumes what is there. If the nearby rungs are missing, the order falls until it finds one.

This is the mechanical reason the Flash Crash produced not only a sharp index move but also bizarre single-stock prints and ETF prints: the book's *shape* changed faster than many participants could react.

Stub Quotes: Placeholder Prices That Became "Real"

One of the most important and least intuitive microstructure concepts for non-professional readers is the **stub quote**.

A *stub quote* is a very far-away bid or offer that is not intended to represent true trading interest near current prices. Historically, such quotes could exist for operational reasons (for example, to technically satisfy a requirement to maintain a two-sided quote, or as a minimal placeholder). In a healthy market, stub quotes are irrelevant because there is abundant liquidity at sensible prices long before the market would ever reach them.

During a liquidity vacuum, the pathologically thin book can expose these placeholders. The market "walks" to prices that were never meant to be used—but once they are the best available prices, the matching engine can execute against them.

In plain English:

> **A stub quote is like an emergency exit sign in a hallway.** You usually do not touch it. But if the hallway collapses, suddenly the exit sign becomes the only visible landmark.

The key is not the stub quote itself. The key is the *absence of real quotes* between the current price and the stub.

The Screen Illusion in Fragmented Markets: One Price, Many Places

Broken prices are made more confusing by fragmentation. Even when you see a single number on a retail screen, the market is actually many venues:

- multiple exchanges,
- alternative trading systems,
- internalizers,

- and routing logic that decides where your order goes.

In calm conditions, competition and arbitrage keep these venues aligned tightly. In a crisis, alignment can degrade:

- Venue A may have a small but real bid at $39.50.
- Venue B may be empty down to $30.
- Venue C may show a stub at $0.01.

If your order routes into the thin venue at the wrong moment, your execution can be dramatically worse than what your screen suggested a second earlier. This is why broken prices are not just about *what* traded, but *where and how* it traded.

A Practical Distinction: "I Saw It" vs. "I Could See It Again"

Another subtlety is that a single print can be both:

- **real** (it happened; it is recorded),
- and **non-repeatable** (you could not reliably trade meaningful size at that level).

This matters because many people interpret a chart as though the market offered everyone the chance to trade at the low. In a crash, the low can be a transient execution for a small quantity. It is closer to catching a falling knife in midair than stepping onto a stable floor.

This is one reason post-crisis narratives can diverge:

- Some participants report "I got filled at an insane price."
- Others report "I couldn't trade at all; liquidity vanished."
- Still others report "I traded fine; my orders were small and my routing happened to find liquidity."

All can be true simultaneously.

Why the Market Produces These Outcomes (and Why It Usually Fixes Them)

It is tempting to ask: why allow absurd trades at all? Why not simply declare that extreme prints "don't count"?

The uncomfortable answer is that markets are designed to be **rule-based and continuous**. A matching engine follows a simple logic: match orders according to price-time priority (or the venue's rules). It does not know whether a price is "reasonable." It knows only whether a willing buyer and seller met.

When the market later repairs:

- liquidity providers return as volatility stabilizes,
- arbitrageurs reconnect prices across venues and instruments,
- and the book refills with orders near the new equilibrium.

The repair creates the familiar V-shape or partial reversal. But the damage during the vacuum is not erased for those who traded at the extremes.

Investor-Level Implications: What Broken Prices Mean for Decision Making

This book is not advocating constant fear. It is advocating accurate mental models. Broken prices teach three practical lessons:

1. **Do not equate "last price" with "tradable price."** In a crisis, the last trade may reflect a thin, momentary book condition rather than broad consensus.
2. **Order type is part of market risk.** A market order is not just "faster." It is a willingness to accept whatever liquidity remains. In a vacuum, that can mean accepting an extreme.
3. **A chart can hide microstructure pain.** A one-minute candle that touches a low does not tell you whether that low was available for meaningful size, or whether it was a handful of shares that printed while most participants could not trade.

Connecting Back to the Case Studies

The Flash Crash timeline showed how the market can transition from orderly trading to a liquidity vacuum in minutes. ETF dislocations showed that when arbitrageurs step back, linked prices can detach and print nonsense. Cross-market contagion showed that the same cascade mechanics appear in Treasuries and FX because liquidity is conditional everywhere.

Broken prices are the visual artifact of those mechanics. They are what happens when

$$\text{liquidity withdrawal} + \text{thin books} + \text{rule-based matching} \rightarrow \text{extreme prin}$$

Is this the market discovering new value, or the market briefly losing the ability to express value through liquidity?

8.5 Lessons Learned: The Anatomy of a Crash

The four case studies in this chapter were intentionally chosen to feel different on the surface. The 2010 Flash Crash is remembered as an equity index free-fall and rebound. ETF dislocations feel like a mechanical betrayal: a product that is supposed to track a basket suddenly prints absurd prices. Cross-market contagion shows that the same instability can appear in U.S. Treasuries and foreign exchange—markets many people assume are too deep to "break." Finally, broken prices forced us to separate what the screen *shows* from what the market can *actually execute* when liquidity goes thin.

When you step back, these stories rhyme. They reveal a universal lifecycle that repeats across modern electronic markets. The details change (equities vs. bonds, exchange vs. dealer network, ETFs vs. futures), but the logic is remarkably stable:

> A modern crash is rarely a single event. It is a **process** that moves through stages: a trigger, a withdrawal of liquidity, a cascade of prices, and a repair driven by arbitrage and stabilization mechanisms.

This section synthesizes the recurring motifs into a practical framework you can use when the next headline arrives.

A Crash Is Not "Panic"—It Is a Sequence of Microstructure Decisions

In movies, a crash is depicted as a crowd yelling "Sell!" In electronic markets, a crash is more often a chain reaction of **rule-based decisions**:

- execution algorithms continue to sell because their rule says "finish the order";
- market makers widen or cancel because their rule says "reduce risk under volatility";
- arbitrageurs pause because their rule says "do not trade when the basket cannot be priced"; and
- risk managers cut exposure because their rule says "lower leverage when volatility rises."

None of these rules is irrational in isolation. The crash emerges when many sensible rules point in the same direction at the same time.

Stage 1: Trigger Event (The Spark)

A trigger is the first shove. It is important, but it is often *not* the main story. In the 2010 Flash Crash narrative, the trigger was a large automated sell program in index futures hitting a fragile market. In other episodes, the trigger might be:

- a surprise macro headline,
- a geopolitical shock,
- a large fund rebalancing,
- an options-hedging wave,

- or even a technical disruption that changes order flow patterns.

A key lesson from every case study is that the trigger does not need to be "big enough" to justify the price move on fundamentals. It only needs to be big enough to push the system into a regime where liquidity providers become defensive.

What to look for in real time. Triggers often show up as:

- a sudden surge in aggressive orders (market orders or marketable limits),
- a sharp, localized move in a price leader (e.g., a futures contract),
- and a quick change in spreads or visible depth.

Stage 2: Liquidity Withdrawal (The Crowd Steps Back)

Liquidity is not a physical substance stored in a vault. It is a behavior: participants displaying willingness to trade close to the current price in meaningful size. During stress, that willingness becomes conditional and can be withdrawn quickly.

In our chapters' stories, liquidity withdrawal took different forms:

- In equities, market makers reduced displayed size and widened spreads.
- In ETFs, the arbitrage link weakened because hedging the basket became too risky.
- In Treasuries and FX, dealers and electronic market makers tightened risk limits and became less aggressive.
- Across venues, fragmentation meant that some pools went thin faster than others.

Liquidity withdrawal is the *hinge* of the lifecycle. Without it, the trigger would have caused a normal, manageable price move. With it, the market becomes fragile: small additional orders can cause large moves.

The most important misconception. Many people assume that "liquidity" equals "high trading volume." The Flash Crash taught the opposite: you can have enormous volume and still have poor liquidity if trades are dominated by hot-potato passing of risk rather than genuine balance-sheet commitment.

What to look for in real time. Liquidity withdrawal often appears as:

- spread explosions,
- depth disappearing near the inside quote,
- quote flickering (rapid cancels and re-posts),
- and difficulty executing even modest size without moving the price.

Stage 3: Price Cascade (The Fall Through Missing Rungs)

Once the book is thin, prices can cascade. The defining feature is not simply that prices move quickly; it is that they move in a way that reflects **gaps** in available liquidity.

This is where the "broken prices" concept matters. In a cascade:

- the next trade can occur far away from the last trade,
- odd prints can appear because orders fall through empty levels,
- and instruments that are usually tightly linked can detach.

Stop cascades and forced selling. A cascade is often accelerated by orders and constraints that activate *because* the price has moved:

- stop-loss orders convert into market orders,
- margin calls force liquidation,
- volatility-targeting strategies reduce exposure,

- and hedgers trade more aggressively to keep risk within limits.

The result is reflexivity: the move creates the conditions for more selling (or buying, in the case of a flash rally).

Fragmentation makes cascades sharper. In a fragmented market, prices are not discovered in one place. During a cascade, the "best" price can be a moving target:

- one venue may briefly have real liquidity while another is hollow,
- routing decisions become more consequential,
- and cross-venue arbitrage becomes harder precisely when it is most needed.

This is why a crash can produce isolated absurd prints without implying that the entire market agreed on that extreme valuation.

What to look for in real time. Price cascades often show up as:

- sharp gaps rather than smooth trading,
- multiple instruments moving together in a tight window,
- a surge in cancellations and short-lived quotes,
- and sudden dislocations between linked products (ETF vs. basket, futures vs. cash, on-the-run vs. off-the-run bonds).

Stage 4: Arbitrage Repair (The System Reconnects)

Cascades do not continue forever. Markets eventually find a floor (or ceiling) because the incentives change. Once prices overshoot and volatility begins to stabilize, the repair crew returns:

- market makers cautiously re-enter when they can manage inventory again,
- arbitrageurs reconnect linked instruments when hedging becomes feasible,

- and protections (pauses, limits, or other mechanisms) slow the feedback loop enough to let liquidity rebuild.

The repair stage is why flash events often exhibit a V-shape. The same connectivity that spreads stress (fast linkages, cross-asset hedging, common signals) can spread stabilization once risk conditions become measurable again.

A subtle but crucial point. Repair does not mean "no harm was done." It means that the market's *ability to trade* has recovered. Participants who executed at the extremes during the vacuum may have experienced real losses even if the market later mean-reverted.

What to look for in real time. Repair often appears as:

- spreads narrowing,
- depth returning near the inside market,
- linked instruments snapping back into alignment,
- and volatility falling from "panic" levels to merely "high."

Recurring Motifs Across All Case Studies

Across the chapter, the same underlying forces repeatedly appeared. These motifs help you understand why the lifecycle is so portable across markets.

Motif 1: Speed compresses human time. The fastest decisions are not made by people watching a screen. They are made by systems reacting to microstructure signals (volatility, order flow, inventory, correlation). In a flash event, the market can transition between regimes before a human can process what is happening.

Motif 2: Liquidity is conditional and can be revoked. Liquidity providers are not obligated to catch a falling market at tight spreads. Their participation is voluntary and risk-managed. When conditions cross thresholds, liquidity can disappear abruptly.

Motif 3: Volume can be a mirage. Heavy trading does not guarantee stability. If the volume is dominated by rapid inventory passing rather than risk absorption, the market can still be thin where it matters.

Motif 4: Linkages are stabilizers until they are stress channels. Arbitrage links (ETF-basket, futures-cash, cross-venue price alignment) usually dampen deviations. In stress, if arbitrageurs step back, those same linkages can transmit imbalance without enforcing alignment.

Motif 5: "The price" is not a single object. In calm markets, we treat price as a fact. In stressed markets, price becomes a set of artifacts: quotes, prints, and executable depth. Broken prices are what happens when the artifacts diverge.

Using the Lifecycle as a Reader's Checklist

When you encounter a dramatic market headline, you can use this lifecycle as a diagnostic checklist:

- **Trigger:** What was the initial imbalance? Was it an order-flow event, a news event, or a structural event?
- **Liquidity withdrawal:** Did spreads widen and depth thin? Did market makers or dealers step back?
- **Cascade:** Did prices gap through levels? Did linked instruments detach? Were there absurd prints?
- **Repair:** Did spreads and depth return? Did relative-value relationships re-align? Was there a sharp reversal?

This checklist will not tell you what the market *should* do. It will tell you what the market is *capable* of doing when its plumbing is stressed.

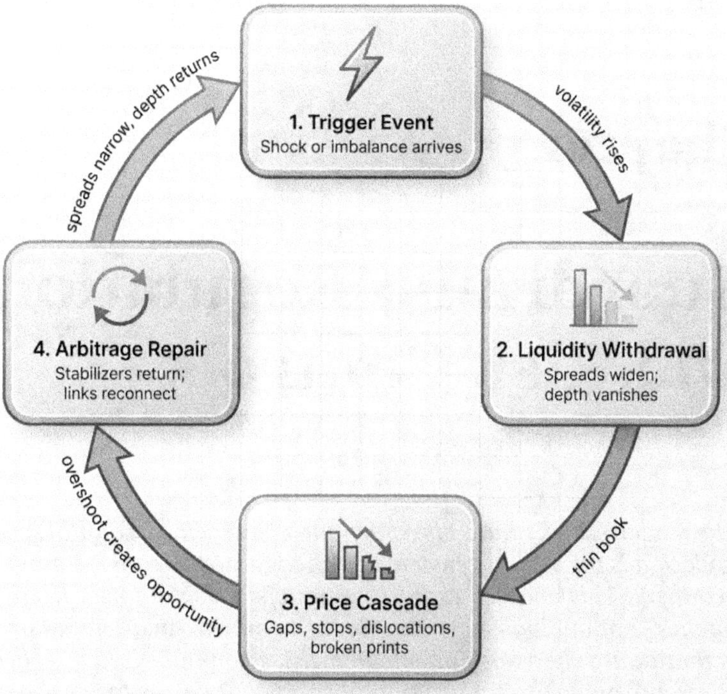
1. Trigger Event
Shock or imbalance arrives
volatility rises
2. Liquidity Withdrawal
Spreads widen;
depth vanishes
thin book
3. Price Cascade
Gaps, stops, dislocations,
broken prints
overshoot creates opportunity
4. Arbitrage Repair
Stabilizers return;
links reconnect
spreads narrow, depth returns

Chapter 9

Guardrails: Regulation and Risk Controls

If the modern stock market is a Formula 1 car racing at digital speeds, regulation is the braking system designed to stop it from spinning out of control. This chapter explores the invisible safety nets-from 'kill switches' that unplug rogue algorithms to market-wide circuit breakers that pause chaos-asking whether these computerized guardrails are strong enough to tame a digital beast that moves faster than human thought.

9.1 The Digital Airbag: Pre-Trade Risk Controls

In the earlier parts of this book, we built a simple picture of how modern markets work: orders flow from humans and algorithms into a fragmented landscape of exchanges and off-exchange venues; trades happen fast; and *liquidity* can look deep and stable right up until it suddenly vanishes. That speed and fragmentation create a paradox. The same technology that makes it easy to trade can also make it easy to make a mistake *at scale*.

This section introduces the market's first line of defense: **pre-trade risk controls**. Think of them as a *digital airbag*. An airbag does not prevent you from driving fast. It also does not decide where you go. But if something goes wrong—a sudden impact, a skid, a simple lapse—it deploys quickly to reduce damage. Pre-trade controls play the same role for trading systems: they try to catch the most dangerous errors *before* an order becomes a market event.

Why the "first line" matters: once an order is released, it becomes everyone's problem

A key idea from earlier chapters is that prices are not "set" by a single authority. They are *discovered* by a continuous process of order matching across many venues. That means an erroneous order is not contained by default. Once it reaches a live order book, it can:

- hit multiple price levels ("sweeping the book"),
- trigger stop orders and algorithmic responses,
- propagate across venues through routing and arbitrage,
- and, in the worst cases, set off a feedback loop where liquidity providers widen spreads or pull quotes.

Pre-trade risk controls exist because the cost of stopping a bad order *after* it is executed is often far higher than stopping it *before* it arrives. Post-trade fixes are messy: you may need busts/corrections, regulatory review, or bilateral negotiations, and the market impact (the temporary or permanent price distortion) may be irreversible.

The basic architecture: order flow through a gauntlet of sanity checks

At a high level, an electronic order is typically created by a person (a trader typing) or an algorithm (software deciding), then handed to a broker's systems, and only then routed to an exchange or other venue. Along that path are checkpoints. Each checkpoint asks a simple question:

> *Is this order plausible and permitted, given the account, the market, and the firm's limits?*

The checks are intentionally simple because they must be fast and reliable. A good pre-trade control does not require deep "understanding" of the world. It only needs to catch the mistakes that are *obviously* dangerous.

The three common "gates"

While different firms implement different rule sets, three families of checks show up almost everywhere:

Price checks ("Does this price make sense?")
A price check compares the order's limit price (or implied price for a market order) to a reference, such as:

- last traded price,
- mid-quote (the midpoint between best bid and best ask),
- national best bid/offer (NBBO) for U.S. equities,
- or a volatility band based on recent trading.

If a buy order is priced far above the current market, or a sell order far below it, the system suspects a fat-finger error (extra zero, wrong decimal, wrong symbol) or a runaway algorithm. The order may be rejected outright or forced into a safer form (e.g., converted into a limit order inside a bound).

Size checks ("Is this order too big?")
Size checks control *quantity*. A quantity may be "too big" relative to:

- the account's typical order size,
- the security's average daily volume,
- a per-order maximum share limit,
- or a notional limit (shares × price).

This is the classic defense against "I meant 10,000 shares but typed 1,000,000." It also limits the blast radius of an algorithm that begins to fire repeatedly.

Credit checks ("Can this account afford it?")
Credit checks determine whether the account has sufficient buying power, margin capacity, or risk budget to carry the position the trade would create. In practice, this can include:

- available cash and margin availability,
- firm-set exposure limits (per symbol, sector, or portfolio),
- concentration limits (preventing one position from dominating),
- and intraday loss limits (sometimes treated as a separate check, but often integrated).

Even a "reasonable" order can be unacceptable if it would breach exposure limits. Credit checks are especially important because an order that cannot be financed can turn into a broker problem, not just a client problem.

A concrete story: the fat finger that tries to escape

Imagine a trader intends to buy 10,000 shares of a liquid stock trading around $50. In a hurry, they type:

Buy 1,000,000 shares, Limit $500

That is a $500 million notional order at a price 10× the current market. If released, it could:

- lift every sell order in the book,
- print trades at absurd prices,
- trigger volatility pauses,
- and set off cross-venue routing that drags multiple marketplaces into the same mess.

A robust pre-trade stack is designed so that this order never becomes "market reality." It should be rejected quickly, *before* it reaches a matching engine.

Order Created (Human or Algorithm)
"Fat Finger" Order Example: BUY 1,000,000 shares @ $500 (intended: 10,000 @ $50)
"Sane" Order Example: BUY 10,000 shares @ $50.10
Pre-Trade Risk "Gates" (Sanity Checks)
Price Check: Is price within allowed band vs. reference (NBBO / last / volatility band)?
"Bad" order is stopped
If Fail: bounce back
Size Check: Is quantity / notional within per-order and per-symbol limits?
If Fail: bounce back
Credit Check: Is buying power / margin / exposure limit sufficient?
If Fail: bounce back
REJECT / BLOCK
Order bounced back to sender with reason code (e.g., PRICE_BAND, SIZE_MAX, CREDIT_LIMIT)
PASS
Order eligible for routing to exchange / venue
"Good" order proceeds to market

What actually happens when a check fails

A rejection is not just a red light; it is information. Modern systems typically return a **reason code** (e.g., PRICE_BAND_BREACH or MAX_ORDER_SIZE) and log the event for compliance and post-mortems.

From a market-stability perspective, the most important feature is *speed and certainty*. A slow, ambiguous rejection can be worse than no rejection because an algorithm might respond by retrying, routing elsewhere, or escalating its behavior. Good systems make failures:

- fast (microseconds to milliseconds, depending on architecture),
- deterministic (the same input yields the same outcome),
- and explicit (clear reason codes, clear counters).

Controls you do not see: throttles, duplicate detection, and kill switches

The "big three" checks (price, size, credit) are the headline items, but practitioners add additional guardrails to stop modern failure modes:

Message throttles (rate limits)
A runaway algorithm may not send one enormous order; it may send *thousands* of small ones. Rate limits cap:

- orders per second,
- cancels per second,
- or total messages per second (orders + cancels + replaces).

These controls matter because exchanges and brokers are not just financial systems; they are also *networked computing systems*. Message floods can degrade market quality by delaying legitimate orders and creating stale quotes.

Self-trade prevention (STP)
Large firms often have multiple strategies trading the same symbol.

Without STP, one algorithm can end up buying from another algorithm at the same firm, generating unnecessary fees and misleading volume. STP rules prevent internal "crossing" through the public book in certain circumstances, reducing noise and operational risk.

Duplicate order detection
If a network glitch causes an order acknowledgment to be lost, a client system might resend the same order. Duplicate detection tries to identify this by IDs, timestamps, and order fingerprints.

Kill switches (emergency stops)
A kill switch is not subtle. It is the trading equivalent of pulling the fire alarm:

- block new orders for a strategy or account,
- cancel open orders,
- and require explicit human action to resume.

The best time to use a kill switch is early. If a strategy is malfunctioning, every additional second can compound losses and market impact.

The hidden trade-off: safety versus speed

Pre-trade controls are protective, but they are not free. Every check adds:

- latency (time),
- complexity (more code paths and configuration),
- and operational burden (limits must be maintained, exceptions managed).

This creates a temptation in ultra-competitive trading: **loosen the filters** or **bypass them** for "trusted" flows. In practice, firms may allow:

- higher limits for certain strategies,
- broader price bands for liquid instruments,

- or specialized paths for market-making systems that must update quotes quickly.

The danger is that exemptions are often designed for normal days—and failures rarely happen on normal days. When volatility spikes and liquidity thins, a band that felt "conservative" at 10:00 a.m. can become permissive at 2:30 p.m.

Configuration risk: the guardrail is only as strong as its settings

A crucial point for non-professional readers is that these controls are not a single universal feature called "risk management." They are *parameters*:

- max order size,
- max notional value,
- allowed price deviation,
- max messages per second,
- max position,
- max intraday loss,
- and dozens more.

Those parameters are set by humans. That means the system can fail in at least three ways even if the code is "correct":

Too loose
If limits are excessively permissive, the controls become ceremonial: present, but ineffective.

Too tight
If limits are overly restrictive, they create false positives that disrupt legitimate trading. Traders then pressure operations teams for exceptions, and exceptions tend to multiply.

Correct yesterday, wrong today
Market conditions change. A static limit calibrated to quiet markets can be inappropriate during earnings, macro announcements, or crisis periods. The challenge is to scale protection with volatility without creating an unpredictable rule set that confuses both humans and algorithms.

Where pre-trade controls sit in the bigger "flash crash" story

Flash crashes and liquidity crises are rarely caused by a single fat-finger mistake. More often, they emerge from **interaction effects**: many fast participants responding to the same signals, pulling liquidity, widening spreads, and triggering cascades. Pre-trade controls cannot prevent all of that. What they *can* do is reduce the probability that one participant's error becomes the spark that lights the room.

In the chapters ahead, we will move from these "before the order" defenses to what happens *after* trading begins to spiral—mechanisms that slow markets down when speed itself becomes dangerous. Pre-trade controls are the airbag; the next set of tools are the brakes.

9.2 Pulling the Plug: Circuit Breakers and Halts

Pre-trade risk controls are designed to stop *bad inputs*—fat-finger prices, oversized orders, or runaway message storms—*before* they become public market events. But not every destabilizing episode starts with an obviously "wrong" order. Sometimes the inputs are perfectly valid and still dangerous in aggregate: thousands of rational, automated decisions all pointing in the same direction, at the same time, in a market that suddenly cannot absorb them.

When that happens, the problem is no longer "one bad order." The problem is **market dynamics**: liquidity thins, spreads widen, price impact grows, and the same price move can trigger more selling (and more risk-reducing behavior) across many strategies and venues. In those moments, the most powerful risk control is not a filter. It is a pause.

Circuit breakers and trading halts are the market's version of *pulling the plug*: a mandatory time-out that forces the system to stop, breathe, and re-form prices in a more orderly way.

Why pauses exist: speed can turn disagreement into a stampede

In calm markets, speed is helpful. It tightens spreads and lets buyers and sellers meet quickly. In stressed markets, speed can turn ordinary disagreement into a cascade.

Here is the intuition, in plain language:

1. A negative shock hits (news, rumor, macro surprise, a large sell program, or a sudden liquidity withdrawal).

2. Prices start to fall.

3. Many participants respond automatically: risk models cut exposure, leveraged traders face margin pressure, volatility-targeting strategies reduce holdings, market makers widen quotes or step back.

4. The order book becomes thinner exactly when more traders want to sell.

5. Thin books mean larger price moves for the same selling pressure, which triggers more automated responses.

A key idea from earlier chapters is that the limit order book is a *queue of willingness*. When fear rises, willingness disappears. The market can transition from "deep enough" to "too thin" in seconds. A halt is meant to interrupt that feedback loop.

Two kinds of brakes: single-stock pauses versus market-wide halts

Not all halts are the same. Regulations and exchange rules typically distinguish between:

- **Single-stock mechanisms** that pause trading in an individual name when its price becomes disorderly.
- **Market-wide circuit breakers** that halt the entire market (or broad swaths of it) when the overall index drops too far, too fast.

Both share the same philosophy: *when the system is moving faster than it can process information, slow it down.* But they are triggered differently and have different side effects.

Single-stock pauses (e.g., "limit up-limit down" style bands)

A single-stock pause is usually triggered when a stock's price attempts to move outside a defined band over a short window. The band is intended to reflect "reasonable" price discovery given recent trading.

Conceptually, imagine a rubber guardrail around a stock's recent price. In normal conditions, trading stays inside it. In stress, orders push the price to the edge. If the next trades would break through, trading is paused.

What this accomplishes:

- **Stops mechanical printing at absurd prices.** When liquidity is thin, one aggressive market order can sweep through many levels and execute at extreme prices. A pause reduces the chance that the market "discovers" a price that is really just an accident of a temporarily empty book.
- **Gives liquidity time to reappear.** Many liquidity providers are not willing to quote in a freefall. A pause can encourage them to return with tighter, more stable quotes once the immediate panic wave slows.

- **Creates a moment for verification.** Participants can check news, confirm whether the move is real, and adjust algorithms that may be reacting to stale or erroneous signals.

What it does *not* guarantee:

- It does not guarantee the price will bounce back.
- It does not guarantee "fairness" in the sense of everyone being able to trade at their preferred price.
- It does not eliminate losses; it tries to reduce *disorderly execution.*

Market-wide circuit breakers (broad "time-outs")

Market-wide halts are triggered by moves in a broad market index (such as an S&P 500-style benchmark). The logic is that when the entire market is dropping rapidly, the risk is not limited to one stock's order book; it is systemic.

Market-wide halts address problems single-stock pauses cannot:

- **Cross-asset contagion.** Index products, ETFs, futures, options, and baskets can transmit stress. Pausing the broader market can reduce the speed of contagion.
- **Correlation spikes.** In crises, everything starts to move together. If every stock is near a disorderly state, halting one at a time becomes a game of whack-a-mole.
- **Operational stability.** During extreme volatility, message traffic can surge and systems can strain. A market-wide pause can reduce the chance of technical failures compounding financial stress.

The drawback is obvious: a market-wide halt is blunt. It is disruptive, and because it affects everyone, it can create a psychological "this is serious" moment that changes behavior.

What a halt feels like: the psychology of a stopped market

A stopped market is not calm; it is *suspended*. During a halt, three psychological dynamics often appear:

Information vacuum

Humans hate uncertainty. A halt can be interpreted as confirmation that something is wrong, even if the true cause is simply volatility. Participants search for explanations, rumors spread, and narratives form quickly.

Frozen intentions

Traders who wanted to sell but could not may become more urgent. Traders who wanted to buy may become more cautious. Everyone recalculates. The result is that the first moments after a halt can be intense.

Coordination problem

In continuous trading, participants can adjust one trade at a time. In a halt, everyone is waiting for the same restart moment. That concentrates decision-making and can create a burst of supply or demand at reopening.

This is why the *reopening process* is just as important as the pause itself.

How reopening works: from continuous chaos to an auction

A common misconception is that trading simply "turns back on" and resumes where it left off. In practice, many venues use an **auction-style reopening**:

1. **Orders accumulate.** During the halt, participants can submit, modify, or cancel certain orders (depending on rules). Interest builds.

2. **A clearing price is determined.** The system looks for a sin-

gle price that best matches buy and sell interest (maximizing executable volume while respecting constraints).

3. **Trading reopens at that price.** After the auction print, continuous trading resumes with a newly established reference point.

Why an auction helps:

- It replaces a potentially chaotic sequence of one-by-one trades with a coordinated price-setting event.
- It reduces the chance that the first trade after reopening is an extreme outlier caused by a temporarily empty book.
- It gives liquidity providers a clearer target: they can re-enter around a known auction price rather than guessing in freefall.

However, reopening auctions can also concentrate risk. If the imbalance is severe (far more selling than buying), the clearing price can gap down sharply. In other words: the pause can *delay* a move without *preventing* it. The goal is orderly discovery, not denial.

Where halts help—and where they can backfire

Circuit breakers are safety devices, and like all safety devices they involve trade-offs.

How they help

They break feedback loops

If automated strategies are amplifying each other, a forced pause interrupts the chain reaction. Models that would have sold again at the next tick do not get that tick.

They reduce execution at "nonsense" prices

In a thin book, a market order can create prints that do not reflect true consensus value. Halts reduce the chance that temporary liquidity gaps become official prices.

They encourage liquidity to return

Many liquidity providers widen spreads or step away when volatility is extreme. A pause can make re-entry less hazardous, because the reopening auction sets a more stable starting point.

How they can backfire

They can concentrate panic

If everyone believes the reopening is the moment of truth, the restart can attract a surge of aggressive orders, producing another sharp move immediately after trading resumes.

They can create "magnet" behavior near trigger levels

When participants know a halt will occur at a threshold, some strategies may change behavior as the price approaches it. That can accelerate moves into the band (or cause liquidity to retreat in anticipation).

They can shift volatility rather than eliminate it

A halt may simply move volatility from continuous trading into the auction and immediate post-auction period. The market still has to reprice; it just does so in a different format.

A practical mental model: halts protect *process*, not *price*

For readers new to market structure, the most useful way to think about halts is this:

> **A halt is not a promise that the price will be higher later.**
> **A halt is a promise that price discovery will slow down when it becomes disorderly.**

Pre-trade controls (from the previous section) try to stop obviously dangerous orders from entering the system. Circuit breakers assume the orders may be legitimate, but the *system* is temporarily unable to process them without destabilizing side effects.

Even with pauses and filters, markets still rely on participants willing to quote and trade in stressed conditions—and modern electronic market makers often have more discretion to step back precisely when their presence matters most.

9.3 Fair-Weather Friends: Market Maker Obligations

Pre-trade risk controls try to stop dangerous orders at the door. Circuit breakers try to slow the entire room down when everyone starts running at once. But neither of those tools directly answers the most uncomfortable question in a liquidity crisis:

> *When everyone wants to sell, who is required to stand there and buy?*

In modern electronic markets, the honest answer is often: *no one, at least not in the way many people imagine.* Liquidity is frequently supplied by firms commonly described as "market makers"—including many high-frequency trading (HFT) firms—but the obligations they carry can be limited, conditional, or absent, especially compared to older systems built around designated specialists.

This section explains why liquidity can feel abundant on ordinary days yet disappear precisely when it is needed most, and how the difference between **duty** and **optionality** lies at the heart of many flash-crash-style events.

Start with the simplest definition: what is a market maker?

A **market maker** is a participant who regularly posts *both* a bid (a willingness to buy) and an ask (a willingness to sell), aiming to earn the spread and manage inventory risk.

In a limit order book, market makers are typically a major source of the *resting* orders you see:

- They quote many times per second.
- They cancel and replace frequently as conditions change.
- They try to stay close to the current price while avoiding being "picked off" by better-informed traders.

For casual readers, it helps to think of market making as running a small shop:

- You post a *buy price* ("I will buy your item for \$X") and a *sell price* ("I will sell for \$Y").
- You earn money if customers buy from you at \$Y and sell to you at \$X, with $Y - X$ covering your costs and risk.
- But if a sudden storm hits and everyone dumps inventory on you at once, your shop can fill up with unwanted stock.

That last point is crucial: providing liquidity is not a charitable act. It is a strategy with risk limits, and those limits bind hardest during crises.

The old world: specialists as *designated shock absorbers*

Historically, many equity markets relied on **designated specialists** (or similar roles) who had:

- privileged placement in the market's structure,
- informational advantages (in some regimes),
- and, importantly, **affirmative obligations** to maintain a fair and orderly market.

The details varied by venue and era, but the spirit was consistent: a specialist was not merely *allowed* to provide liquidity; they were *expected* to. The job came with carrots (benefits, status, sometimes exclusive rights) and sticks (requirements, oversight, reputational consequences).

This mattered most during disorderly selling. A specialist could not simply say, "This is too volatile; I'm done." They might widen spreads and slow trading, but the system treated them as a stabilizing anchor.

Even then, obligations were never magical. Specialists could be overwhelmed, and they were not required to lose unlimited money. But the market's design explicitly included a role whose mandate was to lean against temporary imbalances.

The modern world: fast liquidity, but often optional liquidity

Today's electronic liquidity provision can be extraordinarily deep in normal times, yet fragile under stress. The core reason is that many modern market makers operate with **high optionality**:

- They can reduce quote size.
- They can widen spreads sharply.
- They can cancel quotes and step away.
- They can change models, parameters, and risk limits intraday.

This optionality is not necessarily malicious. It is the rational response of firms that are:

- managing inventory risk in real time,
- trying to avoid adverse selection (trading against someone who knows more),
- and operating within strict loss limits and capital constraints.

The key difference versus the older specialist model is **incentive alignment**. In many modern settings, the market does not grant one firm a privileged franchise in exchange for a strong obligation. Instead, liquidity provision is competitive and decentralized. Competition improves pricing in calm conditions. But during stress, competition can turn into synchronized retreat.

Why market makers pull back in a crisis (and why it is rational)

When markets become disorderly, three forces hit market makers simultaneously.

Spread risk: the "ground is moving"

In stable conditions, the spread compensates the market maker for modest uncertainty. In a crisis, the "true" price can be moving faster than the market maker can update quotes. If you post a bid at $50 and the next piece of news implies the fair price is $47, your bid is suddenly a loss waiting to happen.

Market makers respond by:

- widening spreads,
- quoting smaller size,
- and demanding more compensation per trade.

To outside observers, this looks like "liquidity disappearing." To the market maker, it is simply repricing risk.

Adverse selection: you are trading against urgency (and maybe information)

In calm markets, many trades are routine. In stressed markets, trades are often urgent and informed:

- A forced seller must sell *now*.
- An informed trader may know bad news.
- An algorithm may be reacting to signals faster than you can.

If the flow is toxic (skewed toward informed or forced trades), the expected profitability of providing liquidity collapses. The market maker's best defense is to step back.

Inventory and funding: the warehouse fills up

Market making is inventory management. During a sell-off, market makers tend to accumulate inventory (they buy as others sell). But inventory is not free:

- It consumes balance sheet and capital.
- It increases exposure to continued downside.
- It may trigger internal risk limits.

At the worst moment, the market maker can become the unwilling owner of a rapidly depreciating asset. The strategy then shifts from "provide liquidity" to "survive."

So what are the obligations today? A spectrum, not a binary

It is tempting to ask, "Are market makers required to quote or not?" In reality, obligations exist on a continuum and depend on venue roles and rulebooks.

A useful mental model is a spectrum from **purely voluntary** liquidity provision to **contractual** or **rule-based** quoting requirements.

Arrangement	What the market maker gets	What the market maker must do
Voluntary (ordinary participant)	Ability to trade, earn spread/rebates, compete	No special duty; can widen, reduce, or cancel quotes at will (subject to general rules)
Incentive program (rebates/tiers)	Better economics (fees/rebates), sometimes status benefits	May need to meet quoting metrics (time-at-BO, minimum size, minimum symbols), often with exemptions during extreme conditions
Designated role (formal market maker in a venue)	Potentially enhanced economics, access, or formal designation	Quoting obligations defined by the venue (e.g., two-sided quotes for a fraction of the day), usually bounded by risk parameters and allowed withdrawal conditions

The educational point is not that "there are no rules." The point is that the rules often do not create a guaranteed buyer in a freefall. They are designed to improve liquidity *on average*, not to force firms to absorb unlimited risk during tail events.

How this interacts with the previous section: halts need someone to come back

Circuit breakers and halts can stop the spiral, but reopening requires real buy and sell interest to meet at a clearing price. If liquidity providers remain cautious, the reopening auction can gap down sharply or remain unstable afterward.

In practice, halts work best when they accomplish at least one of the following:

- **Uncertainty drops:** news is clarified, erroneous prints are corrected, or confusion is resolved.
- **Risk budgets reset:** firms widen spreads but re-enter at a price that reflects the new reality.
- **Two-sided interest returns:** longer-horizon buyers step in, not just market makers.

Notice that only one of these is "market makers doing their job." The other two depend on *information* and *investment capital*. Halts can buy time; they cannot manufacture risk appetite.

The uncomfortable truth: liquidity provision is pro-cyclical

A stabilizing force would be counter-cyclical: it would provide more liquidity when liquidity is scarce. But modern liquidity provision is often **pro-cyclical**:

- When volatility is low, spreads are tight and size is plentiful.
- When volatility is high, spreads widen and size shrinks.

This is not a failure of character; it is a feature of risk management. Yet it creates a systemic vulnerability: at the exact moment the market most needs passive buyers, the dominant fast-liquidity suppliers may be reducing exposure.

This is one reason flash crashes can feel like "the floor disappeared." The floor was not a concrete slab; it was a crowd of conditional quotes.

What should a reader conclude?

Three conclusions will help you read future flash-crash stories with clearer eyes:

- **1. "Market maker" does not automatically mean "liquidity guaranteed in a crisis."** Many market makers are businesses with the explicit right to manage their risk by stepping back.
- **2. Regulation can shape incentives, but it cannot repeal risk.** Even strict quoting rules must include exits, exemptions, or practical limits, or they become unsustainable.
- **3. Stability depends on diversity of participants.** The more liquidity is concentrated in one style of fast, risk-limited strategy, the more likely liquidity is to retreat in a correlated way.

In the next section, we will turn to a related debate that sits underneath many policy arguments: whether we should force more trading "into the light" for transparency, or whether hidden venues (dark pools) can sometimes *improve* execution and reduce market impact—even as they complicate trust and oversight.

9.4 Lights On or Off? The Transparency Debate

In the previous sections, we built up the market's "safety stack" from the inside out. Pre-trade risk controls try to prevent obviously dangerous orders from ever reaching a venue. Circuit breakers and halts pause trading when the market's feedback loops become unstable. Market maker obligations (and the limits of those obligations) explain why liquidity can be plentiful in calm weather and scarce in storms.

Now we come to a debate that sits underneath all of those guardrails: **how much of the market should be visible in real time?**

At first glance, the answer seems obvious. Transparency sounds like a pure good. If everyone can see prices and sizes, then markets should be fairer, more competitive, and harder to manipulate. And often, that is true.

But market transparency is not a simple on/off switch. It has a cost: **being seen changes how others trade against you**. For large investors trying to buy or sell quietly, "lights on" can mean getting front-run (legally, through anticipation), paying more, and moving the market against themselves. This is one of the main reasons dark pools and other forms of hidden liquidity exist.

This section explains the core tug-of-war: *transparency supports trust and price discovery*, while *darkness can support execution quality for large orders*. The hard part is that both can be true at the same time.

What does "transparency" mean in practice?

When people say "transparent markets," they usually mean some combination of the following:

- **Pre-trade transparency:** you can see quotes and available liquidity *before* trading (posted bids and asks, displayed sizes, depth-of-book).
- **Post-trade transparency:** you can see that trades occurred (time, price, volume), even if you did not see the order beforehand.

A fully "lit" market emphasizes pre-trade transparency: it displays quotes that other traders can hit or lift. A "dark" venue generally reduces pre-trade transparency: participants may submit orders, but the broader market does not see that interest sitting there in advance.

Trades are typically reported afterward (post-trade), though the timing and detail can vary by market rules.

For non-professional readers, a simple analogy helps:

- **Lit market:** an open auction where bidders hold signs up in public.
- **Dark pool:** a private matching room where participants agree on rules, and the match is announced only after it happens.

Why transparency matters: trust, competition, and price discovery

Transparency is not merely a moral preference; it is a mechanism that creates **competitive pressure** and supports **price discovery**.

Price discovery needs visible reference points

Markets need reference prices that participants can trust:

- Investors mark portfolios to market.
- Derivatives settle off reference prices.
- Risk models and margin systems rely on observable prices.

Lit quotes provide an ongoing "thermometer" of supply and demand. When prices move, everyone can see how the book is changing and adjust accordingly.

Transparency discourages certain forms of abuse

When quotes and trades are observable, it becomes easier (not easy, but easier) to detect:

- manipulation patterns,

- suspicious price moves,
- and discriminatory access.

Even in highly electronic markets, perception matters. If participants believe prices are being set in private rooms they cannot access, confidence can weaken, and liquidity can ultimately shrink.

Transparency can tighten spreads

When liquidity is displayed, multiple market makers and investors can compete to provide the best price. Competition tends to narrow spreads, especially in liquid names, because everyone knows they must post an attractive quote to trade.

This is one of the strongest arguments for "more trading in the light": it can improve execution for the *average* investor by making the market more competitive and harder to game.

Why darkness exists: large orders create footprints

If transparency is so valuable, why do dark pools exist at all?

Because a large order is not just a desire to trade. It is **information**. A big buyer reveals demand; a big seller reveals supply. If that information becomes public too early, other traders respond in ways that can raise the buyer's cost or deepen the seller's loss.

Market impact: the unavoidable cost of being large

Recall a key idea from earlier chapters: liquidity is the ability to trade without moving the price too much. A large order, by definition, risks moving the price.

In a fully lit market, a large order that is displayed can cause:

- **Mechanical impact:** it consumes multiple levels of the order book.

- **Strategic impact:** other traders reposition in anticipation.

The second part is subtle but important. Even if nobody is "cheating," traders can infer that persistent buying means the price may drift up, so they raise offers or buy ahead. The large buyer ends up paying more simply because the market sees them coming.

Information leakage: the market learns your plan

Institutional trading often involves executing a position over time (minutes, hours, or days). If the market detects the pattern, it can respond:

- market makers widen spreads to protect themselves,
- short-term traders lean against the flow,
- and liquidity may "fade" (quotes disappear) at the exact moments the institution needs it.

The more transparent the market is *about the institution's remaining size*, the easier it is for others to play defense—or offense.

Hidden liquidity as a practical compromise

Dark pools and hidden orders can be viewed as a compromise mechanism:

- Price discovery primarily happens in lit markets.
- Some large trades are matched quietly to reduce footprint.
- The trade is reported after execution, contributing to post-trade transparency.

The argument is not "dark is better." The argument is "some darkness can reduce the costs of executing large trades, which can benefit long-term investors such as pension funds."

The iceberg metaphor without the picture: what is "hidden" liquidity?

Even in lit markets, not all liquidity must be displayed. Many markets allow forms of **hidden or reserve** orders (often called *iceberg orders*):

- The trader has a large total size they want to buy or sell.
- Only a small "tip" is displayed at the best price.
- When the displayed portion executes, another small portion refreshes.

This is a key bridge concept: the transparency debate is not only about separate dark venues. It is also about how much of an order's true size should be visible, and when.

For readers, the intuitive takeaway is:

If you show the whole iceberg, the ocean steers around you. If you hide it completely, other ships worry about what they cannot see.

The regulatory tug-of-war: competing definitions of "fair"

Regulators are pulled between two visions of fairness.

Fairness as equal visibility

In this view, fairness means:

- everyone sees the same prices,
- everyone competes on the same lit order book,
- and private dealing is limited so public markets remain robust.

The fear is that if too much trading moves to dark venues:

- lit quotes become less informative,
- spreads widen because displayed liquidity shrinks,
- and the visible market becomes a "thin shell" that can gap violently.

This is especially concerning during stress events, when confidence and visible liquidity matter most.

Fairness as equal ability to execute without being exploited

In this view, fairness means:

- long-term investors should be able to trade large positions without being penalized for their size,
- information leakage should be minimized,
- and the market should not force investors to "announce" their needs to the fastest traders.

The fear here is that a perfectly lit market can become a hunting ground where speed dominates patience. If institutional investors face excessive trading costs, end-investors (retirees, savers) ultimately pay through worse fund performance.

How transparency interacts with liquidity crises

The transparency debate becomes sharper in a crisis because the same mechanisms that help in normal times can amplify stress.

In a crisis, too much visibility can accelerate herding

If everyone sees prices falling quickly and sees liquidity evaporating, many risk systems respond automatically. That can increase correlation and speed up withdrawals of liquidity.

This does *not* mean transparency is bad. It means transparency can make collective behavior more synchronized. In other words, the market becomes a shared dashboard that many automated systems read at the same time.

But too little visibility can destroy confidence

Darkness has its own crisis problem: trust. If participants suspect that:

- the "real" trading is happening elsewhere,
- the public quotes are stale,
- or the best liquidity is hidden behind selective access,

they may step back from providing liquidity in lit markets, worsening the situation.

In fragile moments, confidence in the displayed price is itself a form of liquidity.

A balanced way to think about it: "one price, many places" needs a strong anchor

From earlier chapters on fragmentation, you already know the modern market is not a single room. It is a network. The transparency debate is ultimately about whether that network still has a strong, reliable **anchor** for price discovery.

A practical framework is to separate two functions:

- **Price discovery function (anchor):** where the market forms the reference price that others trust.
- **Execution function (minimizing footprint):** where large investors can transact with less information leakage.

Lit markets tend to be better anchors. Dark mechanisms can improve execution for large orders. The regulatory challenge is ensuring the execution function does not undermine the anchor function.

Where this leaves us heading into the conclusion

Across the chapter so far, a pattern has emerged:

- Risk controls and halts are attempts to make the system safer without destroying its speed and efficiency.
- Market makers provide much of the liquidity, but often with discretion to step back.
- Transparency improves trust and price discovery, but it can increase the cost of executing large trades and can change behavior in stressed moments.

In the concluding section, we will synthesize these tensions into a single question: **Is the system actually safer?** Or have we built a market that is robust against small errors yet still fragile in large shocks—because the very features that make it efficient in good times (speed, optionality, fragmentation) also create new failure modes in bad times?

9.5 Is the System Safer? The Paradox of Resilience

Across this chapter, we have toured a modern market's safety equipment. First came **pre-trade risk controls**: software gates that reject clearly dangerous orders before they touch an exchange. Then **circuit breakers and halts**: forced time-outs that slow trading when feedback loops begin to run faster than human understanding. Then the uncomfortable reality of **market maker optionality**: much of today's liquidity is supplied by fast firms that can step back when volatility rises. Finally, we examined the **transparency debate**: more "lights on" can strengthen trust and price discovery, while some "darkness" can reduce information leakage for large investors.

This final section asks a deceptively simple question:

Is the system safer than it used to be?

The honest answer is nuanced. In many ways, yes: the system is better at preventing obvious mistakes from becoming disasters. But it is also more complex, more interdependent, and more automated. That combination can create a paradox: **we have engineered a market that is resilient to small shocks, yet fragile to certain big ones**.

Safety is not one thing: robustness, resilience, and fragility

To evaluate whether the system is "safer," we need three related concepts:

- **Robustness:** the ability to withstand routine stress without changing behavior much.
- **Resilience:** the ability to recover quickly after disruption.
- **Fragility:** the tendency to fail abruptly once stress crosses a threshold.

A system can be robust in everyday conditions and still fragile in rare conditions. A glass cup is robust enough for daily use; it is fragile if dropped. Likewise, a market can handle ordinary volatility and still experience sudden liquidity breakdowns under extreme, fast-moving stress.

The paradox of modern regulation and risk controls is that many interventions improve *everyday* robustness while leaving (or even shifting) tail-risk fragility into new corners.

How the system *is* safer: fewer "unforced errors"

There is a strong case that modern markets are safer in the sense that fewer disasters are triggered by avoidable mistakes.

Pre-trade controls reduce the "single bad order" problem

Price bands, size limits, and credit checks are extremely effective at catching:

- wrong-price orders,
- extra-zero quantity errors,
- and orders that exceed an account's capacity.

These controls do not merely protect one trader. They protect the market from a brief but damaging distortion of prices that can trigger stop orders, margin events, and cascading algorithmic reactions.

In this sense, the market is more robust against a class of errors that used to cause dramatic disruptions.

Circuit breakers reduce mechanical cascades

Halts and pauses are a direct response to a modern reality: machines can amplify each other. By forcing a pause, circuit breakers reduce the probability that:

- a thin book prints at extreme prices,
- those prints trigger additional automated selling,
- and the market spirals without a moment to reset.

Even when prices continue to fall after a halt, the reopening process tends to be more orderly than a continuous freefall into an empty order book.

More surveillance and clearer rules improve accountability

Modern market structure includes extensive:

- audit trails,
- reporting requirements,
- and monitoring systems.

This does not prevent every crisis, but it helps regulators and firms diagnose what happened and refine controls. Over time, that learning improves operational safety.

Why crises still happen: the system is safer from *errors*, not from *fear*

Here is the key distinction:

Most guardrails are designed to prevent mistakes. Liquidity crises are often driven by rational fear and synchronized risk reduction.

In a liquidity crisis, the market is not necessarily malfunctioning. It is repricing risk rapidly, while many participants simultaneously reduce exposure. The guardrails can slow the process, but they cannot force participants to be brave, solvent, or willing to catch a falling knife.

This is why the same market can be well-defended against fat-finger errors and still experience flash-crash dynamics.

The paradox of resilience: controls can shift risk rather than eliminate it

Safety mechanisms can change *how* stress is expressed. Sometimes this is an improvement; sometimes it is a relocation of risk.

From continuous chaos to concentrated events

Circuit breakers can reduce chaotic price prints during continuous trading, but they can also concentrate pressure into:

- the reopening auction,
- the first seconds after the restart,
- and threshold effects near pause triggers.

In other words, volatility can be "packaged" rather than removed. The market still must find a lower price if fundamentals demand it; the difference is that the discovery happens in bursts rather than a smooth slide.

From obvious failures to subtle configuration failures

Pre-trade controls work only if configured well. This introduces a different type of vulnerability: **configuration risk**.

Examples of configuration fragility include:

- limits set too loose (controls exist but do not constrain),
- limits set too tight (false rejections cause firms to add exceptions),
- inconsistent limits across brokers or venues (orders rejected in one path but accepted in another),
- and stale parameters in abnormal volatility regimes.

A control that is slightly mis-set may not matter for months. Then, during a crisis, it can matter enormously. This is a form of tail-risk: silent in normal times, loud when it finally appears.

From human discretion to model-driven synchronization

Older market structures relied more on human judgment at critical points. Modern markets rely heavily on models:

- volatility estimators,

- correlation matrices,
- value-at-risk limits,
- and automated de-risking rules.

Models improve day-to-day discipline. But models can also synchronize behavior. If many institutions measure risk similarly and respond similarly, they may all sell the same assets at the same time. This can transform a solvable imbalance into a liquidity vacuum.

Paradoxically, "better risk management" at each firm can produce a worse outcome for the system if everyone's risk management is the same.

Market fragmentation: one system, many failure points

Fragmentation is not just an execution detail; it is a resilience issue.

A fragmented market has:

- many venues,
- many routing decisions,
- many different rulebooks,
- and many distinct technology stacks.

That diversity can be a strength: a failure at one venue might not shut down the entire market. But fragmentation also creates multiple ways for stress to propagate:

- latency differences can cause temporary price dislocations,
- routing logic can unintentionally concentrate flow,
- and liquidity can vanish in one venue before others react.

In calm markets, fragmentation often improves competition. In fast crises, it can increase complexity at exactly the moment when simplicity is valuable.

Liquidity provision as a weak link: optionality meets stress

From the previous section, we learned that modern market makers frequently have discretion to step back. This matters because many of the system's safety assumptions quietly presume that:

- someone will quote,
- spreads will widen but not explode,
- and size will shrink but not disappear.

During a true liquidity crisis, those assumptions can fail. If multiple liquidity providers pull back at once, the order book can go from "thin" to "hollow." At that point:

- pre-trade controls still reject obviously wrong orders,
- circuit breakers may still pause trading,
- but prices can gap sharply anyway because the market must clear at a level where real buyers exist.

This is not a moral failing of market makers; it is a structural fact about relying on voluntary, risk-limited liquidity for stability.

The transparency trade-off revisited: trust versus footprint

The transparency debate also feeds into resilience.

- Too little transparency can erode trust in the reference price, encouraging participants to retreat.
- Too much transparency can increase information leakage and intensify strategic behavior around large orders, potentially increasing volatility during stressed execution.

A resilient system needs both:

- a strong, trusted anchor for price discovery (typically lit markets),
- and execution mechanisms that do not punish long-term investors for their size (which can include dark or hidden liquidity under well-designed constraints).

The paradox is that policy solutions that maximize one dimension can degrade the other. This is why the debate persists: the "right" balance depends on what failure mode you fear most.

A checklist for readers: how to diagnose "safer or just different"

When you read about a sudden market break—a mini flash crash, a disorderly open, a violent ETF dislocation—ask four questions. They will tell you whether the guardrails reduced risk or simply moved it.

1. **Was the trigger an error or a legitimate shock?**
   If it was an input error, pre-trade controls and kill switches are the key issue. If it was a legitimate repricing, the issue is liquidity and synchronization.
2. **Did liquidity disappear, or did it reprice?**
   Wide spreads and small size are "repricing." A near-empty book is "disappearance." The remedies are different.
3. **Did a pause help, or did it concentrate pressure?**
   Look at the reopening: did the auction restore two-sided trading, or did it gap and then destabilize again?
4. **Did fragmentation amplify the move?**
   Were there venue-by-venue dislocations, routing anomalies, or cross-product feedback loops?

These questions keep the analysis grounded. They also prevent a common mistake: blaming technology in general, rather than identifying the specific mechanism that failed.

Chapter 10

The Reader's Toolkit: Surviving Market Stress

We have explored the hidden machinery of dark pools and the chaotic mechanics of flash crashes. Now, let's equip you with a survival kit. This isn't about becoming a high-frequency trader; it's about understanding the dashboard indicators when the engine starts smoking. We will replace complex jargon with simple mental models and provide crucial safety rules-like why hitting 'sell' at any price is dangerous-to help you navigate the fragile landscape of modern markets.

10.1 Mental Models for Markets

Most readers have an intuitive sense that markets are usually *liquid*: you can buy or sell without much fuss, and the price you see on a screen feels like a fair, tradable number. In calm conditions, that intuition is mostly correct.

In market stress, however, the intuition breaks. Prices can jump, spreads can widen, and trades that *should* be easy suddenly become difficult or expensive. This is the central puzzle of flash events and liquidity crises: *how can a market be "deep" one minute and "empty" the next?*

This section equips you with two mental models you can carry into every dramatic headline and every scary chart:

- the **Fire Exit** model (why liquidity vanishes when everyone rushes at once), and
- the **Queue** model (how orders stack up, and why the "line" can disappear).

These are deliberately non-technical. They are not meant to replace the formal language of the limit order book, market makers, and order routing; instead, they give you a *feel* for what those mechanisms do under pressure.

The Fire Exit Model: When a Wide Door Becomes a Bottleneck

Imagine leaving a movie theater.

- On a normal night, people stand up, gather their things, and drift toward the doors. The exit feels wide. You barely notice the doorway.
- Now imagine someone yells "Fire!" People surge toward the same exit at the same time. The *same doorway* suddenly feels narrow. The door did not shrink. The crowd changed.

That is liquidity in a single picture.

- **Liquidity in normal times** is like the normal exit: many willing counterparties (buyers and sellers) spread out across nearby prices. Trading feels smooth because not everyone needs to act at once.
- **Liquidity in stress** is like the fire exit: everyone tries to do the same thing (usually *sell*) at the same time, and the "passageway" of trading capacity becomes a bottleneck.

To make the analogy precise, map the pieces:

- **People** → **orders** (your order, other investors' orders, algorithms' orders).
- **The doorway** → **available immediate liquidity** near the current price.
- **A smooth flow through the doorway** → **many small trades executed without moving price much.**
- **A jam at the doorway** → **orders competing for limited bids, forcing price to fall to find buyers.**

Why the "door" feels wide in calm markets

In calm conditions, there are typically many participants willing to provide the other side of your trade:

- long-term investors rebalancing,
- short-term traders capturing small price differences,
- market makers and liquidity providers posting buy and sell quotes,
- algorithms that continuously update quotes.

Crucially, these participants do not all react in the same direction at the same time. Their motives differ, so their orders *spread out* across prices and time. That diversity of motives is a major source of market stability.

Why the "door" jams in stress markets

In a stress event, several things tend to happen together:

- **Crowding:** Many participants suddenly want the same action (sell now, reduce risk now, cancel exposure now).

- **Urgency:** They become less picky about price. Speed matters more than getting a "fair" deal.
- **Retreat:** Some liquidity providers step back—not because they are malicious, but because uncertainty makes quoting dangerous. If you cannot estimate the next price move, posting a firm quote is like standing in a doorway while the crowd runs.

The result is a paradox that is easy to remember:

> *Markets look most liquid precisely when you least need liquidity, and least liquid exactly when you most need it.*

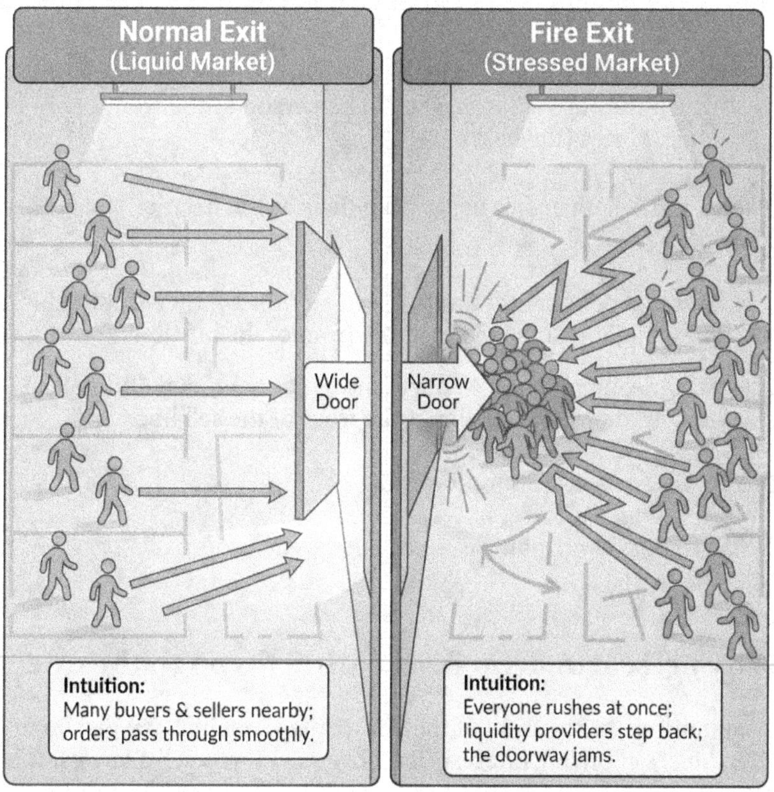

The Queue Model: The Market as a Line of Orders

The fire-exit model explains *why* markets can jam. The queue model explains *how* that jam translates into sudden price moves.

A modern electronic market is not a single person deciding a price. It is a constantly updating set of lines—queues—of buy and sell orders.

A plain-English picture of the order queue

Think of two lines facing each other:

- On the **buy side**, people are standing in line offering prices they are willing to pay. The person at the front offers the *highest* price (the best bid).
- On the **sell side**, people are standing in line offering prices at which they are willing to sell. The person at the front offers the *lowest* price (the best ask).

When a trade happens, it usually happens at the front of one of these lines:

- If someone urgently wants to sell *right now*, they "hit the bid"—they trade with the buyer at the front of the buy line.
- If someone urgently wants to buy *right now*, they "lift the ask"—they trade with the seller at the front of the sell line.

The key idea is simple but powerful:

> *Price is what you get when you reach the front of the queue.*

Why price can drop fast: eating through the queue

In calm markets, the front of the buy queue is not just one person; it is often *layers* of buying interest close together. If you sell a modest number of shares, you trade with the first layer. The price barely moves.

In stressed markets, two queue failures appear:

1) The queue gets thin.

Some buyers step away, and some market makers widen quotes or cancel them. The buy queue becomes shallow near the current price.

2) The queue gets one-sided.

Many sellers arrive at once. They are not calmly negotiating; they are urgently trying to get out. The selling flow *consumes* the thin buy queue quickly, forcing trades to occur at lower and lower bid levels.

That mechanical process is a big part of what people later describe emotionally as "panic." The panic is real, but the price drop is often driven by a very concrete micro-mechanism: a thin queue being rapidly depleted.

Why "liquidity vanishes" is often a cancellation story

A critical nuance for readers: during stress, liquidity does not always vanish because buyers have no money or because a company suddenly became worthless in five minutes. Liquidity often vanishes because *potential* liquidity is not the same as *displayed, executable* liquidity.

Many participants may be willing to buy at some price, but not at *this* price, and not with *this* uncertainty, and not without time to assess what is happening. So they cancel, pause, or demand a larger discount.

In the queue model, this looks like:

- fewer people in line near the front, and
- larger gaps between acceptable prices.

Those gaps matter. If the next buyer is far down the line, the price must fall a long distance to meet them.

Putting the Two Models Together

Use the models together, not separately.

- The **Fire Exit** model tells you *why* the crowding happens: correlated behavior, urgency, and retreat by liquidity providers.
- The **Queue** model tells you *how* the crowding becomes a chart: thin lines of orders get consumed, cancellations open gaps, and the next executable price can be far away.

Once you internalize these two pictures, many "mysteries" of market stress become less mysterious:

- Why prices can gap down without any single "new" piece of information.
- Why you can see a price on a screen but be unable to trade anywhere near it in size.
- Why a market can recover quickly once the crowd stops rushing and the queue refills.

The next step is practical: if liquidity can vanish and queues can thin, how can a non-professional reader detect that the market is entering the fire-exit phase *in real time*? That is the purpose of the next section's toolkit for reading market stress as it happens.

10.2 Reading the Tape in Real-Time

The previous section gave you two mental models—the *Fire Exit* (crowding turns a wide door into a bottleneck) and the *Queue* (prices are where you reach the front of the order line). Now we convert those pictures into a practical skill: recognizing, in real time, when the market's "doorway" is narrowing and the "queues" are thinning.

You do *not* need a professional terminal to do this. You need a small set of observable signals—the market's equivalent of dashboard lights. None of these signals is perfect on its own. But together they answer a crucial question:

> *Is the market currently functioning like a normal exit, or is it turning into a fire exit?*

What "Reading the Tape" Means (in Plain English)

Historically, "the tape" referred to printed trade reports on ticker tape: the live stream of transactions and prices. Today the tape is digital, but the idea is the same: **watch what is actually trading and how it trades**, not just what the last price used to be.

Reading the tape during stress is less about predicting the future and more about diagnosing the present:

- Is liquidity *available* or merely *implied*?
- Are prices moving because of new information, or because the market's plumbing is struggling?
- If you *had* to trade, would your order likely execute cleanly—or fall into a gap?

To keep this practical, we will focus on four high-signal indicators that are widely visible even on free charting sites or most brokerage apps:

- **1. Bid–ask spread** (your first stress gauge),
- **2. Depth/quotes behavior** (is the queue refilling or disappearing?),
- **3. Volatility and gap behavior** (how "jagged" is the path?),
- **4. Halts and limit states** (when the market hits the brakes).

Indicator #1: The Bid–Ask Spread (The Market's Pulse)

If you learn only one microstructure signal, learn this one.

What the spread is

At any moment there is usually:

- a **bid**: the highest displayed price someone is willing to pay, and

- an **ask** (or offer): the lowest displayed price someone is willing to sell for.

The **bid–ask spread** is:

$$Spread = Ask - Bid.$$

Why spreads widen in stress (linking back to the models)

In the *Queue* model, the bid and ask are simply the front of two lines. A narrow spread means the two lines are close together and confident. A wide spread means the lines have pulled apart.

In the *Fire Exit* model, a widening spread is a warning that the doorway is narrowing:

- Liquidity providers become less willing to stand in the doorway with firm prices.
- They demand more compensation for uncertainty.
- Some quotes disappear entirely, which makes the best remaining quotes look farther apart.

A practical way to remember it:

> *When the spread widens, the market is charging you a higher "toll" to cross the bridge from buyer to seller.*

What to watch (even without level-II data)

Even if your screen only shows last price plus a bid/ask, you can still observe:

- **Spread relative to normal:** Is it noticeably larger than what you typically see for that asset?

- **Spread relative to price:** A 1-cent spread on a $10 stock is different from a 1-cent spread on a $0.20 stock. In percentage terms:

$$\text{Spread\%} \approx \frac{Ask - Bid}{(Ask + Bid)/2}.$$

- **Spread behavior during moves:** In a healthy market, spreads may widen slightly during fast moves but then *snap back*. In a stressed market, spreads widen and *stay* wide.

A key interpretation rule (to avoid a common mistake)

A widening spread does *not* automatically mean:

- someone knows bad news you don't, or
- the asset is "going to zero."

It often means something more mechanical:

> *Market participants are uncertain about the next price, so they step back from offering tight, executable quotes.*

This distinction matters because it changes your next step. If it's primarily a liquidity problem, patience and safer order types (covered later) can matter more than "getting out immediately."

Indicator #2: Depth and Quote Behavior (Is the Queue Refilling?)

The spread is the headline number; *depth* is the supporting evidence.

Depth in plain English

Depth is simply: **how much can trade near the current price before the price has to move a lot?**

In the queue model, depth answers: how many people are standing close to the front of the line?

What a casual observer can actually see

Not everyone has full order-book depth. But many brokerage platforms show at least some version of:

- "bid size" and "ask size,"
- top-of-book quotes that update rapidly,
- a time-and-sales list (prints of recent trades),
- or a chart with volume bars and rapid tick movement.

Even without professional tools, you can still notice patterns that strongly suggest thinning depth:

Quotes that flicker or vanish

If the bid/ask updates so quickly that it feels unstable—or if you see moments where the quote becomes "weird" (suddenly far away)—that is often the market trying to find a stable clearing level. In the fire-exit model, it's the crowd pressing forward while doorway guards keep stepping aside.

Sudden "air pockets" (gaps)

If price jumps from one level to another with little trading in between, that hints at missing orders in the middle—the line has gaps. In calm markets, you typically see more continuous trading across adjacent prices.

The "one print moves the market" feel

When individual trades seem to move the price more than usual, that often indicates reduced depth. The same-sized order now consumes a larger fraction of the available queue.

A simple diagnostic question

When you see a fast move, ask:

> *After the price moves, does the market quickly re-form tight quotes and trade normally again, or does it look hesitant and jumpy?*

Quick re-formation is a sign of resilience. Hesitation is a sign that liquidity is not confidently re-entering.

Indicator #3: Volatility Shape (Smooth Slide vs. Staircase Drop)

In a healthy market, price changes often look like a relatively smooth path: many trades at many nearby prices. In stressed markets, price changes often look like a **staircase**:

- long pauses with little trading,
- sudden drops to a new level,
- brief rebounds,
- followed by another sudden drop.

This "staircase" shape is consistent with the queue model: the front of the line gets eaten, then price must jump to the next cluster of available bids.

A practical cue: speed plus jaggedness

Fast moves happen in healthy markets too, especially around major announcements. The danger sign is the combination of:

- **speed** (large moves in short time), and

- **jaggedness** (gaps and abrupt steps).

When both appear, you are often watching liquidity withdraw in real time.

Volume is informative, but not always in the way you think

Many people assume high volume always means high liquidity. In stress, high volume can mean the opposite: *a crowded fire exit*.

Volume answers "how many people are trying to get through." Liquidity answers "how wide is the door." During panic, you can have huge volume *and* poor liquidity, because participants are urgently trading *through* a narrow doorway.

So use volume as a contextual clue:

- **High volume + tight spreads** often looks like healthy activity.
- **High volume + widening spreads + staircase price action** often looks like stress.

Indicator #4: Trading Halts and Limit States (When the Market Hits the Brakes)

At some point, stress can become severe enough that the market itself forces a pause. These mechanisms are often called **circuit breakers** or **trading halts**. To a casual observer, a halt can feel alarming—as if something has "broken." But conceptually, it is the market acknowledging that the fire-exit conditions are getting dangerous.

What a halt usually means (and what it does not mean)

A halt usually means:

- the market is trying to slow down an extreme move,

- allow participants to update orders and reassess,
- and reduce the risk of trades occurring at absurd prices due to momentary gaps.

A halt does *not* automatically mean:

- the asset is worthless,
- you are "trapped forever,"
- or that a bankruptcy was just announced.

In the mental-model language:

> *A halt is the venue temporarily controlling the doorway so the crowd can re-sort into lines again.*

Why halts can feel chaotic when trading resumes

When trading restarts, you often see:

- a burst of activity,
- a jump to a new price level,
- temporarily wide spreads,
- and then, if the situation stabilizes, a gradual return to tighter quoting.

This is consistent with the queue model: during the pause, participants cancel and replace orders. When the gate reopens, the "front of the line" may be at a very different price.

A Minimal "Market Health Checklist" You Can Use Anywhere

Here is a compact checklist you can apply in seconds.

- **1. Spread:** Is the bid–ask spread noticeably wider than normal for this asset?
- **2. Stability:** Do quotes look steady, or do they flicker and jump?
- **3. Path shape:** Is price moving smoothly, or in steps and gaps?
- **4. Speed:** Is the move unusually fast for the time of day and the asset?
- **5. Interruptions:** Are there halts, limit states, or repeated "pauses" in trading?

If several of these lights turn red at the same time, you should assume you are in a fire-exit regime: liquidity is thin, queues are unstable, and the cost of immediacy is rising.

What This Means for a Non-Professional Trader

The point of reading the tape is not to turn you into a day trader. It is to prevent a very common and very costly mistake: behaving as if a stressed market is still a normal market.

When spreads widen and the tape turns jagged, standard assumptions fail:

- "I can always get out near the last price" becomes false.
- "A market order just means immediate execution" becomes dangerous.
- "Stops will protect me" becomes unreliable in fast gaps.

That sets up the next section, which is the most actionable safety lesson in the chapter: **how order types behave when the market is in a fire-exit condition**, and why certain common orders can become financial self-sabotage during a flash event.

10.3 Order Safety for Individuals

The previous section taught you how to *diagnose* market stress in real time: widening bid–ask spreads, flickering quotes, jagged price paths, and occasional halts. This section is about what to do with that diagnosis.

When the market shifts from "normal exit" to "fire exit," your main risk is no longer being wrong about direction. Your main risk is **execution**: the gap between the price you *think* you are trading and the price you *actually* get.

This is the part of market stress that surprises casual investors most. They assume:

> *If I click sell, I sell at about the current price.*

In a stressed market, that assumption can fail dramatically—not because the broker is cheating, but because the market's order queues have thinned and gaps have opened. In other words, the *queue* is sparse, and you may be forced down the line farther than you expect.

The Core Principle: In Stress, Price Certainty Beats Speed

Order types are best understood by the trade-off they make between:

- **speed/certainty of execution** (getting filled), and
- **certainty of price** (knowing the worst price you will accept).

In calm markets, the difference between these two goals is small, so many order types feel interchangeable. In stress markets, the difference becomes huge. Your objective should usually shift to:

> *Control the price, even if it means you might not trade.*

That sounds counterintuitive until you remember the fire-exit model: in a jam, forcing your way through "at any cost" is exactly how you get hurt.

Market Orders: "Fill Me at Any Price" (A Hidden Promise You May Not Want)

A **market order** is simple: *execute immediately at the best available price.* The dangerous phrase is "best available," because in stress the best available might be far away.

Why market orders can become financial self-sabotage in a flash event

A market order does *not* mean:

- "fill me near the last traded price," or
- "fill me near the midpoint," or
- "fill me within some reasonable range."

It means: **take whatever liquidity is sitting at the front of the queue, and if it is thin, keep walking down the line until the entire order is filled.**

If there is an air pocket—a gap where few or no bids exist—your order can fall through it, executing at prices that look absurd in hindsight.

The most common market-order misconception

Many investors treat the last traded price as if it were a posted guarantee. It is not. The last price is merely the price of the *most recent* transaction, which could have been:

- small in size,
- executed milliseconds ago,
- in a moment when the queue briefly looked healthier than it does now.

In a fast selloff, the last price can be stale almost immediately. A market sell order submitted into a collapsing queue can get filled at a much lower price than the last print.

Limit Orders: The Seatbelt (You Choose the Worst Price You'll Accept)

A **limit order** is a boundary:

- A **limit buy** says: "Buy *no higher* than L."
- A **limit sell** says: "Sell *no lower* than L."

This changes the trade-off:

- You give up guaranteed execution.
- You gain control over the worst-case price.

In a stressed market, this is often the correct bargain.

Why limit orders matter specifically in flash-crash conditions

Flash events are defined by **speed** and **thin liquidity**. When both are present, the biggest danger for an individual is getting executed at the wrong end of a temporary vacuum.

A limit order is a hard rule that says:

> *I will not run through the fire exit if the doorway becomes a cliff.*

The correct mental model for a limit order

A limit order is not a prediction. It is **risk management**. You are not saying, "The price will definitely trade at my limit." You are saying, "If the market cannot trade at a reasonable price, I refuse to participate in the panic."

That refusal can be valuable. In many microstructure-driven drops, the worst prices occur when the queue is most distorted. If you are not forced to trade at that moment, you often avoid the most pathological prints.

Market vs. Limit: A Two-Path Outcome Diagram

The following diagram summarizes the difference in one picture: a market order keeps moving until it finds a fill, even if it falls through a gap; a limit order stops at a pre-set boundary.

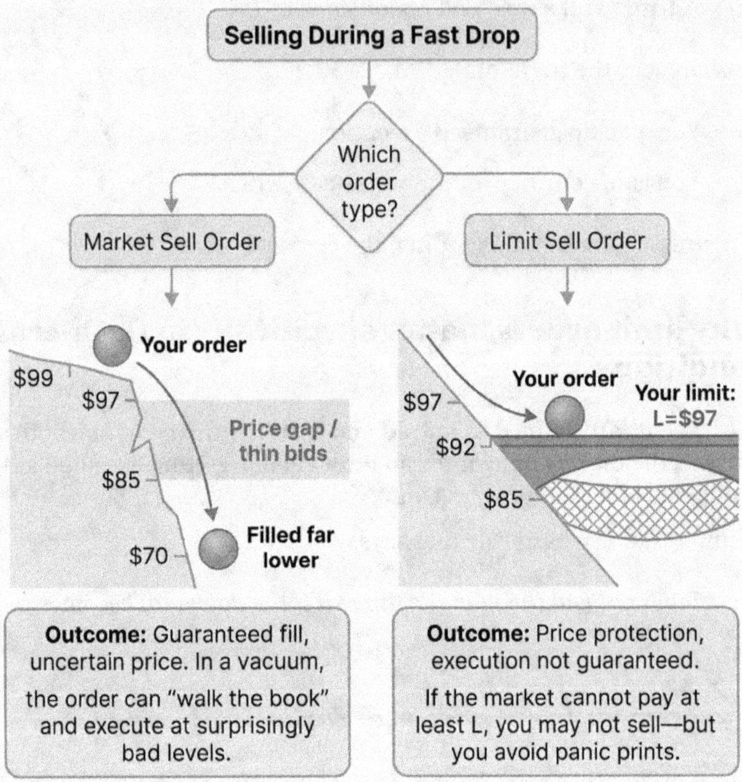

Stop Orders: Why They Often Trigger at the Worst Moment

Stop orders are widely used by individuals because they sound like insurance:

- A **stop-loss sell** says: "If the price falls to S, sell."

The hidden detail is what happens *after* the stop triggers.

Stop-market: a stop that turns into a market order

On many platforms, the default stop-loss is a **stop-market** order: once the stop price S is touched, your order becomes a *market order*.

That means in a fast drop:

1. the price hits S (often during a liquidity vacuum),
2. your stop converts to a market sell,
3. and it can execute *well below* S if the queue is thin.

This is why stops can feel like they "trigger at the bottom." Often, they are not magically choosing the bottom. They are mechanically converting into the most dangerous order type at the most dangerous moment.

Stop-limit: safer, but with a trade-off

A **stop-limit** order tries to fix the problem by adding a limit. It says:

> If the market trades at S, then sell, but *no lower than* L.

This can reduce the worst-case price, but it reintroduces non-execution risk: if the market gaps below L, you may not sell.

That is not a flaw; it is the unavoidable trade-off. You cannot have:

- guaranteed execution *and*
- guaranteed price

during a discontinuous move. Stress reveals the constraint that calm markets hide.

Practical Rules of Thumb (Designed for Flash-Event Conditions)

The goal here is not to dictate a single "best" order for all situations. The goal is to prevent catastrophic mismatches between your intention and the market's condition.

Rule 1: If spreads are wide, treat market orders as hazardous

When your diagnostic lights (spread, instability, jaggedness) flash red, interpret a market order as:

> *Permission for the market to choose my price.*

In a fire-exit moment, the market may choose a bad price quickly.

Rule 2: Use limit orders as a default seatbelt, especially for less-liquid assets

If an asset is thinly traded, volatile, or currently in stress, a limit order is often the safest baseline tool for an individual.

A simple way to choose a limit for a *sell* in a stressed tape is:

- look at the current bid and ask,
- decide the worst acceptable price,
- place your limit near that boundary rather than "hoping" the spread behaves.

This does not guarantee an optimal fill; it prevents a disastrous one.

Rule 3: Don't confuse "risk control" with "guaranteed outcomes"

A limit order is not a magic shield. During extreme moves, you may not get filled. But that "failure" can be a form of protection: it keeps you from trading at the most distorted, lowest-liquidity prints.

Rule 4: Understand what your stop order becomes

Before relying on stops, confirm whether your platform is using:

- stop-market (becomes a market order), or
- stop-limit (becomes a limit order).

Then match it to your real objective:

- If your priority is **must exit at all costs**, you are choosing execution certainty and giving up price certainty.
- If your priority is **avoid an extreme print**, you must accept the possibility of not exiting immediately.

The Big Picture: Your Order Type Is Part of Market Structure

It is tempting to view order types as personal preferences, like choosing a lane on the highway. In stress, they are more like choosing whether to drive into fog at full speed.

When many participants use marketable orders (market orders, stop-market triggers) at the same time, they collectively *consume* the queue. That accelerates the fire-exit jam:

- more aggressive selling eats bids,
- the best bid falls rapidly,
- spreads widen further,
- liquidity providers retreat more,
- and the next round of stops triggers.

This is one reason flash events can cascade: not because everyone is irrational, but because many "reasonable" automated instructions become dangerous when the door narrows.

Bridge to the Next Section

By now, you can:

- recognize stressed conditions in real time, and
- choose order types that reduce the risk of catastrophic execution.

The next section extends the toolkit beyond your trading screen and into your news feed. During a panic, headlines can push you toward the very behaviors that worsen outcomes. We will learn to separate **liquidity crises** (a temporary jam in the plumbing) from **solvency crises** (a fundamental collapse), so you can interpret scary narratives without being pulled into the crowd at the fire exit.

10.4 Interpreting Headlines

In the previous sections you built a working survival kit:

- mental models for why liquidity vanishes (the *Fire Exit* and the *Queue*),
- real-time stress gauges (spreads, instability, jagged price paths, halts),
- and execution seatbelts (especially the disciplined use of limit orders).

Now we address the other force that drives bad decisions during a fast market: **the news feed**.

Headlines are not neutral. They compete for your attention under time pressure. During a sharp move, many headlines blur together:

> *"Bloodbath." "Rout." "Panic." "Traders flee." "Something is breaking."*

Sometimes those words describe a genuine fundamental crisis. Sometimes they describe a *market plumbing event*: a temporary, mechanical breakdown in how orders meet liquidity. If you cannot tell the difference, you are vulnerable to exactly the behavior the fire-exit model warns about: rushing for the door because everyone else is rushing.

This section gives you a simple filter to keep your head when the tape is chaotic and the headlines are loud.

The Headline Problem: Narratives Arrive Faster Than Explanations

Markets move in milliseconds. Journalism moves in minutes. Careful analysis moves in hours or days. That timing mismatch creates a predictable pattern:

1. Price moves violently (often for microstructure reasons).
2. A headline appears explaining the move with a confident story.
3. Later, details emerge: liquidity was thin, a large flow hit at once, quotes were pulled, stops triggered, an auction mechanism kicked in, a halt occurred, or a venue had an outage.

The key lesson is not that journalists are dishonest. It is that **a market move demands a story immediately**, even when the true cause is still unclear. In the first minutes of a flash-type event, the correct answer is often:

> *We don't know yet, and the market is struggling to match buyers and sellers.*

Your job as a reader is to recognize when the "story" is being written over missing information.

The One Question That Cuts Through Noise

When you see a dramatic headline during a sharp move, ask:

> **Is this a liquidity crisis or a solvency crisis?**

These words sound technical, but the distinction is intuitive.

Liquidity crisis: the plumbing is jammed

A **liquidity** problem means the market's *ability to trade smoothly* is impaired:

- quotes widen or disappear,
- depth thins,
- orders walk through gaps,
- price overshoots and later rebounds.

This fits the Fire Exit model perfectly: the door is the same, but everyone rushed it at once, and some "doorway staff" (liquidity providers) stepped back to avoid getting crushed.

In liquidity crises, the most important word is **temporary**. Temporary does not mean harmless; it means the mechanism can normalize once participants regain confidence and queues refill.

Solvency crisis: the structure is unsound

A **solvency** problem means the underlying entity (a company, a bank, a fund, sometimes a country) may be fundamentally unable to meet obligations:

- too much debt,
- collapsing cash flows,
- legal or regulatory shocks,
- fraud or catastrophic losses.

Solvency crises can also produce fast price moves. But they are driven by a different reality: **the thing being traded may truly be worth much less.**

In solvency crises, the most important word is **permanent**. Permanent does not mean immediate bankruptcy, but it means the valuation may be changing for fundamental reasons.

A Practical Headline Filter: Four Checks You Can Do Quickly

You cannot fully diagnose a crisis from a single headline. But you can do quick checks that reduce the odds of making a reflexive mistake.

Check #1: Does the headline cite a concrete, verifiable trigger?

Treat these as higher-quality signals:

- earnings release with numbers,
- guidance change with specifics,
- regulatory action with a named agency and document,
- credit downgrade with a named rater and rationale,
- a confirmed outage or rule-based halt with timestamps.

Treat these as lower-quality signals in the first minutes:

- "on fears of ..."
- "amid uncertainty ..."
- "as traders digest ..."
- "after risk-off mood ..."

The second group may become true later, but in the moment it often functions as a placeholder story for a mechanical move.

Check #2: Does the price action look like a queue problem?

Bring back the real-time tape cues:

- Were spreads unusually wide?

- Did price move in steps and gaps?
- Were there halts?
- Did the move partially reverse quickly?

A sharp move *with* these features often has a strong microstructure component. It may still reflect genuine information, but execution conditions are clearly degraded, which should affect how you trade (or whether you trade at all).

Check #3: Is the move broad and correlated, or isolated and specific?

A single stock collapsing on an earnings miss is often a fundamentals-driven revaluation.

A large synchronized move across many unrelated names can be:

- macro news (rates, inflation, geopolitics), *or*
- a deleveraging/positioning event (forced selling, margin calls, risk-parity de-risking), *or*
- a liquidity event (spreads and depth deteriorate everywhere).

For a casual observer, the key is not to guess which of these is "the truth" instantly. The key is to recognize that broad correlated selling increases the odds of fire-exit dynamics: everyone is trying to use the same door.

Check #4: Is the explanation about value, or about mechanics?

Learn to spot two different languages:

Value language (points toward solvency or fundamentals).

- profits, cash flows, debt, default, dilution,

- demand collapse, competitive damage,
- legal judgments, fraud, asset impairments.

Mechanics language (points toward liquidity and market structure).

- spreads, depth, order imbalance,
- halts, auctions, circuit breakers,
- "thin liquidity," "air pocket," "stop cascade," "liquidity pulled."

A common failure mode in stress coverage is mixing the two: treating a mechanical disruption as if it were a revelation about value. That confusion pushes readers toward unnecessary panic.

Why Sensational Headlines Are Dangerous: They Push You Toward the Worst Order Types

The last section's advice about order safety becomes relevant here.

Under emotional pressure, a reader is more likely to:

- slam a market order ("get me out now"),
- rely on stop-market orders ("my protection will trigger"),
- or chase price ("I need to catch up").

But remember what your tape diagnostics mean: when spreads widen and gaps appear, the market is explicitly telling you that **immediacy is expensive and execution is hazardous**. Sensational headlines increase the probability you will pay that cost at the worst moment.

A disciplined interpretation process therefore protects you in two ways:

1. it improves your understanding, and
2. it reduces the chance you will choose an unsafe execution method.

A Calm Response Protocol (Designed for the First 10 Minutes)

Here is a simple protocol for the initial phase of a fast market. It is intentionally conservative.

1. **Separate diagnosis from action.** First ask: is this fire-exit behavior (liquidity) or structural damage (solvency)?
2. **Check the spread.** If the spread is wide relative to normal, treat any immediate trading decision as high-risk.
3. **Look for halts or limit states.** If trading is repeatedly paused, the market is admitting that price discovery is impaired.
4. **Demand a concrete catalyst before believing a confident story.** If the headline is vague, assume uncertainty is high.
5. **If you must trade, prioritize price control.** Avoid turning urgency into a blank check (market orders) in a thin queue.

This protocol does not tell you to never trade. It tells you not to let a headline force you into the worst microstructure conditions.

A Note on "Liquidity Crisis" Headlines: Don't Confuse the Label with the Mechanism

Sometimes the media will explicitly use the phrase "liquidity crisis." Even then, be careful: the phrase is used loosely.

In this book, a liquidity crisis means a specific mechanism:

- displayed liquidity retreats,
- the order queue becomes thin,
- aggressive orders consume the remaining depth,
- and price gaps to find the next available counterparties.

When you see that label, your follow-up question should be:

> *Liquidity crisis where, exactly? In which instrument, at which venues, and visible through which signals (spreads, depth, halts)?*

That question keeps you anchored to observable reality rather than narrative momentum.

10.5 Conclusion: The Fragile Balance

This chapter has been a survival manual for moments when markets stop behaving like the calm, continuous charts we are used to. We began with two mental models:

- the **Fire Exit** (liquidity feels abundant until everyone rushes at once), and
- the **Queue** (prices are determined by the order line, and the line can thin or vanish).

We then translated those models into practical tools:

- real-time health indicators such as spread widening, quote instability, jagged price paths, and halts,
- and execution safety habits that keep individuals from turning urgency into a blank check—especially by preferring price control (limit orders) when the tape looks stressed.

Finally, we stepped away from the trading screen and into the news feed, learning to filter headlines by separating **liquidity** explanations (plumbing jams) from **solvency** explanations (structural damage).

Now we close by addressing the deeper lesson underneath all of these tools: modern electronic markets are a **delicate trade-off**. They are extraordinarily efficient most of the time—and unusually fragile some of the time.

The Modern Market's Bargain: Speed and Efficiency

Electronic markets have delivered real benefits to everyday participants:

- **Lower explicit costs:** commissions and fees have generally fallen.
- **Tighter spreads in normal conditions:** competition among liquidity providers can reduce the "toll" you pay to trade.
- **Faster execution:** your order can be matched almost instantly.
- **More continuous price discovery:** information is reflected in prices quickly.

These improvements are not abstract. For a long-term investor who trades occasionally, they often mean better fills and less friction in normal markets. In the Fire Exit model, it is as if the building has many doors, excellent signage, and efficient crowd flow on a typical day.

The Hidden Cost: Fragility Under Crowd Behavior

The same features that create efficiency can create fragility.

Speed compresses decision time

When prices move quickly, human decision-making becomes the slow part of the system. This matters because stress is often a *race* between:

- participants who can cancel and re-quote instantly, and
- participants who react with a delay.

In a fast market, a quote that looks available can disappear before you reach it. The queue can change faster than your intuition can update.

Liquidity is conditional, not guaranteed

A crucial takeaway from this book is that liquidity is not a permanent feature of an asset. It is a behavior of other participants:

- In calm times, many are willing to provide two-sided quotes.
- In uncertain times, many become one-sided, or step back entirely.

This is not necessarily wrongdoing. It is risk management. When the next price move is highly uncertain, standing in the doorway becomes dangerous.

Fragmentation can improve competition—and complicate stress

Modern markets are fragmented across venues. In normal times, this can be beneficial: multiple places compete to offer better execution.

In stress, fragmentation can complicate the picture:

- liquidity may be thin in each venue even if total volume is high,
- routing and quote updates may lag during extreme bursts,
- and the "one price" you see can temporarily become "many prices," depending on where and how trades are executed.

For the casual participant, the practical implication is simple: the market you imagine as a single room is often a *network* of rooms connected by fast hallways. In a fire-exit moment, those hallways can become crowded too.

Fairness vs. Efficiency: A Permanent Tension

At the heart of modern market design is a tension between two ideals:

- **Efficiency and speed:** make trading fast and cheap in normal times.

- **Robustness and stability:** make trading orderly in abnormal times.

You can improve one at the expense of the other. For example:

- Allowing instant cancellation and rapid re-quoting can tighten spreads in calm conditions, but it can also cause displayed liquidity to vanish quickly during stress.
- Adding more "speed bumps," pauses, or constraints can reduce runaway cascades, but it may increase costs and reduce immediacy in ordinary trading.

This is why the chapter's toolkit matters. You are not trying to "solve" market structure as an individual. You are learning to live safely inside a system that sometimes prioritizes efficiency over robustness.

The Practical Bottom Line for Readers

This book is not arguing that markets are rigged beyond participation, nor that technology is inherently harmful. It is making a narrower, more useful claim:

Modern markets are usually smooth, but they can become discontinuous. Your safety depends on recognizing the regime and choosing actions that match it.

In concrete terms:

- When spreads are tight and the tape is smooth, many order types behave similarly and execution is forgiving.
- When spreads widen and the tape becomes jumpy, execution becomes the risk. Market orders and stop-market triggers can behave like stepping into the fire-exit jam.
- When headlines are loud, your job is to separate plumbing problems from structural problems before you act.

A Final Reminder: You Cannot Control the Crowd, Only Your Footwear

In a true stress event, you cannot personally restore liquidity. You cannot force other participants to stand in the doorway. You cannot make the queue deeper by sheer will.

But you can do something that is surprisingly powerful: **avoid the choices that reliably cause damage to individuals during flash conditions.**

If you remember only three things from this chapter, remember these:

- **Liquidity is a behavior.** It can retreat suddenly when uncertainty spikes.
- **The spread is a warning light.** Wide spreads are the market telling you that immediacy is expensive.
- **Limit orders are seatbelts.** In a fast market, price control is often more important than instant execution.

That is the fragile balance of modern markets: extraordinary speed and efficiency most days, punctuated by moments when the same machinery becomes sharp-edged. The goal of the reader's toolkit is not to make you fearless. It is to make you *prepared.*

www.ingramcontent.com/pod-product-compliance
Lightning Source LLC
LaVergne TN
LVHW052033200926
848481LV00005B/1660